WINDOWS
on the
Old Testament: Year C

an anthology to amplify the
Old Testament readings
for Year C of Common Worship

Ronald W. Dale

kevin
mayhew

First published in 2003 by

KEVIN MAYHEW LTD
Buxhall, Stowmarket, Suffolk IP14 3BW
E-mail: info@kevinmayhewltd.com

KINGSGATE PUBLISHING INC
1000 Pannell Street, Suite G, Columbia, MO 65201
E-mail: sales@kingsgatepublishing.com

9 8 7 6 5 4 3 2 1 0

ISBN 1 84417 150 7
Catalogue No 1500640

Cover design by Angela Selfe
Typesetting by Simon Loxley

Printed and bound in Great Britain

Contents

Foreword

For me the Old Testament is full of wonderful treasure, with many well-known stories that still resonate today. For instance, the story of Joseph and his coat of many colours; how he was sold into slavery but became the 'saviour' of his own family and the nation of Egypt by rescuing them from seven years of famine.

Then there is David, the shepherd lad, who slays the giant Goliath to rescue his people from oppression, later becoming the greatest of all Israel's kings. Other great leaders in Israel are the prophets, such as Elijah and Elisha; Isaiah and Jeremiah; Amos and Hosea, among many more who spoke 'the word of the Lord', fearlessly denounced evil and pointed to the coming of a messiah that was fulfilled in the coming of Jesus. The Psalms also are rich treasure for all who will read and ponder them. Such as Psalm 23 – The Lord is my shepherd – Psalm 51 that speaks of the need for divine pardon and pleads for mercy and a cleansing from all evil, and psalms that tell of God's omnipresence – as in Psalm 139 – along with psalms of thanksgiving and praise to God, such as Psalm 107 which opens with the words: 'O give thanks to the Lord, for he is good; for his steadfast love endures for ever', and Psalms 146 and 148 that begin on a note of worship, the first line of each saying 'Praise the Lord', and Psalm 150, the final psalm, that ends with the words 'Let everything that breathes praise the Lord! Praise the Lord!'

As we read the Old Testament we need to remember that it cannot be understood in isolation from the New Testament; indeed, it finds its fulfilment in the New. Likewise we cannot understand the New Testament in isolation from the Old. We must notice also that our Lord Jesus was steeped in the Old Testament. He loved the psalms and frequently alluded to the Old Testament, the Scripture of his time. Sometimes it was the way Jesus interpreted the Old Testament that caused outrage among his contemporaries. My hope is that this volume of interpretation and comment will enrich the reader, give a deeper insight into each passage and show something of the relevance for today of this great book.

Ron Dale, July 2003

First Sunday of Advent

Jeremiah 33:14-16

God is a God of righteousness . . . He can be relied upon never to change, never to let us down.

These verses from Jeremiah are located in the context of a series of announcements of salvation. The chapter begins with an introduction that attributes the words that follow to Jeremiah, 'while he was still confined in the court of the guard' (33:1), during the Babylonian siege of Jerusalem. However, there are numerous allusions in the chapter to the circumstances of the Babylonian Exile or even later. References to the city and nation as already destroyed (33:7, 10, 12) are followed by these unconditional promises of restoration. Moreover, the fact that our reading is part of a section (33:14-26) not found in the ancient Greek version of Jeremiah is further indication that it comes from a period later than that of the prophet Jeremiah.

Verses 14-26 in fact contain an exact quotation of lines already found in Jeremiah 23:5-6. They apparently are quoted here to provide a text for the explanation and interpretation that follow in Jeremiah 33:17-26, in the same way that preachers cite a biblical text as the foundation for a sermon. Thus, in the context of our reading, an earlier promise concerning the line of David is called to the attention of a new and later group of hearers who are assured that the hope will one day be fulfilled. The major addition to the text of Jeremiah 23:5-6 is the line 'when I will fulfil the promise I made to the house of Israel and the house of Judah' (verse 14). Those to whom these lines were addressed must have lived in a time when there was no king in the line of David on the throne in Jerusalem, but it is not clear whether the 'righteous Branch' was expected in the near or distant future.

These verses reach to the heart of the Old Testament expectations, assuming the promise, recorded in 2 Samuel 7, of a perpetual kingship in the line of David. The 'messiah' (or 'anointed one') was the title applied to each new monarch. The Davidic monarchy and the assurance that it would be permanent were gifts of divine grace intended to guarantee the peace and security of the people of God (2 Samuel 7:10-13). Because the people experienced rulers who were less than just and righteous, the promise of a 'righteous Branch' was heard through the prophets and was reiterated after the Babylonians brought an end to the Davidic dynasty.

In Jeremiah 33:14-16 it is the Lord who will fulfil the

promise and 'cause a righteous Branch to spring up from David.' Divine intervention is expected, but through a human figure. The language that characterises this figure occurs also in Isaiah 11:1 (cf. also Isaiah 4:2). In Zechariah 3:8 and 6:12, 'branch' may refer to a particular individual in the time of that prophet.

Most important here are the functions of the one whom the Lord will 'cause . . . to spring up'. 'He shall execute justice and righteousness in the land . . . Judah will be saved and Jerusalem will live in safety' (verses 15-16). This language has become such a part of our abstract religious vocabulary that we must remind ourselves of its concreteness. Justice and righteousness – the most familiar pair of terms from the Old Testament prophets – refer to fair and equitable relationships among people, impartial law courts, the protection of the weak from the strong (justice), and the personal characteristics (righteousness) that make such conditions possible. To 'save' Judah and cause Jerusalem to 'live in safety' do not refer in the first instance to religious experiences or practices, but to specific political circumstances: Judah will be free of foreign domination and Jerusalem from fear of invasion.

The functions, then, of the righteous Branch are in the realm of what we would call governmental, political concerns, both domestic and foreign. If the Old Testament lesson has a contribution to make to the beginning of Advent, it is to keep before us God's concern for such matters. The reign of God comes not only beyond time and this world, but also in history and in this world. The righteous Branch, the anointed one of God, comes in human form into a human world. That is not just an ancient Israelite hope, but the Christian expectation at Advent as well.

Gene M. Tucker
Preaching Through the Christian Year: Year C

Mr Righteous

One of the greatest days in my annual diary is Maundy Thursday. For that is the day when I have to attend the Queen at the service of the Royal Maundy. As Lord High Almoner (a somewhat Gilbertian title) it is my duty to arrange the service in a different cathedral each year and to stand alongside the Queen as she gives the red and white purses containing the silver Maundy money to the elderly recipients. As you can imagine, it is a very moving occasion but for me there is nothing quite so spine-tingling as the moment when the chapel royal choir begins to sing Handel's beautiful anthem 'Zadok the Priest', culminating in its repeated cry, 'God save the king, long live the king'. It is enough to set the whole place alight.

But who was Zadok and what did he do to merit being set to music? In the Old Testament, he was probably the most influential priest in King David's court in Jerusalem, and with Nathan the prophet he was responsible for the coronation of Solomon as David's successor. Hence his place in Handel's coronation anthem.

What interests me, however, is his name, Zadok, meaning 'righteous'. Fancy being called Mr Righteous! What a name to have to live up to. I always feel sorry for children who are given virtuous-sounding Christian names that they may not be able to exemplify. Names like Charity, Faith or even Christian. Fortunately Zadok was righteous. He lived out justice and loyalty and was rewarded by being the forerunner of a long line of high priests in Israel.

Going Straight

Hebrew has a number of words associated with the idea of justice and *zedeq* is one. It is translated as either 'righteousness' or 'justice' and one of its adjectives is *zadoq*. In origin it means 'to be straight', like a plumb-line. Then it comes to mean conforming to a norm, and so from there to the qualities we associate with the word 'righteous'. The 'paths of righteousness for his name's sake' that we sing about in the 23rd Psalm are really 'straight paths' along which we ask God to lead us. If we stray from these paths we go wrong and fall into sin.

God is a God of righteousness, he is utterly straight and undevious. He is described in the letter of James as 'the Father of lights with whom there is no variableness, neither shadow of turning' (James 1:17 KJV). He can be relied upon never to change, never to let us down.

And he looks to his people to live similarly, with an uprightness, a moral integrity, a reliability that shows. 'A righteous man who walks in his integrity – blessed are his sons after him!' is how the Book of Proverbs sums it up (Proverbs 20:7). But it is never easy.

I think of the prisoner who is released from prison who makes up his mind that he has had enough of the life of crime and punishment. He declares his intention to 'go straight'. He usually means it when he is talking to the prison governor or chaplain, and they congratulate him (and themselves) that he has learnt his lesson. His words sound less confident when spoken down at the local pub with his old associates and far too frequently he gets drawn back to crime because the weakness that led him there has never been addressed and jobs for ex-prisoners are few and far between. His desire for *zedeq* is praiseworthy. We need to ask ourselves what responsibility we have to help him be more successful in achieving it.

John B. Taylor
Preaching on God's Justice

Second Sunday of Advent

Malachi 3:1-4

Advent is the season of preparation not only for the first coming of our Lord, but also for the second.

That Advent is a time of preparation is clear to all who take the season seriously, especially to all who take seriously the biblical texts associated with Advent. Yet the sense of preparation with which many Christians approach these first four weeks in the church's liturgical year consists of the joyful anticipation of the events of the Bethlehem manger. 'For God so loved the world that he gave his only Son' is perhaps as apt a text as any to summarise our Advent readiness. 'Joy to the world' is as appropriate a hymn as any. Love and joy thus become the watchwords of the season.

While there is no denying the persistent reality of these qualities as Advent themes, it is easy to overlook another reality, and that is that Advent is also a season of anticipation, or even apprehension, over the coming of Christ the Judge, the One who will set straight all the world's wrongs by presiding in glory and in justice over a sinful humankind. In other words, Advent is the season of preparation not only for the first coming of our Lord, but also for the second.

The lection from Malachi 3 brings to the forefront of our thinking these 'other' images of Advent.

Because we have virtually no idea of the historical context in which Malachi lived and worked (or, indeed, whether 'Malachi' is a person's name or simply a euphemism ['my messenger'] for some anonymous prophet or prophets), we are in the dark concerning the immediate object of the prophetic words. Perhaps Malachi is expecting some military figure to be raised up by God to purge evil out of the life of God's people. Or perhaps – and more likely – the prophet is describing some eschatological agent of God who will usher in a final, righteous era in the history of Israel and humankind.

Be that as it may, the church has traditionally interpreted these verses as a statement about John the Baptist and has linked them with Malachi 4:5. A new Elijah will arise, or, in the view of the church, has already arisen in order to judge the people and in order to usher in the coming kingdom of God.

In spite of the fact that John himself is recorded as denying this association (John 1:21), and in spite of other early interpretations that connected the Elijah role with Jesus himself (Matthew 16:14; Luke 9:8), the church has continued to consider the ministry of John as fulfilment of the words of Malachi 3:1-4; 4:5-6.

Our text for this day begins on a note of great good news: the messenger of the Lord of hosts, the God of Israel, is about to appear. The coming of this noble figure is by no means unexpected, for this is the one 'whom you seek,' the one 'in whom you [the people] delight.' (Note carefully here that the 'Lord' [*Adon*] of Malachi 3:1 is not the same as the 'LORD [YHWH] of hosts' of that same verse. The first figure is the messenger of the Lord, the second is the very God of Israel.) Nevertheless, he comes 'suddenly,' and his role is that of the 'messenger of the covenant'. Whatever else this title may represent, it is surely a sign that the work of this messenger, this *Adon*, involves the life of the community of faith, for it is with none other than the faithful people that the Lord holds covenant.

But the glad tidings with which the lection opens are soon transformed into a mood of apprehension. The messenger may be a news bringer, but the news that he brings is a word of judgement. The justice of God, which this coming one represents, is so thorough in its determination that it is doubtful that any may survive unscathed. 'Who can endure the day?' 'Who can stand?' (verse 2). The reason for this tension is announced without equivocation. (The manner in which NRSV divides verse 2 into parts of two paragraphs is not sustained by the Hebrew text nor by the conceptual flow of the passage. It would be preferable to include all of verse 2 in the second paragraph of our lection.)

The messenger of the covenant, as the Lord's agent, will consume human impurities in the same manner in which a metallurgist's fire consumes the dross, and in the same way that a strong detergent eliminates contaminants. The people of God will be reshaped into the image that the Lord intends for them, an image of righteousness. Then and only then will they be able to present righteous offerings to their Lord.

(The specific object of the Lord's judgement would seem to be the priesthood, the 'descendants of Levi' of verse 3. But it is likely that in the prophet's mind the priests are representatives of all Israel.)

Thus, in this text the church is confronted by the reality that the Advent expectation is not just a longing for the 'sweet little Jesus boy' of the wonderful old spiritual. It is also the anticipation that with the coming of God's messenger the world is put on notice that things are about to change, that old wrongs are about to be uprooted and replaced with the values of God. This new day will, in reality, be a return to a former time, the 'days of old' of verse 4, when the world was younger and human life was lived nearer the heart of God.

James D. Newsome
Texts for Preaching: Year C

Justice at Last

There is a saying in the Book of Proverbs, 'He who justifies the wicked and he who condemns the righteous are both alike an abomination to the Lord' (Proverbs 17:15). It sounds so obvious that one wonders why it was necessary even to mention it. But as usual there is more to the proverb than meets the eye. In Hebrew the words 'wicked' and 'righteous' need not in certain contexts refer to a person's moral character. Instead – and this is particularly true in matters of justice – they become technical terms for the person who is in the right (the righteous) and the person who is in the wrong (the wicked or the guilty). In all other respects their characters may be impeccable, or the reverse . . .

The task of judges, whether they are specialists in administering justice, or the disputants' fellow-citizens trying to sort out a quarrel, is to justify (i.e. find in favour of) the person in the right, and to condemn the person in the wrong. As Deuteronomy 25:1 puts it: 'If there be a controversy between men, and they come unto judgement, that the judges may judge them; then they shall justify the righteous and condemn the wicked' (AV). The person who has done nothing wrong cries out to be justified – declared publicly to be what he is: innocent, guiltless. And the judge's job is to do that without being swayed by outside pressure.

This talk of the justification of the righteous leads us naturally on to the New Testament where in his letter to the Romans Paul writes of the one who justifies the ungodly (Romans 4:5). This is an astonishing enlargement of what the Old Testament has been insisting upon; indeed it almost turns it upon its head. But the criterion of judgement has changed through the life, death and resurrection of Jesus Christ. He has died for sinners, not for the righteous. 'God shows his love for us in that while we were yet sinners Christ died for us' (Romans 5:8). As a result of his sacrificial death, sinners may be given the verdict, declared to be innocent before God's judgement seat – not because they are no longer sinners but by reason of their reliance upon the God who in Christ justifies the ungodly.

. . . The cross of Christ . . . is the place of God's justice, the only one available.

There was no other good enough to pay the price of sin:
He only could unlock the gate of Heaven and let us in.

John B. Taylor
Preaching on God's Justice

Third Sunday of Advent

Zephaniah 3:14-20

For as long as God's people can remember, they have been seeking the way home.

No emotion is more welcomed into human life than that of joy. Joy is the realisation that deeply held hopes have been or shortly will be fulfilled. Joy is also the dawning of an understanding that those events which have been most feared will not occur. But if joy is always one of the sweeter sensations of life, especially exultant is that joy which is completely unexpected, or which breaks suddenly into the midst of our gloom.

The present lection from Zephaniah speaks of such joy. Surely those scholars are correct who view Zephaniah 3:14-20 as a post-exilic addition to the corpus of sayings (or writings) of a prophetic individual who lived early in the reign of King Josiah (circa 640–609 BC). Yet in its canonical setting this passage stands as a sudden and not completely anticipated shout of great gladness. It is as if a deep and imponderable cloud had been pierced by a ray of sunlight! A funeral dirge punctuated by a carol of hope!

Would that the historical record had left us more information about the person whose name is associated with this brief anthology. The suggestion of the editorial introduction to the book (Zephaniah 1:1) is that Zephaniah was the great-grandson of Judean King Hezekiah (circa 715–687 BC), of whom the Deuteronomistic historians record that 'he did what was right in the sight of [the Lord]' (2 Kings 18:3). But things had deteriorated to a sorry state by the time of the accession to the throne of Hezekiah's descendant (and thus Zephaniah's cousin) Josiah. During the interim, evil Manasseh had occupied the throne for almost half a century (687–642 BC), with a resulting decay in faithfulness and morality (note 2 Kings 21:1-16). To be sure, Josiah would eventually set things straight (2 Kings 22-23), but that would take time. For the moment, faithful persons like Zephaniah could only lament the terrible realities of their world.

Those realities were so dreadful that the prophet concludes that the Lord has no option but to destroy all creation (Zephaniah 1:2-9). The Lord will invade the darkness of Judah's heart like a person with lamps who ferrets out secret and hidden sins (1:12). The result will be a terrible day of judgement, a 'bitter' day 'of distress and anguish', 'of ruin and devastation', 'of darkness and gloom', 'of clouds and thick darkness', 'of trumpet blast and battle cry'! (1:14-16).

How astonishing, then, to reach the climax of this prophetic anthology and to discover words, not of despair, but of hope and great joy. It is as if the prophet, or someone writing in the prophet's name, has drawn us back from the chasm of judgement at the very last minute, so that our joy is rendered all the more intense because of the hopelessness out of which it has come. In historical terms, it would be more accurate to say that the joy of which 3:14-20 speaks has been generated by the sense that a terrible price has now been paid for the sinfulness of the nation, for almost surely our lection was written from the standpoint of a nation that had survived and recovered from exile. Yet, to return to the shape of the text as the tradition has presented it to us, we cannot escape the remarkable conclusion that that word from God which began as irredeemable judgement has been transformed into trans-cendent gladness. That which once anticipated the silence of the people (1:7) now celebrates their choruses of joy (3:14)!

It goes without saying that the roots of this joy do not lie in the strength or sudden goodness of the people. It is, rather, vested in the grace and benevolence of God. The God who is Israel's judge is also Israel's lover and partner in covenant. 'The king of Israel [the Lord], is in your midst' (verse 15). The people should replace their fear with confidence and strength (verse 16), because the Lord is like a mighty warrior who has championed the cause of the people (verse 17). Since Israel's warrior-God will now 'rejoice' and 'exult', so may Israel be caught up in the same emotions. Since the Lord will 'renew' Israel 'in his love' . . . Israel may accept this love in gladness.

The power of this text as an Advent lection lies not only in its words of joy, but in the particular context in which these words are found. The church's 'ordinary time', that extended season observed before Advent, is, among other things, a reminder of the mundane character of much of life. 'Ordinary time' exists – in part, at least – as a paradigm of a sinful world to which the church is called by God to minister and to witness. The painful reality is, however, that the work of the kingdom is shot through with our own incompetence and sin and, if we were left to our own devices, we would be trapped in the midst of those very forces of darkness against which the church labours.

Advent, then, is the signal that in the midst of human darkness the light shines. The coming One draws near not to condemn the people, but to redeem them and to cast their lives into new patterns and shapes. 'The king of Israel . . . is in your midst' (verse 15) is as sure a message for those who anticipate the birth of the Child as it was for those to whom the prophet spoke long ago.

The result is identical: profound joy and gladness!

James D. Newsome
Texts for Preaching: Year C

Zephaniah 3:20 records God saying to his people, 'At that time I will bring you home,' so a quotation from a sermon by Barbara Brown Taylor which she calls 'None of us is home yet':

My home is a promise I make to myself when I get too tired to go on. 'You can go home soon,' I tell myself, and the knowledge spreads through me like sun on a cold day, so that I *can* go on, for a little longer at least. Several months ago I acted on that promise, leaving the church a little before dark after a long, hard day. Looking out into the parking lot I saw my lone car. I also saw Luther, a homeless man who spends his days walking between the big downtown Atlanta churches in shoes that do not fit. He drinks, and he has lung cancer, and he loves churches.

'Hello, Luther,' I said. He was sitting in the bushes with a bottle in a paper bag. 'Hello, Barbara,' he said. I asked him how he was and got the full answer. None of it made much sense, but then the bottle was empty and things never seemed to get any better for Luther. Finally I wearied of his monologue and said, 'Luther, I've got to go home now.' No sooner had I said it than I regretted it. What a thing to say to someone who did not have one! What an excuse to use with him. The word hung between us for a moment until Luther brushed it aside. 'This is my home,' he said, waving his arm toward the church. 'This is the only home I have.'

Home. What a compelling, elusive word that is. What a strong hunger the human heart has for home, and what a hard thing it is to find and keep a home – not just a building, but a place to belong – a place to be *from* and a place to *go to*. A safe place where one is known and a safe place from which to know the world: a nest, a family, a stable fortress in a vast and often frightening universe.

I had lots of homes, growing up. My family moved eleven times during my first fourteen years; I lived in six different states and went to eight different schools. I left the state where I was born when I was six months old and have never been back. When people ask me where I am from, I hesitate. Shall I lie, or bore them to tears with the truth? 'I am not from anywhere, really.' That is what I usually say. 'We moved a lot.'

And I was not alone. We live in a transient society, full of corporate nomads with children who are good at memorising new addresses and telephone numbers, children who grow up with plenty of houses but no clear sense of home. But it is not necessary to move a lot to lose track of home these days. You can stay put where you are and still feel the ground shift under your feet.

The neighbourhood where you have lived all your life begins to change complexion; property values go way up or way down. Where did home go? The marriage breaks up and the children become commuters, living part-time with each parent. Where did home go? Or your own parents die, and the house you grew up in is taken apart piece by piece. Where did home go?

None of our sanctuaries is invincible. Even the church – the one place that *should* be safe – is subject to the diverse and fractured world in which we live. Brought together by our wish to belong to one family, we sit down around the dinner table and find that we do not agree about what to believe, or how to worship or even about who belongs to the family. We confess that there is one head of our household, but our descriptions of who that is bear little resemblance to one another. Where did home go?

For as long as God's people can remember, they have been seeking the way home. 'A wandering Aramean was my father . . .' That is how the story of Israel begins in the book of Deuteronomy, and that is the story every Hebrew learned to repeat when presenting first fruits to the Lord. However settled God's people became, however prosperous they became in their promised land, they were not to forget the long roundabout journey by which they had been delivered there. Wanderers once, they would be wanderers again, but wherever they went they were to remember: their destination was never Egypt or Jerusalem or Babylon but God, always God.

Barbara Brown Taylor
The Preaching Life

Fourth Sunday of Advent

Micah 5:2-5a

The peace that the world can give is different from that which God bestows . . . the world promises peace, but never gives it.

The prophet Micah was active in the eighth century BC and was a contemporary of Isaiah of Jerusalem, Amos, and Hosea. He was a Judean whose theological perspective closely paralleled that of Isaiah. Both prophets believed that the dynasty of David was God's means of care for the people and that the city of Jerusalem was God's holy place. Micah's message stressed judgement upon the people because of social injustice, especially in high places (see Micah 3:9-12).

On the other hand, the message of the book of Micah is more complicated: God will indeed judge the people and punish them with military defeat and exile; but later, as an act of grace, the Lord will bring them back and establish a reign of perpetual peace, with its centre in Jerusalem and its leader a king in the line of David. The most vivid statement of that promise is Micah 4:1-5, which is virtually identical to Isaiah 2:2-5. This message with salvation as the last word is the result of the history of the book's use and growth through the centuries after the time of the original prophet. Consequently, the book as we have it is the product of generations who heard the word of God in ever new circumstances.

It is not certain whether our reading for the day comes from the time of Micah or later. Because of the reference to the Assyrians in 5:5-6 one must keep open the possibility that the unit as a whole is from Micah in the eighth century. In that case the promise would be the prophetic response to the Assyrian invasions of Israel and Judah and the siege of Jerusalem. On the other hand, the announcement of coming salvation may stem from a time when there was little room for hope, the postexilic period in Judah. The slightly veiled promise of a Davidic ruler would then have been heard by people who no longer had their own king but lived under Persian rule.

Micah 5:2-5a (verses 1-4a in Hebrew) are best understood as part of the immediate unit, verses 1-6. The lectionary doubtless means by verse 5a only the first line of the verse, although it is not even a complete sentence. The unit follows a pattern familiar in the surrounding sections of the book, moving from a description of the present trouble to an announcement of salvation. The present trouble is characterised as a siege of Jerusalem and the abuse of its ruler (verse 1). Salvation is coming first (verses 2-4) through a new ruler who will care for the people 'in the strength of the Lord' so that their security is assured. Second (verses 5-6), peace will be established when 'seven shepherds and eight installed as rulers' are raised up to deliver the land from the Assyrian threat.

The heart of the promise is the expectation of a new ruler in Jerusalem from Bethlehem. Although the promise certainly is messianic – that is, it expects an anointed leader – there is no explicit reference to the promise to the dynasty of David, as in 2 Samuel 7. However, the new ruler, like David, comes from Bethlehem (1 Samuel 17:12). As in the stories of the elevation of David, we hear of the irony that the one who will be 'great to the ends of the earth' (verse 4) comes from the one who is so little among even the clans of Judah (verse 2). The divine destiny of the anticipated ruler is expressed in the phrase 'whose origin is from of old, from ancient days' (verse 2). The reference in verse three to the birth of the ruler – 'when she who is in labour has brought forth' – echoes Isaiah 7:14. But before this one can come, the people must be given up to their enemies and then return – probably an allusion to the Exile and the return from Babylon.

It is the role of the new ruler that most closely expresses both the Old Testament understanding of the function of the Davidic kings and the New Testament hope at the time of the birth of Jesus. The one who comes is sent by God, rules in the Lord's strength, and fulfils God's purpose. That purpose is the care and feeding of the flock and the establishment of peace to the ends of the earth. Just as the kings were seen as God's means of care for the people, so Matthew 2:6 can apply this passage to the birth of Jesus.

Gene M. Tucker
Preaching Through the Christian Year: Year C

'Peace I leave with you: my peace I give unto you, not as the world giveth.' – John 14:27.

All men seek for peace, but they do not seek it where it is to be found. The peace that the world can give is as different from that which God bestows, as God is different from men; or rather, the world promises peace, but never gives it.

It presents some passing pleasures to us, but these cost more than they are worth. It is only the religion of Jesus that can give us peace. This sets us at peace with ourselves; it subdues our passions, and regulates our desires; it consoles us with the hope of everlasting good; it gives us the joy of the holy Spirit; it enables us to be happy; it gives us peace of mind in the midst of outward trials; and as the source from whence it springs is inexhaustible, and as the recesses of the soul which it inhabits are inaccessible to the malignity of man, it is to the righteous a treasure that can never fail.

True peace is the possession of the favour of God. This is to be found only in submission, faith, and obedience to his laws; it is the result of a pure and holy love for him. Resign every forbidden joy; restrain every wish that is not referred to his will; banish all eager desires, all anxiety. Desire only the will of God, seek him alone, and you will find peace; you shall enjoy it in spite of the world. What is it that troubles you? Poverty, neglect, want of success, external or internal troubles? Look upon everything as in the hands of God, and as real blessings that he bestows upon his children, of which you receive your portion. Then, the world may turn its face from you, but nothing will deprive you of peace.

Mrs Follen (translator)
Francois de la M. Fenelon: Selections from the Writings of Fenelon

Christmas Day 1

Isaiah 9:2-7

*In the Christ-child
are the wisdom,
the strength, the
compassion and
the peace of God
himself.*

The scene is a royal coronation. The prophet sees in the young king a child of promise, who will walk in the steps of his great ancestor, David, and fulfil the hopes and aspirations of the nation. The time of war and oppression and suffering is over. On his accession to the throne, the king is acclaimed as God's son and heir. He is given 'throne names', royal titles for the royal task:

Wonderful Counsellor: he will be a wise political leader.

Mighty God (better translated 'Divine Warrior'): he will be strong in battle.

Everlasting Father (better translated 'Father for ever'):
he will care for the welfare of his people.

Prince of Peace: his reign will bring stability, with prosperity. Never again will the nation's security be shattered.

In fact, not even the 'good kings' were able to live up to this ideal. But each Christmas we celebrate the birth of the child who *does* fulfil the prophet's promise. In the Christ-child are the wisdom, the strength, the compassion and the peace of God himself. Faith and hope are renewed as we work and wait for his rule to be established throughout the world.

Revd Preb. Gill Summer
The Ministry of the Word

This is one of the best-known messianic prophecies in the Old Testament and, in its present context, it stands as the impressive climax to Isaiah's memoirs (6:1-9:7). Just as the first series of judgement prophecies (chapters 2-4) ended with a glorious prophecy of hope (4:2-6), so now after the prophet's terrifying vision of the heavenly court (chapter 6), his failure to convince the house of David that God is with us (chapter 7) and his final predictions of distress and darkness (8), there comes this superb dynastic poem picturing the birth of a royal saviour who will establish a kingdom of justice and righteousness.

The continuity of the poem with what goes before is unmistakable. Chapter 8 ended with a picture of darkness that has no dawn and then, with that leap of faith that characterises so much of this book, the text goes on: But there will be no gloom for her that was in anguish; the people who walked in darkness have seen a great light. Whether or not the poem was originally composed by Isaiah, and how early it was placed in its present context, we shall look at in a moment. It certainly fits, as Matthew 4:13-16 illustrates.

As our English versions usually indicate, the messianic poem in verses 2-7 has a structure and a style that prove it was originally an independent poem, whatever its present connection with verse 1. It is obviously written in royal dynastic language and was probably composed for a coronation in Jerusalem. Isaiah himself must have been in Jerusalem for three coronations, those of Jotham (741 BC), Ahaz (736) and Hezehiah (725), and it would make good sense to date it to the last of these celebrations. Not only was this the start of a new reign in Jerusalem; in the previous year the long and oppressive reign of Tiglath-Pileser, whose punishing campaigns in the north have left their mark on Isaianic tradition as we saw, also came to an end. So there were at least two new beginnings to celebrate, and every reason to sing of victory and the end of oppression.

On the other hand, the language and imagery of the poem, the legendary day of Midian, the transcendent names of the new king, the picture of everlasting peace and justice might equally suggest that the poem has no connection with any historical period, but envisages a messianic age far beyond the present, and such a poem might have been composed in Jerusalem at any time from the reign of David onwards. However that may be, no poem would fit more perfectly into the context of Isaianic tradition: light for those in darkness, military imagery, the son of David, and the picture of justice and righteousness in his kingdom are all typically Isaianic themes.

The recent death of Tiglath-Pileser may have given rise to the belief that oppression, symbolised by yoke, staff and rod, was finally over (verse 4). It seemed as if God had stopped beating Israel with the rod of his anger (10:5). The day of Midian is an allusion to the sensational victory of Gideon and his 300 men over 120,000 Midianites (Judges 6:8). No doubt in 612 BC, when Assyria's capital Nineveh fell and her empire came to an end, verses 4 and 5 became even more meaningful (cf. Nahum 3). It might also be significant that Gideon's victory was one in which light, suddenly and decisively, shone in the darkness (Judges 7:20).

John F. A. Sawyer
Isaiah: Volume 1

Darkness in the spiritual life may be due to several causes. It may be psychophysical, that is, the result of illness or over-strain. Here common sense, rest and refreshment, coupled with quiet confidence in God, is the only line to take. It may be due to sin: to self-will or to lack of love or truth. This cause can soon be discovered by one who is sensitive to the voice of the spirit; the only way back is through repentance, followed by the humble effort to wait for God, to follow at his pace, and not to try to force ours. But the darkness of which writers like St John of the Cross speak with such authority is a normal experience, and must be patiently endured. For, just as we cannot look directly at God, who is Light, the glare would be too much for us; we must direct our gaze to him indirectly. The whole principle of the spiritual life is this: that progress will be measured by what is felt to be defeat; that the blind who walk in the darkness of prayer are those who are really seeing most; that light doesn't make things clearer but less clear; that knowledge is perfected in ignorance. In the words of St John of the Cross: The soul makes greatest progress when it travels in the dark, not knowing the way. The truth is that the nearer the soul comes to him it perceives that the darkness is deeper and greater because of its own weakness. So the further a penitent advances, the further from himself he must go, walking by faith and not seeing.

In such darkness there is nothing to fear. The trial is severe, it is true, and there is no getting away from the fact that the darkness is real, and the way seems hard. Often we feel as though we were travelling in the wrong direction; but by faith we know that we are not alone; that God is with us, leading and sustaining us all the time. Gradually, as we learn to adjust ourselves to this new way of living, we begin to understand why God must work in this secret way; he has to do so, because if we could see what he was doing we might become far too much interested in the process, and then we would spoil his work by looking at ourselves instead of at him. All we are asked to do is to keep moving: some run swiftly; some walk; some creep painfully; but everyone who keeps on will reach the goal.

Olive Wyon
On the Way

Christmas Day 2

Isaiah 62:6-12

The prayer of perseverance keeps us following and suffering, not triumphing consciously but just weathering the storm, learning our weakness more and more, being grounded in humility more and more.

The last verse of the chapter translates the metaphor into the classical biblical language of covenant:

> They shall be called, 'The Holy People,
> The Redeemed of the Lord';
> And you shall be called, 'Sought Out,
> A City Not Forsaken . . .'
> (Isaiah 62:12)

The assurance of God's protection and blessing that run throughout the chapter are interwoven with the motif of urgent appeal to the Lord to act. Verse 6 develops a picture of sentinels posted on the walls of Jerusalem who are to 'take no rest' in giving God 'no rest' until God completes the salvific act. The command of God to God's divine assistants to prepare a highway through the wilderness upon which the exiles could return to their homeland is echoed in verse 10, but the new setting gives the words a different significance. The journey, in the literal sense, has been completed; they are in Judah. But in a metaphorical sense, they have a long way to go. The Master's word becomes an admonition to persevere in both faith and hard work as instruments of God's redeeming purpose, never losing sight of the fundamental fact that hope ultimately resides not in human strength but in divine grace. Words taken again from Second Isaiah make the point:

> See, your salvation comes;
> His reward is with him,
> And his recompense before him.
> (Isaiah 62:11; cf. 40:10)

At a point when the pain of delay and the burden of perseverance becomes heavy upon the people, a vision is reformulated in chapters 60-62 and placed at the heart of the struggling community. Lofty in its holy fantasy and elaborate in its hope, it nevertheless gives hints of the struggle of which it is a part, especially in chapter 62. It is entirely fitting that this beautiful heartening vision should have been made the centrepiece of the Third Isaiah corpus. It saves this section of the Bible from becoming hopelessly entangled in the vindictiveness that increasingly grew amidst the hardships and struggles of the restoration community. Even at the most bitter points of the battle, such as the portrait of the Lord as bloody warrior slaying the nations in 63:1-6 or the description of the curse placed upon those perceived to be enemies within the community itself in 65:11-15, chapters 60-62 shed divine light upon a dark human situation. In fact, where the situation becomes the most bleak, the light is seen to shine most brilliantly.

Paul D. Hanson
Isaiah 40-66

Isaiah 62:6-7 tell of sentinels posted on the walls of Jerusalem who are never silent and who remind God and 'give him no rest until he establishes Jerusalem'; sentinels who persevere in their inter- cessory prayer for Jerusalem; hence a short quotation from the writings of Father Andrew on persevering in prayer:

The prayer of *perseverance* keeps us following and suffering, not triumphing consciously but just wea- thering the storm, learning our weakness more and more, being grounded in humility more and more. The fruit of this prayer will be a very humble constancy in the following of our Lord. Supplication and per- severance will bring about in the soul at last a condition of silent contemplation, as the development of the life of prayer issues increasingly in the death of self, the passing from the thought of self, all selfish wants, irritations, resentments, vanities, to the thought of God, his righteousness, his interests. By the way of meditation we are led at last to this prayer, and this is the prayer without ceasing about which St Paul the Apostle speaks.

Father Andrew, SDC
In the Silence

Christmas Day 3

Isaiah 52:7-10

What every man looks for in life is his own salvation and the salvation of the men he lives with.

Zion stands ready, expectant, dressed for the celebration of her release from bondage. But there are two movements in the drama the Teacher wishes to describe before concluding his lesson.

The first comes in 52:7-10, beginning with a jubilant shout from the prophet:

> How beautiful upon the mountains
> Are the feet of the messenger who announces peace,
> Who brings good news,
> Who announces salvation,
> Who says to Zion, 'Your God reigns.'
>
> (Isaiah 52:7)

To those sublime words one commentator replied, 'How strange this mention of feet, one of the ugliest parts of the human body.' Wrong! Human feet in fact are not only beautiful but remarkable. Think for example of the bare feet of a Nigerian Olympian sprinter! But the point regarding the messenger's feet seems to be a different one than a lesson in podiatric aesthetics. Considering the geography and customs of the Near East, we can assume that the messenger's feet, after the long journey over the mountains, were not only dusty but very calloused and perhaps bleeding. To those feet the witness exclaims, 'How beautiful!' For these are feet that bring words that thrill the heart longing for just this announcement, 'Your God reigns.' It is like the old man peering into the still sparkling eyes of his ninety-year-old wife, eyes bordered by wrinkles enfolding the wisdom of a thousand revelations, and exclaiming, 'How beautiful!' It is like the loving husband stroking the stomach of the mother of his children, gently tracing the stretch marks that memorialise her maternal labours, and exclaiming, 'How beautiful!' Yes, indeed, how beautiful these feet bruised on behalf of the blessed mission of proclaiming the coming of salvation.

Who is the messenger, coming with lightning speed, to announce, 'Your God reigns'? Likely it is one of the divine messengers commissioned by God in 40:1-2, 'Comfort, O comfort my people . . . Speak tenderly to Jerusalem.' For the sentinels who observe this remarkable event respond,

'The Lord has comforted his people, he has redeemed Jerusalem' (52:9).

What precisely is this event which is described in 52:8 as 'the return of the Lord to Zion'? Second Isaiah is drawing on a pattern that is very familiar to his audience, it being found in the mythology of all ancient Near Eastern culture. Responding to an attack on the divine realm by ferocious agents of chaos, the warrior God goes forth into battle. After a fierce struggle that threatens to cause the collapse of the divine habitation into primordial formlessness, the warrior God slays monster Chaos, restores order to the life of the gods, and then with the carcass of the slain beast demonstrates consummate artistic skill in fashioning the universe. The mythic drama culminates with watchmen announcing the Warrior's return and with everyone joining in a festival of rejoicing and celebration of the restoration of celestial harmony.

As not infrequently in the Bible, we here find echoes of this mythic drama. In 51:9-10 the battle against the chaos monster Rahab was described. In verses 51:17 and 52:1 Jerusalem/Zion was summoned to rouse herself and prepare herself for a celebration of victory by clothing herself in beautiful garments. The celebration itself breaks forth in 52: 7-10 with the announcement to Zion that the victorious God has returned to the capital city. True to the universal scope of the ancient pattern, the victory is witnessed by all nations, for the restoration thereby accomplished affects the ends of the earth (52:10).

Paul D. Hanson
Isaiah 40-66

What every man looks for in life is his own salvation and the salvation of the men he lives with. By salvation I mean first of all the full discovery of who he himself really is. Then I mean something of the fulfilment of his own God-given powers, in the love of others and of God. I mean also that he cannot find himself in himself alone, but that he must find himself in and through others. Ultimately, these propositions are summed up in two lines of the Gospel: 'If an man would save his life, he must lose it,' and, 'Love one another as I have loved you.' It is also contained in another saying from St Paul: 'We are members one of another.'

The salvation I speak of is not merely a subjective, psychological thing – a self-realisation in the order of nature. It is an objective and mystical reality – the finding of ourselves in Christ, in the spirit, or, if you prefer, in the supernatural order. This includes and sublimates and perfects the natural self-realisation which it to some extent presupposes, and usually effects, and always transcends. Therefore this discovery of ourselves is always a losing of ourselves – a death and a resurrection. 'Your life is hidden with Christ in God.' The discovery of ourselves in God, and of God in ourselves, by a charity that also finds all other men in God with ourselves is, therefore, not the discovery of ourselves but of Christ. First of all, it is the realisation that 'I live, now not I, but Christ liveth in me', and secondly it is the penetration of that tremendous mystery which St Paul sketched out boldly – and darkly – in his great Epistles: the mystery of the recapitulation, the summing up of all in Christ. It is to see the world in Christ, its beginning and its end. To see all things coming forth from God in the Logos who becomes incarnate and descends into the lowest depths of his own creation and gathers all to himself in order to restore it finally to the Father at the end of time. To find 'ourselves', then, is to find not only our poor, limited, perplexed souls, but to find the power of God that raised Christ from the dead and 'built us together in him into a habitation of God in the spirit' (Ephesians 2:22).

Thomas Merton
No Man Is an Island

Because salvation and redemption are the main themes of Isaiah 52:7-10, one final quotation; some wisdom from Paul Tillich:

Who shall be saved, liberated, healed? The fourth gospel says: The world! The reunion with the eternal from which we come, from which we are separated, to which we shall return, is promised to everything that is. We are saved not as individuals but in unity with all others and with the universe. Our own liberation does not leave the enslaved ones alone, our own healing is a part of the great healing of the world. Therefore, two other petitions of our Lord's Prayer also ask the same: Save us from the evil one, and thy Kingdom come! This Kingdom is his creation, liberated and healed. This is what we hope for when we look from time to eternity. Deliver us – heal us – that is the cry of everything that is; of each of us in unity with all mankind and in unity with the whole universe. The divine answer is: I shall return to me what is separated from me because it belongs to me. I am liberating you today as I did before and will do in the future. Today, when you hear these words, 'I am liberating you, I am healing you,' do not resist!

Paul Tillich
The Eternal Now

First Sunday of Christmas

1 Samuel 2:18-20, 26

Hannah enabled Samuel to fulfil his God-given work.

I once read a news item in my newspaper that interested and intrigued me, it also raised all sorts of questions in my mind to do with the nature of motherhood.

Apparently a mother and son were both directors in their family owned business. Mother was Managing Director, son was simply a director.

One day the son told his mother that he had met the girl of his dreams and was going to marry her. Mother, who seemed to be quite possessive, absolutely refused to countenance such a marriage. It would be, as it were, over her dead body. Because neither would give way, the mother sacked her son from the Board of Directors and the son took her to court claiming 'unfair dismissal' and won his case, winning thousands of pounds damages from his mother. I forget what later transpired, but it struck me at the time as a very good example of a mother who could not let go of the 'apron strings' in order to let her son have freedom to make his own decisions. The marriage went ahead, but I do not remember what happened to the company and its Managing Director.

By contrast, today's Old Testament lection tells part of the story of Hannah who WAS prepared to let her son go, indeed she dedicated her son Samuel to God from his early childhood. As his story unfolds it is made quite plain that Samuel became a very great prophet in the land with not one of his words 'falling to the ground,' that is, failing to come true. In letting him go, Hannah enabled Samuel to fulfil his God-given work, and no doubt enjoyed a good relationship with him all her life; though that is my imagination, for nothing is said of how mother and son related.

Hannah's story always reminds me of my own mother who was fiercely possessive of her three sons, but who, at the same time, allowed us enormous freedom to be and do and become what we ourselves chose; and all within the context of a firm but loving discipline within the family.

When I finally left home, my mother burst into tears, but knowing that I was going to become a Christian minister, she told me with tears in her eyes that within the church family I would be blessed by many women who would take a kind of mothering role towards me. My mother was absolutely right, for that is how it turned out over a period of thirty-five years ministry. A lot of hospitality, food, friendship, wisdom and help was given me over the years, and because my mother's love was not a possessive one, I was able to respond to God's call and enjoy a very satisfying and fulfilling ministry.

Ron Dale

Second Sunday of Christmas

Jeremiah 31:7-14

*In every season,
including ours,
the oracle of God
breaks the dread of
exile . . . The only
ground for
newness is God.*

The exile of Israel smells of defeat, despair, and abandonment. Moreover, it is a place of deadly silence. All the voices of possibility have been crushed and nullified. Our capacity to make this text available depends on making two daring connections.

1. The *deadliness of exile* is the context into which Jesus is born and in which Christmas is celebrated. Christmas is an act against exile.

2. The *deadliness of exile* continues to be a metaphor through which to understand *our own social, cultural situation* of defeat, dehumanisation, and despair.

Thus all three settings, in the exile of Jeremiah 31, in the New Testament, and in our time, are closely parallel in their hopelessness. In all three scenes, the gospel flings this strident speech of God.

In the first part of our text, God addresses the exilic community and invites it to a new reality, which is rooted only in God's faithful resolve (verses 7-9).

1. God issues an invitation to Israel in exile filled with glad imperatives (verse 7). In characteristic hymnic fashion, Israel is invited to sing aloud, raise shouts, proclaim, praise, say. These are all acts of joyous assertion which muted Israel thought it could never voice. The reason for the rejoicing is in the substance of the saying, which might be paraphrased: 'The Lord has *saved* the covenant partner!' God intervenes to liberate and new life begins, new life that was not at all expected. The reason for singing is that the deathly grip of Babylon is broken!

2. Verses 8-9 give the reason for the singing. The introductory 'see' invites Israel to notice something utterly new. Now God speaks in the first person. Moreover, God is the willing subject of active verbs that will transform the life of Israel: 'I am going to bring, I will gather, I will lead, I will let them walk.' The poet conjures a great pilgrimage of people headed home, the ones who thought they would never have a home. In that pilgrimage are included the ones who are vulnerable and dependent, the blind, the

lame, the pregnant women. These are the ones who are always at risk. Now, however, that risk is ended; they are safe, kept, and guarded on the way.

Now God addresses the nations (verses 10-14).

1. The speech of God puts the nations on notice (verses 10-11). They will have to yield to God's deep resolve. They will have to release their hostages and forgo their supply of cheap labour. God will be the faithful shepherd who values every sheep, even the lost, even the ones in exile. The nations can do nothing to stop God from this daring resolve.

2. The poet then conjures for us what new life will be like when the exiles come home and the power of fear and death is broken (verses 12-14).

(a) Creation will flourish; there will be extravagant material goods (verse 12). In an arid climate that has only marginal supplies of water, to be by reliable 'brooks of water' (see verse 9) is a powerful image of material well-being. Death is fended off.

(b) Social life will resume (verse 13a). Young people can have their loud, boisterous parties. No one will mind; older people can join in, because such noise is a song of confidence, stability, freedom, and well-being.

(c) Restored creation (verse 12) and restored community (verse 13a) are rooted in God's transformative power. It is God, only God, but surely God, who transforms mourning to joy, exile to homecoming, death to life, sorrow to gladness (verse 13b – compare John 16:20).

(d) An ordained religious community will live in utter well-being (verse 14). People will prosper, priests will prosper. Priests and people together will live in well-being, where blessings abound.

In every season, including ours, the oracle of God breaks the dread of exile. Exiles are those who live in resignation, believing no newness is possible. That gripping hopelessness is not explained by the psychology of modernity, but is a deep theological crisis. The only ground for newness is God. Here God speaks unambiguously, against all our presumed death. It is by the power and faithfulness of God that life begins again.

Walter Brueggemann
Texts for Preaching: Year C

A soul in commerce with her God, is heav'n;
feels not the tumults and the shocks of life;
the whirls of passions, and the strokes of heart.
A Deity believ'd, is joy begun;
a Deity ador'd is joy advanc'd;
a Deity belov'd is joy matur'd.

Edward Young
Night Thoughts

Lord, 'in your presence is the fullness of joy',
for 'the gods whom earth holds sacred are all worthless'.
The gods of status and power and success,
the images that attract our reverence and worship,
all are emptied of ultimate meaning.

On this I make my stand, though you know full well
the strength of their hold on me.
'Enlarge my boundaries.'
Widen my horizons.
'Show me the path of life.'
Let us dwell together so that your joy may be mine,
and my joy complete.

Rex Chapman
A Glimpse of God

Consider first, that although the kingdom of heaven abounds with all that can be imagined good and delightful, yet there is but one sovereign good, in the enjoyment of which consists the essential beatitude, and that is God himself, whom the blessed ever see as he truly is, face to face; and see him in the very centre of their own souls; and by the eternal contemplation of his infinite beauty and truth, together with all his divine attributes and attractions, they are quite ravished and set on fire with seraphic flames of eternal love. By means of this contemplation and love they are closely united by a most pure and amiable union with this sovereign and infinite good, and they eternally enjoy him. He surrounds and penetrates them on all sides with inexpressible delights; he fills their whole souls with himself, the overflowing source of all good; he gives himself to them to be their joy, their treasure, their never-ending bliss; he transforms them in manner to himself, as when brass or iron in the furnace is perfectly penetrated by fire it loseth in a manner its own nature, and becomes all flame and fire. O happy creatures! What can be wanting to complete your joy, who have within and without you the immense ocean of endless felicity?

Richard Challoner
Meditations

Epiphany

Isaiah 60:1-6

God's presence creates newness for the entire world.

Israel has had a long season of darkness (the despair of exile). Now comes its season of light. The light is not self-generated by Israel. It is a gift given by the Lord. In the liturgical life of Israel, God's powerful coming is often presented as the coming of light, though the word used for such light is 'glory'. God's glory 'shines'. And when God's glory (powerful, magisterial presence) 'shines', Israel lives in the glow, and is itself a presence of light in the world. Thus the text that moves Israel from darkness to light is a dramatic move from absence to presence, from despair to hope, from dismay to well-being.

God's coming will decisively transform Israel's circumstance of despondency (Isaiah 60:12). Israel is addressed with an imperative: 'Arise.' The imperative, however, is in fact an invitation. The imperative is not a burden, but good news. The imperative is an invitation for Israel to return to the land of the living.

The ground for the imperative is introduced by 'for' (= because). Israel can arise because 'your light has come.' The words are wondrously and deliberately ambiguous. 'Your light' is in fact the Lord who is Israel's only source of hope and possibility. At the same time, however, 'your light' refers to Israel's own 'glow', which is a gift from the Lord that changes the very character of Israel. Thus 'your light' is both *intrusion from the Lord* and *restored Israel*.

These poetic lines are constructed so that an affirmation of 'God's glory' is stated in verse 1b and reiterated in verse 2d. Between these two affirmations is a statement about darkness and thick darkness, gloom and despair. Thus the 'glory' brackets and comprehends, contains and overwhelms, the darkness.

The poet waxes eloquent and extravagant about the magnet of Jerusalem among the nations (verses 4-7). Something new is happening that Israel could not have expected or believed. When Israel finally lifts its eyes from its despair, it will not believe what it sees! There is a huge procession from all over the known world. Jerusalem had thought itself abandoned; now all the others are making the journey to be in Jerusalem.

On the one hand, 'your sons' and 'your daughters' will come, cared for, protected, valued (verse 4). These are the exiles that have been scattered far from Jerusalem. They have remained scattered long after the 'official return', either because they were restrained by their 'hosts' from coming home, or because they had lost their will and desire and resolve to come home. The light ends the exile. The poet imagines a world in which the abused and nearly forgotten now are drawn back to their proper habitat among God's beloved people.

On the other hand, the procession also includes more than the scattered Jewish exiles. It also includes the 'wealth of the nations' (verse 5). Israel was rarely if ever one of the affluent nations. Most often Israel, in its disadvantage, stood in awe of its more powerful, prosperous neighbours. The poet plays on Israel's long-established sense of disadvantage, of being a rather second-rate people. Now, in this scenario, realities are reversed. The exotic material of the nations, long coveted from a distance, is given to Israel who is the locus of the light in the world. The exiles are not coming home empty-handed. The exiles bring all that the nations can offer – camels, gold, frankincense, and flocks. Damaged Jerusalem has become the pivot and possibility for a new world.

The rhetoric of the poem is double-focused, in a quite careful way. On the one hand there is no doubt that Israel gains as a political, economic power and is assured security and prosperity. On the other hand, that assurance is passionately theological. The exiles bring this much wealth, not to prosper Jerusalem, but to worship the Lord (verse 7). The passage begins in God's glory (verses 1-2) and ends in God's glory (verse 7). Israel's new reality of prosperity exists exactly in the envelope of God's glory.

Whenever the nations bring such exotic gifts, they are in fact submitting themselves to God's new future. That is what is happening with the bringing of 'gold, frankincense, and myrrh' (Matthew 2:11). When God is thus worshipped, Israel prospers, Jerusalem glows, the nations come to their proper existence, all bask in the glow of God's well-being. God's presence creates newness for the entire world. In this poem, all – Jerusalem, the exiles, the nations – receive the gift of life.

Walter Brueggemann
Texts for Preaching: Year C

Isaiah 60:1-6 tells of kings and gold and frankincense, a perfect lead in to the story of the Magi, the Wise Men or as tradition says, Three Kings. So here is Barbara Brown Taylor with her ideas of them in a sermon called 'Home By Another Way':

The story of the magi ranks right up there with the Christmas and Easter stories in terms of snaring the human imagination. Poets as distinct as William Butler Yeats and William Carlos Williams have wrapped words around the visit of the wise men. Longfellow even gave them names: Melchior, Gaspar and Balthasar. Hundreds of artists have painted the scene, including Botticelli and Fra Angelico. Have you ever seen Ghirlandaio's 'Adoration', painted in 1487? In it, the eldest magus kneels before the Christ child, who coyly lifts up his own loincloth to let the old man admire his full humanity.

In more recent years, Garrison Keillor has told the story on National Public Radio's 'Prairie Home Companion,' and James Taylor has written a lilting song from which the title of this sermon comes. So much has been made of this story about which we know so little. They were not kings, of course, and there were not three of them, at least not according to Matthew. We do not know who they were, where they came from, or how many of them there were. We do not know how long it took them to get to Bethlehem or how old Jesus was when they got there. We are not even sure about that famous star.

It is not that the facts don't matter. It is just that they don't matter as much as the stories do, and stories can be true whether they happen or not. You do not have to do archaeology to find out if they are genuine, or spend years in the library combing ancient texts. There is another way home. You just listen to the story. You let it come to life inside of you, and then you decide on the basis of your own tears or laughter whether the story is true. If you are in any doubt, it is always a good idea to watch other people who have listened to the story – just pay attention to how the story affects them over time. Does it make them more, or less human? Does it open them up or shut them down? Does it increase their capacity for joy?

After her own imaginative telling of the Wise Men's story, and after they had presented their gifts to the infant Jesus, Barbara Brown Taylor concludes:

In the morning, the wise men could not find their stars anywhere. They looked in all the corners and under the chairs. The baby's mother even shook out his blankets but after an initial panic the wise men said never mind, they did not need them any more. They had found what they were looking for and they could not lose that. As much as they hated to, they guessed they had better be on their way.

No, they would not be going back through Jerusalem, they said. All three of them had had a dream that said steer clear of Jerusalem, as if they needed to be told. If anyone in Jerusalem knew anything at all they would be here instead of there. Besides, none of their old maps worked anymore. They would find a new way home. So the wise men picked up their packs, which were lighter than before, and then they lined up in front of the baby to thank him for the gifts he had given them. 'What in the world are you talking about?' the baby's mother laughed, and they told her so she could tell him later.

'For this home and the love here,' said the first wise man, who could not remember how to say it in runes.

'For baby flesh,' said the second wise man, who had no interest in living on herbs any more.

'For a really great story,' said the third wise man, who thought telling it would do a lot more for him than walking on coals.

Then the wise men trooped outside, stretched, kissed the baby goodbye, and went home by another way.

Barbara Brown Taylor
Home by Another Way

First Sunday of Epiphany
Ordinary Time 1

Isaiah 43:1-7

God does not cease to comfort his people and to gently soothe their sorrows, so that amid the utmost despair they may preserve their hope firm and unshaken.

1. 'But now, this is what the Lord says – he who created you, O Jacob, he who formed you, O Israel: "Fear not, for I have redeemed you; I have summoned you by name; you are mine."' It is hard to say whether this is a different discourse or the same one as before. The prophets whose writings have come down to us did not separate their discourses into distinct chapters, so as to enable us to know what they spoke each day. For my own part, I think it is probable that this doctrine is connected with the preceding one; he had spoken severely against the Jews and threatened destruction to them, and now he wished to moderate that severity. The Lord always cares for the godly; and wickedness never abounds to such an extent that he does not at the same time preserve his people and provide for their safety, that they may not be involved in similar destruction.

   This passage ought to be carefully noted. It might seem as if everyone is in league to destroy us and that the Lord's anger is burning fiercely and that we are very near destruction. But if just two or three godly people are left, we should not despair, for Jehovah tells them, *'Fear not.'* God does not cease to comfort his people and to gently soothe their sorrows, so that amid the utmost despair they may preserve their hope firm and unshaken.

   'I have summoned you by name.' The verb here means to admit into close relationship, as when we are adopted by God to be his children.

2. 'When you pass through the waters, I will be with you; and when you pass through the rivers, they will not sweep over you. When you walk through the fire, you will not be burned; the flames will not set you ablaze.' This is an anticipation by which the Lord declares that those who rely on his immediate assistance have no reason to sink under adversity. It is stated more fully here than in the preceding verse, because while he shows that the church will not be exempt from calamities and afflictions but must maintain a constant warfare, he encourages patience and courage. In other words, 'The Lord has not redeemed you so that you

might enjoy pleasures and luxuries or so that you might abandon yourself to ease and indolence, but rather so you should be prepared to endure all sorts of evils.'

By *fire* and *waters* he means every kind of miseries to which we are liable in this life. We must contend not just with one kind but with infinitely diversified calamities.

3. 'For I am the Lord, your God, the Holy One of Israel, your Saviour; I give Egypt for your ransom, Cush and Seba in your stead.'

    He confirms the preceding statement by the experience of the past: The Lord had formerly assisted his people in such a manner that it was reasonable and proper for believers to rely on his grace now.

4. 'Since you are precious and honoured in my sight, and because I love you, I will give men in exchange for you, and people in exchange for your life.' By these words God through Isaiah excludes all personal worth on the part of the people, so they would not boast of having obtained anything by their own merit. Indeed, the cause of salvation, and of all the blessings that we receive, is the undeserved love of God. It is also the cause of all our excellence, for if he judged us according to our own qualifications, he would not value us even as straw. We must therefore set aside every idea of merit or of personal worth, of which we have none, and must ascribe everything to the grace of God alone.

5. 'Do not be afraid, for I am with you; I will bring your children from the east and gather you from the west.' Isaiah frequently repeats the exhortation '*Do not be afraid*,' but we ought not to look upon it as being superfluous, for we know and feel how prone we are by nature to fear and distrust. Scarcely any words can express the church's great alarm at that time. As soon as we begin to call God's promises into question, our minds are distracted by various thoughts; we are alarmed and continually tormented by the greatness and diversity of the dangers, until at length we are stupefied and have no perception of the grace of God.

6. 'I will say to the north, "Give them up!" and to the south, "Do not hold them back." Bring my sons from afar and my daughters from the ends of the earth.' These four parts [*east* and *west* in verse 5, *north* and *south* in this verse] include the whole world, as is usual in all languages. But Isaiah speaks in somewhat loftier language than Moses and others, because he wished the people to view the event as if

it had actually occurred. This purpose is admirably served by the lifelike descriptions that bring it before our eyes. He might, indeed, have said it in fewer words, but this manner of address is far more forcible. He represents God as commanding, with supreme authority, all creatures and every part of the world to set his people free.

By *my sons* he means that not all Israel will be gathered, but only that which is the true Israel. Not all who are the physical descendants of Abraham are true Israelites – many of them are illegitimate (see Romans 9:6-7).

7. '. . . everyone who is called by my name, whom I created for my glory . . . ' The Lord testifies that the salvation of his people concerns himself, and he can no more throw away the care of his people than he can expose his name to reproach and disgrace, which he will never do. In a word, his *glory*, of which he is the continual defender, is intimately connected with the salvation of his people.

'*Whom I formed and made.*' God repeats the same thing in many different ways, to amplify it so that they may be more fully convinced that he wishes to carry through to the end the work he has begun.

This passage, therefore, recommends to us the extraordinary grace of God, by which we not only have our human birth but also are renewed in his image.

John Calvin
Isaiah

Isaiah 43 verses 1 and 5 record God saying to his people, 'Do not fear,' and in the New Testament Jesus urges his listeners to 'fear not' (cf. Luke 12:32); so now a story about dealing with fear:

I'm going to begin the story 'Once upon a time . . .', though this story begins, in fact, at the time of the French Revolution, and takes place in France. The central character of the story is Blanche de la Force, and the story begins with her birth – or, rather, it begins with her mother, her aristocratic mother, expecting her birth, travelling home in her carriage, when, for whatever reason, the carriage was overturned. The horses panicked. Rumour had it that Blanche de la Force was born in the half-wrecked carriage. But that was not true. Her mother was confined prematurely, and died soon afterwards. Blanche survived, but only just, the circumstances of her birth.

Not only superstitious people, but also qualified physicians later associated the temperament of Blanche with her birth. She was a fearful child from her first days – fearful if a dog barked, or at the sight of a snail, fearful always that something near her would collapse on her. It was no use explaining there was no cause for alarm. Her proud name – de la Force – was a mockery.

Her father, the Marquis de la Force, engaged an excellent governess to look after her. He himself was an unbeliever, but realised from the first that Blanche, unlike himself, had profound needs of a religious nature. She was by no means unintelligent, and her governess saw to her religious instruction with diligence. So it was not altogether surprising that, after the passage of years, the governess had to inform the Marquis that Blanche had no desire to marry. What she wanted above everything was to become a nun. The Marquis, of course, at first objected, but soon realised his objections would be in vain.

Blanche was immediately happy in the Carmel de Compiegne. That does not mean that all her fears were at an end. Soon after her entrance into the nunnery the Prioress died. Her death struggle was painful beyond words, and for long hours that part of the convent where she lay dying – which was the part where Blanche had her cell – was rent with her cries of agonising pain. Blanche was bewildered and shocked, and asked why God permitted so holy a daughter of his to suffer such pain, and began to fear her own death.

But this was not her most immediate fear. In the year 1789 the National Assembly was taking action against all religious orders, to relieve financial pressures on the state. Blanche dreaded the death of her convent even more than her own death, because it was clearly so close at hand. When Blanche, because of the approaching secular forces, was hurriedly admitted as a postulant into the order, she was given the name of Blanche of the Agony in the Garden.

Blanche was, as we've said, not without intelligence. Some of her questions were profound. One day she asked the Reverend Mother: 'Must fear and horror always be evil? Is it not possible that sometimes they may sometimes be deeper than courage? Is there not virtue in something which is so close to reality: to the terrifying powers of the world – and indeed to the reality of our own weakness and vulnerability?' One of the sisters was scandalised by the very question. 'Poor child,' she said, 'she has come to the convent like a bird seeking a nest. We should have made it clear she will not find it here. This is a place for strong souls. It is certainly no place for waverers.' Meanwhile Blanche, who had shuddered a little when she heard the name that was to be given her, prayed daily: 'O Lord Jesus, in this Garden of Gethsemane, I give myself with you, alongside you, for you and to you.'

It was not long before the agents of the government made themselves known in the neighbourhood. When they arrived at the convent, they soon went from cell to cell interrogating abrasively each of the nuns. Most of them withstood the questioning with boldness and courage. Blanche was so terror stricken she could not utter a word. Indeed, she flew to the arms of her novice mistress, so that her interrogator, an uncouth, humourless sort of fellow, gave a guffaw. He quickly turned his attention to the Reverend Mother, and asked her: did she not fear what the forces of the state had it in their power to achieve? 'How can we fear anything but the thought of displeasing Christ,' she replied: 'Christ, whom you are giving us the honour to proclaim.' When the interrogator departed, the Reverend Mother said to the nuns that she felt 'a tall solemn funeral taper had been lit within her and was bright with light'.

But Blanche was at the end of her tether. Nowadays we would describe her condition as one of near breakdown. She accused herself endlessly of weakness and failure, and begged the forgiveness of the sisters and for their prayers that she should be able to set a stronger example; but she showed her real self in anxiously enquiring again and again where the latest robbery of a convent had taken place.

Reverend Mother went on exhorting her sisters. 'Now is the great hour of the Carmelite Order,' she said. The soldiers were not long in coming, but, before they arrived, one of the sisters had left the convent like a frightened rabbit. They noticed, of course, when one morning Blanche was not at communion; but it was after Mass that they realised she had fled. They were dismayed, but not surprised.

It was the very next day that the sisters were led into the cobbled square of Compiegne. The crowd had gathered before the town hall. They marvelled to see the sisters: their bodies more upright than the soldiers, as they were led to the steps of the scaffold. The crowd stood still at first and for a long time there was virtual silence, save for the soldiers' boots on the cobbles and the sound of them shouting their orders.

Suddenly there was the sound of a single voice singing, a frail, quavering treble voice singing: 'Veni Creator Spiritus.

Come, Holy Ghost, our souls inspire.' As suddenly, the whole crowd took up the sound, full and clear. It was the voice of Blanche of the Agony in the Garden that had begun the singing and inspired every other voice in the crowd. And as the last of the nuns ascended the scaffold it was Blanche who came to join them. There was little sign of courage or defiance about her as she approached the final sacrifice. She looked at best, a reluctant, almost unintentional victim.

Eric James
In Season, out of Season

Second Sunday of Epiphany
Ordinary Time 2

Isaiah 62:1-5

I can't explain it without God . . . when there is pain, I think of him, and when there is joy, I remember.

A City not Forsaken

More painful than captivity or losing one's way is the mental anguish caused by the thought that those able to help have abandoned the search. A prisoner captured by the enemy, a child separated from parents on a wilderness outing, a sailor lost at sea – in each case dread sets in at the thought that the rescuer has given up the search.

The exiles had endured the hardships of exile, had undertaken the risk of returning to a devastated land, had put shoulders to the task of rebuilding the ruins of their nation. All this they endured through the assurances of Second Isaiah that God was present among them fulfilling the promises made through the prophets. But now evidence was mounting that the dawn of the new era of peace and justice was fading in the face of insurmountable obstacles. The resolve necessary to keep the restoration effort on track was being broken by a crescendo of doubts regarding the credibility of Israel's God.

The God who had not prevented the Babylonians and their gods from destroying Jerusalem was still powerless to re-establish the security of the nation. Or perhaps God was indifferent, lacking in resolve or commitment to this small struggling community. All of the talk about God coming as Redeemer was mere wishful thinking. A chill was beginning to encircle the hearts of many within the struggling community.

During the exilic period, Second Isaiah had already confronted the charge of divine indifference within the context of the processions of the Babylonian gods whose devotees boasted of the superiority of Marduk and Nebo over the Lord. The prophet satirised those gods as mere blocks of wood incapable of speech or movement and showing warmth only when cast into the fire for burning. In contrast, Second Isaiah described the Lord as a God filled with passionate concern for the abandoned people:

> For a long time I have held my peace,
> I have kept still and restrained myself;

49

> Now I will cry like a woman in labour,
>   I will gasp and pant.
>
> (Isaiah 42:14)

Effete pride and regal aloofness do not characterise the biblical God. Passion for justice, tender loving care that hurts at the sight of suffering, vulnerability, accessibility, involvement – all of these are of the nature of the God who reaches down to heal and restore. Second Isaiah searched for metaphors that convey this divine passion, and the result is language that can shock and offend, language invoking images of fearless warrior, disappointed lover, angry father, mother in the throes of labour pains.

Third Isaiah faces a community for whom the doubt concerning God's commitment to the well-being of the people has taken another form: They are in their own land, far from the Babylonian gods now humiliated before the superior might of the Persians, but their land is withholding its blessing. The old doubts rise again: 'Is the Lord's hand too short to save, his ear too dull to hear?' (59:1 cf. 50:2)

Disciple again takes cue from Master: Third Isaiah is drawn into action in imitation of the divine passion for the cause of captive Israel earlier described by Second Isaiah in the latter half of chapter 42. The people's cry, raised up to God by an angel in Zechariah 1:12, had to be answered: 'O Lord of hosts, how long will you withhold mercy from Jerusalem and the cities of Judah?' The situation is far too urgent to justify continued restraint!

> For Zion's sake I will not keep silent,
>   and for Jerusalem's sake I will not rest,
> Until her vindication shines out like the dawn,
>   and her salvation like a burning torch.
>
> (Isaiah 62:1)

The Lord's righteous impatience in 42:17 had taken form in a powerful counter attack on the forces of evil (see also verse 13) and in personal involvement in the deliverance of the captives from their oppressors. If we are correct in placing chapters 60-62 at a point early in the activity of Third Isaiah, chronologically not long after the return of the exiles in 538 BC, chapter 62 can be seen as a turning point. The optimism conveyed in the reaffirmation of Second Isaiah's vision of restoration in chapters 60 and 61 is tempered in chapter 62 by another feeling. Sombre intimations of impending crises begin to lead the prophet to a different posture, a more aggressive stance vis-à-vis those perceived as opposing God's purposes. The products of that stance have already been encountered in chapters 57, 58, and 59. They will be found as well in the final four chapters of the book. They do not offer light reading, but neither was the situation of a disintegrating community facing the prophet a light situation.

An aura of urgency runs throughout chapter 62. The change to come will be incisive, discontinuous with the oppressive structures of the past. 'You shall be called by a new name,' Zion is told. The old names recall the suffering and humiliation of defeat and exile.

> You shall no more be termed Forsaken,
>   And your land shall no more be termed Desolate.
>
> (Isaiah 62:4)

Third Isaiah follows Hosea, Jeremiah, and Ezekiel in utilising the marriage metaphor to express the new name, that is, the new status of the people in relation to God:

> You shall be called My Delight Is in Her,
>   And your land Married.
>
> (Isaiah 62:4)

Paul D. Hanson
Isaiah 40-66

In my sermon 'There Is Still God' . . . I began with a reference to my twelve-year-old son's budding agnosticism and to Lorraine Hansbury's play *A Raisin in the Sun* in which Mama, the head of a black household in Chicago's South Side, deals with an agnostic daughter by making her repeat, 'In my mother's house there is still God.' In the body of the sermon I appealed to the evidences for God's existence in two major areas of life – our pains and our joys – neither of which can be fully understood apart from God. I moved quickly from the second area to the conclusion:

I can't explain it without God. Sometimes when I am too busy, or when things are going too smoothly for me, I don't think about him. I don't bow my head and say 'Thank you,' or stop what I am doing and say 'You,' as if he had surprised me again. But when there is pain, I think of him, and when there is joy, I remember. Whenever I get off dead-centre of myself, I see him, and know that he sustains the world I live in, the real world, the world beyond the world of my comfort and forgetfulness.

Then I understand a remark which Tom Stoppard put into his play *Jumpers*, that atheism is only 'a crutch for those who cannot bear the reality of God'. And I remember why the medieval philosophers called him the *ens realissimum*, the 'most real thing there is'. And I recall St Paul's way of putting it, that 'in him we live and move, in him we exist' – *esmen*, in the Greek – 'in him we live and move and ARE'.

And I say, THERE IS STILL GOD IN THIS HOUSE.

John Killinger
Fundamentals of Preaching

My own comment on the above reading is that the House of Israel needed many prophets and wise men (Isaiah among them) to remind them when they strayed and went their own way, when they disobeyed their God, when they resorted to idolatry or when they cried in anguish because of being conquered, exiled and enslaved; they needed a powerful reminder that 'THERE IS STILL GOD IN THIS HOUSE'. Ron Dale

Third Sunday of Epiphany
Ordinary Time 3

Nehemiah 8:1-3, 5-6, 8-10; Corinthians 12:12-31a;
Luke 4:14-21

... the word does for us what it did for ancient Israel. It gives life.

(The following reading by N. T. Wright differs from others I have used in this book in that it expounds the Old Testament, Epistle and Gospel for the day. This means that the Old Testament lection is not as fully expounded as all the rest. Nevertheless I hope each exposition will prove helpful. RWD)

Read the text, and give the sense. Both matter. The first is given, there on the page. The second is risky, a matter of prayer and the Spirit, a deep breath and taking the plunge.

History warns of wrong, sometimes dangerous interpretations. But interpretation is not inevitable; not to interpret is still to interpret. History also remembers defining moments when text and interpretation together create a new world. Ezra and his colleagues read the law and explained it, creating not only post-exilic Judaism but, in a measure today's rabbinic Judaism.

Jesus read Isaiah and interpreted it, setting the stage not only for his own career but also, in a measure, for his followers to our own time. What could be more dramatic than reading the law code to a community, defining them as God's people in a new way, causing simultaneous tears and rejoicing? Perhaps only this: reading prophecies which spoke of future blessing, and declaring that it was already starting to happen.

Ezra's message called forth weeping and celebrating; Jesus' sermon produced both antagonism and loyalty. Luke says that Jesus was already acting 'in the power of the Spirit'; when he applied Isaiah 61 to himself he wasn't simply promoting himself, but explaining what he had been doing. As with other prophecies, being misunderstood came with the package. Ezra had the governor's backing. Jesus stood alone, with Herod not far away, Rome on the horizon, and hostile listeners waiting to pounce.

Whatever reception today's expositor may expect, the vocation is the same. Read the text and explain it. Expect it to create and define the community to evoke joy and sorrow, opposition and enthusiasm. The text may be forgotten, needing to be dusted down and re-presented. It may be well known, needing to be seen in a new light.

Paul's exposition of the unity of Christ's body provides a case in point. If it were read and expounded before the mutually suspicious churches and Christian groupings of our own day; if it were applied in the power of the Spirit to our bizarre and often anachronistic divisions; should we weep in sorrow at our failure to live by it, or throw our hats in the air at the recognition of our real identity and mutual belonging? If someone declared that it was time at last for this Scripture to be fulfilled, would we reject the proposal as dangerous and unworkable, or would we sign up, take the risks, and go with the new movement?

Paul grounds the unity of the Church in the one baptism into Christ's body. If we find it hard to explain the meaning of baptism today, perhaps this is because we are so used to thinking of a variety of different bodies that we can no longer hear what Paul is talking about. Where are today's Ezra's, called to read and teach? Where are today's prophets, prepared to say, 'Now is the moment for this to be fulfilled'?

N. T. Wright
Twelve Months of Sundays: Reflections on Bible Readings: Year C

I vividly remember a number of occasions when I became conscious of 'living between the times'. As a young boy, living through the Second World War, I remember reading newspapers which spoke of 'decisive' battles being fought that would ensure victory for Allied forces fighting Nazi Germany; El Alamein was one such battle, decisively changing the whole course of the war in North Africa. But, in spite of that the 'not yet' of peace was not experienced until some time later. So Vera Lynn would sing: 'There'll be blue birds over, the white cliffs of Dover, *tomorrow* when the world is free.' And in the same song she sang of 'peace ever after,' it was not yet reality, but on its way. An 'in between time'.

Years later, as a teenager and working every night after my 'day job' at my local variety theatre as a stage hand, I remember seeing many of the great music hall stars such as Vic Oliver, Norman Wisdom, Arthur English, Two Ton Tesse O'Shea, and many, many more. The sad thing was that audiences were in steep, and as it proved, terminal decline. People seemed to want something different and so turned to television and the cinema. I sensed that the wonderful people who made their living on the variety stage knew in their heart of hearts that big changes were coming, things could not continue because the crowds were leaving. But in the late 1940s and early 1950s neither cinema nor television had quite got the upper hand; so the old shows and stars battled on. It was again an 'in between time'. Such times are very difficult to live through because everybody knows change is needed, but not many know what that 'change' will require to attract a new audience. The irony is that for a number of years after the demise of the music hall, I saw many of the same faces and acts doing their work of entertaining people on the television and in the cinema. But I still miss the wonderful intimacy, joy and camaraderie of the old time music hall.

Ron Dale

Fourth Sunday of Epiphany
Ordinary Time 4

Jeremiah 1:4-10

*And what
does the Lord
require of you
but to do justice,
and to love
kindness,
and to walk
humbly with
your God?*

In one fashion or another, each of the 'major' prophetic books in the Old Testament, Daniel excepted, contains an account of the Lord's call to the personality whose name the book bears. Isaiah 6:1-8 and Ezekiel 1:1-3:3 thus offer intriguing parallels to the present passage – the account of Jeremiah's call – and, whilst exhibiting a number of important differences, these texts also present several arresting similarities. These include (1) an initial statement by the Lord in which the individual is summoned to speak the prophetic word, (2) a negative reaction by the individual that stresses his weakness or sin, and (3) an infusion of the Spirit of God, symbolised by the Lord's energising of the lips or mouth of the new prophet. (Only in Ezekiel – who is largely a passive personality in the account of his call – is the second feature somewhat muted.)

The Lord's opening statement to the lad Jeremiah would certainly be intimidating to almost anyone. Given what we gather from other passages (see Jeremiah 15:17-18), Jeremiah appears to have been the kind of reflective, private person for whom the hard public life of a the Lord prophet was absolutely repulsive. So it is little wonder that he shrank from the Lord's terrifying summons and from the knowledge that the very God of Israel has intended the prophetic role for him even before the moment of his conception. Yet it was doubtless this cosmic dimension to his self-understanding that enabled Jeremiah to withstand the sufferings and deprivations that were to come (note Jeremiah 20:9).

In some ways, the idea that God has ordained a person for a particular function or vocation strikes a dissonant note in many modern ears. It appears to be the kind of predestination that stifles personal freedom and that portrays God as relating to individuals primarily in terms of their functions in life. Most women and men feel the need to exercise much more initiative in their responses to God's call and, what is more, feel that God has many roles for the faithful person to play over a lifetime. Even ordination to the ministry no longer possesses the kind of finality for many Protestants that it once had.

So how, then, does a modern reader or hearer of this text

understand the uncompromising nature of God's call to Jeremiah?

Perhaps two propositions may be offered as food for thought. The first is that some persons are indeed so inextricably connected with what they do in life that their function, their vocation, is an essential – perhaps *the* essential – expression of their inner being. It is also an outpouring of their very freedom! Can one imagine Leonard Bernstein *not* writing music or conducting an orchestra? Or Bob Hope *not* telling jokes before howling audiences? Or Chuck Yeager *not* flying an airplane? If some persons appear to be 'born' artists or scientists or whatever, those individuals who believe in the power of the Spirit of God would not be surprised to discover that, assuming their work contributes to human well-being, these persons have been 'called' to do what they do by that very Spirit – even if they themselves may not be aware of the work of the Spirit. (Compare the statement about Cyrus' call in Isaiah 45:4-7.)

A second matter is that even though freedom-loving modern women and men often view lifelong commitments with suspicion, this is precisely the nature of the commitments to which God calls us. This is not to suggest that one must hold the same job all one's life or, even less, to suggest that God so 'programmes' individuals that our own wishes and goals are of little importance. It is to suggest, however, that (1) God's ideals for human life – justice and compassion, notably – are also to be lifelong ideals for God's women and men and that, by whatever vocation we earn our bread, we are to shape our lives and to help shape the life of our world according to those ideals. It also means that (2) a life orientated toward justice and compassion is also a life committed to certain persons: God, family, others within the community of faith, and others within communities of our nation and our world. In the thought of the prophets, commitment to ideals and commitment to persons cannot be separated:

> And what does the Lord require of you
> but to do justice, and to love kindness,
> and to walk humbly with your God?

If, then, we are not surprised that Jeremiah shrank from God's call, we should not be surprised that God persisted. In Jeremiah 4:10, as well as in the texts from Isaiah and Ezekiel mentioned above, the prophet submits to an act of God that not only symbolises the prophet's new ability to do the work of God, but also symbolises the internal presence of God's word in the prophet's life. The Lord touches Jeremiah's mouth (verse 9), the seraph brands Isaiah's lips with a hot altar coal (Isaiah 6:6-7), and the unidentified bearer of the divine voice offers Ezekiel a scroll to eat (Ezekiel 3:1-3). In no case has the Lord violated the free will of the individual; the Lord has simply summoned the individual to make his will the Lord's own.

The matter of one's personal call from God will always have about it the aura of mystery, in that we can no more explain why God summons certain persons to do and be what they are than we can explain God's very nature. But there can be no mystery about the reality that God embraces certain hopes for each person and, if we are willing to listen, God will share with us what those hopes are.

James D. Newsome
Texts for Preaching: Year C

When I look back over the years to my own divine call to the Christian ministry within the Methodist Church I realise that whilst I was about 23 years old (not quite like Jeremiah, part of whose response to the call of God was to say to him 'I am only a boy'); the divine call to me was the culmination of many experiences, good and bad, that went before. It has also been a call that has been continually renewed with each passing year.

I regard myself as being extremely fortunate in that the call of God in Christ to me was so vivid and wonderful, something that I can never ever forget, a call that has sustained me over nearly forty years. But before that call was 'given' I went through many difficult times and asked many seemingly unanswerable questions of myself and of God in Christ.

One set of questions that bothered me for twelve long years was, who am I, why am I here, and, where am I going in life?

And then, many experiences in life helped prepare the way for my call to ministry; industrial life in the electrical trade, National Service, mainly in North Africa as a police killer dog handler and the terrible threat of death on more than one occasion, getting to know the Bible by reading it every day. At the outset that meant from cover to cover year in year out with not much guidance because in my ignorance I did not know what a commentary was. The first ones I read proved a real joy as they opened up new worlds for me. Then there was a year of full-time theological and biblical education to pass the necessary examinations to become a local preacher. All of these experiences and much more I believe paved the way for the time when the risen Christ said to me, 'For to this end have I appeared to you, to make you a minister.'

Unlike Jeremiah, Moses and Isaiah who, when called felt their inadequacy, I was assured that Christ the Lord would always strengthen me and also use me. However he has also made me feel my own weakness and constant need of him in ministry. Without him I can do nothing, with him all things are indeed possible, and so it has proved as the years have flown.

Ron Dale

Fifth Sunday of Epiphany/Proper 1
Ordinary Time 5

Isaiah 6:1-8 (9-13)

Together we can hear our calls, and together we can answer them, if only we will listen for the still, small voice that continues to speak to us in the language of our lives.

It is natural to assume that 'the year that King Uzziah died', probably 736 BC, was a turning point in the life and experience of the prophet, since it represents a turning point in the history of Israel. In the first place, it marks the end of a long and prosperous reign, associated with military successes, impressive building operations, agricultural advances – 'for he loved the soil' (2 Chronicles 26:6-15). The year of Uzziah's death also marked the beginning of the Assyrian threat, which hung over Israel and Judah for the rest of the century (2 Kings 15:17-31 – Uzziah is sometimes called Azariah). As early as 738 we hear of the first campaigns of Tiglath-Pileser III (744-727 BC) into Syria and Lebanon, and by 736 he had annexed Gilead and Galilee (2 Kings 15:29). For the prophet, of course, Uzziah's long reign represented a time of decadence, and Tiglath-Pileser was the stick with which the Lord of hosts was going to punish them (10:5).

News of the approaching threat of Assyrian invasion was thus one of the frightening factors in the situation that sparked off his visionary experience described in chapter 6. Maybe another factor in the prophet's terror in the Temple 'in the year that King Uzziah died' was the familiar story of how Uzziah became a leper; for it was in the Temple, before that same altar of incense, that 'leprosy broke out on his forehead' (2 Chronicles 26:16-21). The holiness that made Uzziah a leper can kill and maim; Isaiah discovered it could also cleanse and forgive (6:7).

What the prophet is saying to us, in the context of his terrifying vision, is that holiness is at the heart of his message: the holiness of God, the holiness of men, the holiness that can kill, the holiness that can also forgive. Throughout the sixty-six chapters of the Book of Isaiah, this moment of revelation is alluded to in the continually repeated title 'The Holy One of Israel'. Perhaps it was the eighth-century prophets, especially Isaiah, who discovered the true nature of holiness. A vision of God's perfect holiness, high and lifted up, surrounded by perfect attendants, served to highlight the imperfection and inadequacy of human efforts to achieve holiness, in the Temple and elsewhere. We have heard of the hypocrisy of Judah's leaders, carrying out all the ritual regulations with impeccable devotion, but leading lives of immorality and corruption: 'Even though you make many prayers, I will not listen' (1:15), says the Holy One of Israel. Holiness and justice are inseparably connected: you cannot have one without the other.

In ancient legend people were struck dead for disobeying ritual rules and regulations like the two sons of Aaron (Leviticus 10:1-3) or poor innocent Uzzah (2 Samuel 6:6-7), or indeed King Uzziah himself, although in Uzziah's case ritual disobedience is coupled with arrogance and bad temper (2 Chronicles 26:16-21). But, for Isaiah, holiness is an ethical matter, and uncleanness is not ritual uncleanness, like that of the various forbidden meats (Leviticus 11), or of a leper (Leviticus 13-14), but moral uncleanness – as the preceding five chapters make very clear. The sin for which the prophet is forgiven is his involvement with and contamination by an unclean people, that is to say, arrogant, decadent, dishonest, greedy drunkards and the like, not people who had either accidentally or deliberately offered the wrong sacrifice or missed a solemn assembly.

The other theme in the hymn of the seraphim is the glory of the Lord of hosts. This is creation language, reminiscent of Psalm 8 or Psalm 19 or Isaiah 40 (a chapter which has many connections with chapter 6), and this too has ethical implications as we saw. Before the vast beauty and order of creation, how can people dare to behave with such high-handedness? What is more, this is God's world: let no one forget that, when lands or people are under their care and protection. As we have seen, many of the vices criticised by the prophet can be understood as the misuse of property for selfish ends, and the neglect or exploitation of people in need. The whole earth is God's; if you harm it in any way, you are insulting its Maker (see 5:12).

Verse 4 describes the effect of the vision on the prophet and on the Temple. It seemed to him as if the whole building shook, like Mount Sinai when the Lord descended onto it in fire (Exodus 19:18); and it was filled with smoke, again like Mount Sinai (Exodus 19:18). Like Moses, the prophet was close to God, and the experience was shattering. He uses a rare word probably meaning 'I am doomed' and again the emphasis is on morality. Such a terrifying visionary experience is fairly common in the prophetic literature. Jeremiah describes it as a 'burning fire shut up in my bones' (20:9) and Isaiah speaks elsewhere of 'pangs like the pangs of a woman in travail (21:3). Often the first words spoken by God (or his angels) are therefore 'Fear not!' (e.g. Exodus 20:20; Judges 6:23; Luke 1:13,

30; 2:10). Isaiah, however, can only answer: 'I am a man of unclean lips' (verse 5).

But unlike the sons of Aaron or poor Uzzah or King Uzziah, Isaiah's experience ends with cleansing and forgiveness, not death. The use of a burning coal for the purposes of ritual cleansing is not found anywhere else in the Bible. The idea of cleansing by fire does occur in Malachi (Malachi 3:2-3) and, by implication, in those comparisons of judgement to a furnace in which people are refined (e.g. Isaiah 1:25).

But these passages describe something very different from Isaiah's experience in chapter 6. More to the point may be the idea of punishing 'lying lips' and 'a deceitful tongue' with 'red-hot charcoal' which appears in Psalm 120 (see verse 4). If this was a traditional way of thinking about slander in ancient Israel (James 3:5-6 may be relevant too), then the prophet's vision could be standing it on its head: for Isaiah holiness was an ethical quality, not cultic, and fire on the lips brought him forgiveness and hope, instead of 'staining the whole body, setting on fire the cycle of nature . . .' (James 3:6). Or maybe this was the moment when the fire that later burned in Jeremiah's bones (20:9) entered into Isaiah: Jeremiah 1:9 suggests a connection, as do the verses which follow here.

When the prophet has been forgiven, he overhears a dialogue between God and his heavenly court (just as in 40: 1-8), which he is immediately inspired to interrupt and answer by offering himself, like Moses (Exodus 3:10-11), and indeed Jeremiah (1:4-8), faced with an impossible task as a prophet of the Lord.

The Prophet's Message to a Sinful People

The bitter content of the prophet's message is then spelt out to him in two prophecies of judgement: the first declares that it is too late for repentance (verses 9-10), the second foretells destruction (verses 11-13). The two are linked by the prophet's pathetic attempt to intercede for his people – 'How long, O Lord?' – a cry from the heart that belongs to the language of lamentation. A look at some familiar Psalms will give an idea of what it means:

How long, O Lord? Wilt thou forget me for ever? . . .
How long must I bear pain in my soul,
And have sorrow in my heart all the day?
(13:1-2; cf. 74:10; 90:13)

Like Christ's 'cry of dereliction' on the cross (Psalm 22:1; cf. Mark 15:34), it is not really a question, expecting an answer, but a cry for help: 'Do not let this go on for ever! Do not forsake us!' Amos pleaded for his people when he learnt of the fate that awaited them (Amos 7:2, 5), and Moses offered his life for them (Exodus 32:33). In Isaianic tradition this theme is taken up supremely in chapter 53, where the Servant of the Lord is represented as one who 'bore the sins of many, and made intercession for the transgressors' (verse 12).

This little 'How long, O Lord?' in chapter 6 reveals Isaiah's love for his city, his land and his people, and how hard a task lay before him. But like Jeremiah (7:16) he is not to pray for his people: they are doomed. First he is to tell them to 'hear but not understand, to see but not recognise'. He is to give them ignorance, make them blind and unreceptive; to do all he can to prevent them from seeing the error of their ways and repenting. The irony is unmistakable: whereas, in the normal course of events, a prophet might be expected to teach wisdom and impart knowledge to his audience, and to arouse in their hearts the stirrings of spiritual renewal, Isaiah is instructed to condemn them. In other words they are beyond redemption. This is surely a perfectly understandable view for an eighth-century prophet to come to, and one which was borne out by the tragic events of the latter part of that century. Later writers sought to identify the seeds of hope in many passages (even this one: see below), and there were often other prophets who stood for the exact opposite. Think of Jonah, for example, who protested at the idea of offering the opportunity to repent and the possibility of forgiveness to the Assyrians, or indeed of the author of chapter 40 of the present book. There is no need to agonise over the morality of a God who does not allow repentance. The stern justice of this passage matches the moral horrors of the preceding five chapters, and must surely be contained within the nature of God. Nor need we explain the passage as retrospective, influenced by the prophet's failure to get through to his people. It is the bitter irony of a just God addressing people who mock him (5:19).

Notice how the sarcastic 'this people' is repeated twice rather than the more affectionate 'my people'.

Verse 10 describes the fatal disease with which the prophet is instructed to afflict the people. Three organs are affected: the mind (Hebrew *leb*, 'heart', is the seat of the intellect, not the passions), the eyes and the ears, and according to the last words of the verse, there is no cure. The distinction between the prophet who has 'eyes to see and ears to hear' and his blind insensitive people reappears in the New Testament where these verses are quoted to explain the purpose of the parables: 'To you has been given the secret of the kingdom of God, but for those outside everything is in parables; so that they may indeed see but not perceive . . . ' (Mark 4:11-12).

The description of judgement in verses 11-13 contains several familiar images and ideas, but also some unusual features. Verse 12 seems to refer to deportation and may not go back to the earliest form of the prophecy. This is also suggested by the fact that 'the Lord' is referred to in the third person, while in the rest of the passage he is the speaker. The picture of a deserted land is a familiar one in later parts of the books where for example Zion is triumphantly told:

> You shall no more be termed Forsaken,
> And your land shall no more be termed Desolate,
> But you shall be called My Delight Is in Her,
> And your land Married . . . (62:4)

The rest of the description carries on where chapter 5 left off. The whole land – cities, people, houses – will be devastated. It will be like a forest fire destroying everything in its path, even the mightiest and most ancient trees. This is what 'terebinth' and 'oak' are intended to suggest: the one (often also translated 'oak') is especially mentioned in connection with ancient sanctuaries (Joshua 24:26; Judges 6:11, 19), and the other occurs more than once as a symbol of proud strength (e.g. Isaiah 2:13; Zechariah 11:2). Even they will fall before the fire of God's judgement.

The next part of verse 13 is hard to understand, as you will see if you compare the various English versions:

> 'whose substance is in them, when they cast their
> leaves' (AV)
> 'whose stump remains standing when it is felled' (RSV)
> 'a sacred pole thrown out from its place in a hill-shrine'
> (NEB)

Obviously the key word is the one translated 'substance/ stump/sacred pole', because it is the remnant, it stands for what is left after the disaster. Whatever it means it is identified with the 'holy seed' in the final words of the prophecy, and that is the important thing. However total the devastation, something – be it a mere stump or stick – would survive, and from it would grow 'the noble stem of Jesse' (cf. 11:1), the 'righteous Branch' (Isaiah 4:2; Jeremiah 23:5; 33:15) of David's family tree which would produce, in the fullness of time, 'a Saviour who is Christ the Lord' (Luke 2:11).

Now it is most unlikely that the explanatory note at the end of the chapter, the ray of hope in the midst of judgement, goes back to the original prophecy. As we have seen, Isaiah held out no hope at all to his people. But, building upon the pleading in verse 11 – 'How long, O Lord?' – which shows the prophet still had some sympathy for them, it transforms total gloom into a prophecy of hope. The fire will purify Israel, and in place of former corruption a new king will arise to bring justice and peace, wisdom and understanding into the land (11:1-9). Such was the faith of later Judeans in their Davidic messiah, that a mere 'stump', symbol of total destruction, could be transformed into a sign of hope. The dissident sect, whose writings are nowadays known as the Dead Sea Scrolls, ridiculed this Judean interpretation: their text reads: 'How could this stump be the holy seed?' But for Jews and Christians, ancient and modern, the coming of a son of David who shall be called 'Wonderful Counsellor, Mighty God, Everlasting Father, Prince of Peace' (9:6), the meaning is clear enough.

John F. A. Sawyer
Isaiah (Volume 1) The Daily Study Bible

One of the main themes of Isaiah 6 is the call of God to Isaiah to be his servant. Here is part of an account of the call of God to Barbara Brown Taylor, an American scholar and very fine preacher:

Over the next five years I struggled with the ordination question. I read books, prayed, made appointments with my bishop and cancelled them. I entered diocesan programmes and dropped out of them. I worked as a seminary admin-istrator and a hospital chaplain. I took part-time jobs at churches. I moved a thousand miles away and back again in eight months. I listened for voices in the night and searched the sky for signs. If lasting preoccupation with the church constitutes a call, then I was called, but called to what? One midnight I asked God to tell me as plainly as possible what I was supposed to do.

'Anything that pleases you.' That is the answer that came into my sleepy head.

'What?' I said, waking up. 'What kind of an answer is that?'

'Do anything that pleases you,' the voice in my head said again, 'and belong to me.'

That simplified things considerably. I could pump gas in Idaho or dig latrines in Pago Pago, as far as God was concerned, as long as I remembered whose I was. With no further distress, I decided that it would please me to become a priest, and to spend the rest of my life with a community willing to help me figure out what that meant. It did not strike me as an exalted idea at the time, nor does it seem so now, almost ten years later. The one true turning point in a person's life is when he or she joins the body of Christ, however that comes about – by sprinkling or by immersion, by proxy or by confession. That is the moment we join ranks with God. That is when we become the flesh and blood of God in the world. The decision to become ordained does not supercede that moment; it is simply one way of acting it out, one among very many others.

If my own experience can be trusted, then God does not call us once but many times. There are calls to faith and calls to ordination, but in between there are calls to particular communities and calls to particular tasks within them – calls into and out of relationships as well as calls to seek God wherever God may be found. Sometimes those calls ring clear as bells and sometimes they are barely audible, but in any case we are not meant to hear them all by ourselves. It was part of God's genius to incorporate us as one body, so that our ears have other ears, other eyes, minds, hearts, and voices to help us interpret what we have heard. Together we can hear our calls, and together we can answer them, if only we will listen for the still, small voice that continues to speak to us in the language of our lives.

Barbara Brown Taylor
The Preaching Life

Sixth Sunday of Epiphany/Proper 2
Ordinary Time 6

Jeremiah 17:5-10

The way that leads to life is the way of trust and fruitfulness.

This is an uncompromising passage and one of the Bible's challenges about the two ways. The language and imagery particularly recall Psalm 1. We have no way of knowing who influenced whom, though it is likely that the collection existed in some form at an early stage in Israel's history.

What Jeremiah presents is not two alternative lifestyles; the imagery used, especially that of water, shows that this is a matter of life and death. The personal urgency of the passage suggests that the prophet himself has experienced times of dryness and deadness, his 'dark nights of the soul'. He has survived these and is anxious that others should choose life.

The way that leads to death (verses 5b-6) is one of dryness and fruitlessness. It is one of pride and complacency, relying on human achievement and turning away from God. It leads not only to barrenness, but to a solitary and dehumanizing existence.

By contrast, the way that leads to life (verses 7-8) is the way of trust and fruitfulness. It is part of the creating love of God which causes the desert to bloom as a rose, and is independent of hostile forces represented by heat and drought.

Verses 9 and 10 underline the dependence of all this on the Lord. He cannot be deceived, however much the human heart, fertile in stratagems, tries to deceive him. There is a day of reckoning which is both certain and utterly fair. Here we have both warning and assurance.

Revd Dr Robert Fyall
The Ministry of the Word

I can still remember the excitement I felt when I watched the evening news on television and learned of an amazing surgical operation in South Africa.

It was December 1967 and Doctor Christiaan Barnard had just completed the very first human heart transplant and the television news gave it a huge amount of coverage. It reported how a new heart had been given to Louis Washkansky and mentioned some of the drugs being given to prevent his body rejecting his new heart; but his story inspired me to write a new sermon on the biblical meaning of the word heart.

When I researched the Bible for the sermon and all the commentaries I could use, I found that the word heart in the Bible has nothing to do with the human ticker and everything to do with the mind and the will, so that the heart is the seat of reason and the will. The heart is above all the central place in man to which God turns, where religious experience has its root, which determines conduct. [See TWNT: *Theologisches Worterbuch zum Neuen Testament* edited by G. Kittel]

So when Jeremiah records that the heart is desperately sick, who can know it? In chapter 17:9 he is basically saying that a new mind-set is needed, a purity that Jesus bestows in his Beatitudes when he says: Blessed are the pure in heart, for they will see God. He is saying, among other things, that communion with his heavenly Father is only possible when the thoughts we have are pure and the will accepts what he desires as set forth in the teaching of Jesus and the Ten Commandments. Above all, Jesus calls us to love God and our neighbour with all our heart; in doing so the Law and the Prophets' teaching are fulfilled. Only then will we have not just a fleeting vision of God but complete fellowship with him and living in full accord with his will for us mortals in that realm which is called the Kingdom of God; something which the prophet Jeremiah must have yearned for in his day.

Ron Dale

Seventh Sunday of Epiphany/Proper 3 Ordinary Time 7

Genesis 45:3-11, 15

God takes initiatives for our lives which may run counter to our own best intentions.

Our capacity to know and understand, to decode and analyse bewitches us. We imagine that we can see our life whole and clear, and know how to act wisely. We think we can do it in foreign policy, and we identify where our interests are and make decisions. We can do it at work, for we know who are our allies and our adversaries. We can even do it psychologically, do enough therapy to see clearly and to act differently. Such a capacity for clarity seduces us into being very sure. We end up knowing exactly who we are and who God is and what God wants. It makes us sure and often strident – frequently so sure as to be destructive.

Into the midst of that clarity which gives us control, there is another reality that I announce to you, which is true, whether we like it or not. It is this: There is something hidden, inscrutable, playful, and unresolved about our human lives that warns us not to be too sure. Such a claim is odd and uncomfortable for us, because it robs us of deep certainty and ultimate control. We may say even more: That hidden inscrutable, playful dimension of our life is an arena in which the purposes of God may be at work among us in ways we do not even recognise. This hiddenness must be honoured and taken seriously, because it is a way in which God does for us more than we can do for ourselves. The big word for this hidden power of God is providence. It means that God sees before (*pro-video*), that God knows well ahead of us and takes the lead in our lives. This is not the same as being 'fated', or having our life settled in the stars. It is rather a claim that God is a real power in our lives and is not simply a shadow or mirror of our own good intentions. God takes initiatives for our lives which may run counter to our own best intentions. Faithful people pay attention to this hiddenness and are willingly led by it.

In the Old Testament, the case is Joseph in the book of Genesis. He was deeply resented by his older brothers because he was the family pet. In their resentment, the older brothers sold him off into slavery and pretended he had been killed. He ended up in Egypt. There, after being in prison for a time, he came to great power and influence in the Egyptian government. He turned out, after many years, to be the one who would give food to his needy, starving family. They received help from him, although they did not know who he was. When Joseph finally identified himself to his brothers, they did not recognise him right away. And then, when they recognised him, they were afraid. And with good reason, because he had a lot of unsettled grudges and angers to work out with them. He now had it in his power to banish them, or even to kill them, if he wanted to get even.

If Joseph's life had been only his private story that he could work out according to his loves and his hates, he would have been justified in killing his brothers, for he owed them a good bit of retaliation and getting even.

He does not do that, however, because he does not act out of his own, private inclination. On the face of it, his brothers had maltreated him, and he needed now belatedly to settle accounts. But Joseph, man of faith, takes a second hard look at his life. He is willing to host the hidden, inscrutable, unresolved purpose of God for his life that is beyond his control. He is willing to trust that there is a larger purpose being acted out in and through him, which he must honour and to which he must respond, even if it means denying his first raw inclination of anger and hate.

Thus, after he announces his name, 'I am Joseph', he does two things. First he gives assurance to his brothers that he is not going to kill them. He is not going to continue the vicious circle of fear and hate and violence that they had begun. He is willing to break the vicious circle and act in kindness toward his brothers. He is able to break the vicious circle only because he is willing to trust a purpose for his life that is larger than his own horizon.

Second, he tells his brothers exactly why he is willing to act in such a generous, unexpected way. He says it three times so that they do not miss the point:

God sent me before you to preserve life. (verse 5)
God sent me before you to preserve for you a remnant. (verse 7)
It was not you who sent me here, but God. (verse 8)

God sent, not you, not I, God sent. On that basis, Joseph embraces his brothers, gives them food, welcomes their father, gives them land, and permits them to begin a new life under his protection. He does a complete reversal from his deep resentment to an act of generosity, because he knows God has been at work well beyond him.

No doubt the brothers in their guilt must have thought,

'No, we sent you here, because we hated you and we feared you.' No doubt Joseph answered his brothers, 'I thought that too. But then I became aware that a larger purpose was at work, transcending these petty quarrels, looking far into the future, and I became aware that my life was more than the sum of my little fears, my little hates, and my little loves. My life is larger than I imagined, and I decided to embrace that largeness that is God's gift for my life. I acted differently because I acted in ways befitting God's odd way with my life.'

In his teaching in Luke 6, Jesus seems to take the Joseph narrative as a case in point. In the small, contained world where we live most of the time, we know whom to trust and whom to fear, whom to love and whom to hate. We get it all mapped out into good guys and bad guys, and everything is scheduled and predictable.

Jesus cuts through it all with four abrasive imperatives in verses 27-28:

Love your enemies.
Do good to those who hate you.
Bless those who curse you.
Pray for those who abuse you.

Do what Joseph did. Jesus' teaching is not a scolding. And it is not a little romantic lesson in feeling good about everybody and acting silly. It is rather a rich, evangelical statement that there is more to life than our capacity to contain it all in our little moral categories, whereby life is reduced to a simple set of black/white, yes/no moral choices. For, says Jesus, if you reduced your life to the simple practice of loving your friends and hating your enemies, of being generous only to those you like and trust, and resistant whenever there is risk, what's the big deal? Anybody can do that. Any thief, any sinner, any atheist, any deal cutter, anybody who can count and remember and keep score can do that. But you, says Jesus to his disciples, are not part of that pitiful bunch of frightened people. You know more and you know differently, and you have freedom to act differently. You know about the large purposes of God, and you are called to act concretely as though the purposes of God really did make a difference in your life. For that is what it comes down to: whether God is a real player in our lives, or whether we are in fact fearful, hate-filled atheists who must manage everything on our own, and who in fact love our fear and our anger and our hate and enjoy them a lot. It is wondrous, that right in the middle of all this talk about hate and love and enemies, Jesus speaks about the power of God:

Take another look and consider 'the Most High'.
Take a second look, and see that God is kind to the ungrateful and to the wicked.
Take a painful second look, and see that your Father is merciful, and be merciful.

Act in the world as though the large purposes of God were operative. Then Jesus adds for his disciples three quick imperatives:

Do not judge; you do not have to label and categorise everyone.
Forgive, and you will be forgiven.
Give and it will be given you.

Do not judge . . . forgive . . . give. Forgive, give, share, yield, be generous – because God's powerful generosity moves through and over and in all our categories of control. Our faith invites us to be open to God's generosity, to receive it for ourselves and then for the others. And, like Joseph to his brothers, we break out of our tight, little control that makes us small, and petty, and fearful, and violent.

I am sure it crossed the mind of Joseph that if he was large-spirited, his brothers would take advantage of him. But then he reasoned, it does not matter, because God gives and intends more than the brothers can either give or withhold. In his trust, Joseph decided not to let the smallness of his brothers dictate the terms of his future.

These texts come up in the lectionary, and that is why they are before us here. But I will also tell you why I want to talk about them with you. There is something small and dangerous and brutal happening in our society that is meanspirited. We Christians who know about the merciful, generous God are the ones who must resist and counter that meanspiritedness which is so hateful and killing. I will cite three dimensions of that danger which you know very well.

In terms of *religious morality* it is scary that we are willing and able to sort people out like good potatoes and bad potatoes, and dismiss everyone of whom we disapprove. We act as though we know fully, too fully, the mind of Christ. Such a neat little morality does not allow for the largeness of God's hidden way, which is more generous and more merciful than we can imagine.

In terms of the *economy*, we are on our way to a more and more dangerous division of 'haves' and 'have nots.' We have lost most of our capacity for compassion in our society, and social care that has long been conventional in our history has become an ugly 'liberal' idea. We are on the edge of concluding that poor people are wicked, undeserving people unloved by God, and we lucky ones must be God's chosen. And we construct our economic policies as though these 'enemies' are of no positive interest to us. But these texts cut through our fearful habits, to assert that God's hidden generosity requires us to look again, so that we can escape these comfortable little categories which keep us slotted in hostility.

In terms of *our families*, there is now an epidemic of stress on families. Old resentments surface, unresolved abuses linger – kids who don't act right, mates who behave badly, children that are unproductive embarrass us. Our families, like that of Joseph, become adversarial. The family becomes a powderkeg of hate and fear and resentment that too often ends in abuse, alienation, and violence. And now we, like Joseph, belatedly learn that the family is an area where God's power purposes redefine reality.

When we live according to our fears and our hates, our lives become small and defensive, lacking the deep, joyous generosity of God. If you find some part of your life where your daily round has grown thin and controlling and resentful, then these texts are for you. Life with God is much, much larger, shattering our little categories of control, permitting us to say that God's purposes lead us well beyond ourselves to give and to forgive, to create life we would not have imagined.

This story of Joseph is an affirmation about providence. 'Providence' is scary to 'can-do' Americans. We fear we will lose free will and moral responsibility and all of that. But consider, it will not do to reduce life to our moral calculus, because we become grim and selfish and too sure, and then we die. The counterword on the lips of Joseph and in the life of Jesus in the very heart of the gospel is this:

You need not die, God has sent me to keep you alive.

The terms of life, however, are other than our own. They are the terms of the generous, merciful, giving, forgiving, God. This God invites us to that new life, a second look, and a second life, forgiving, forgiven.

Walter Brueggemann
The Threat of Life: Sermons on Pain, Power, and Weakness

Eighth Sunday of Epiphany
Second Sunday before Lent
Ordinary Time 8 (Alt)

Isaiah 55:10-13

The goal is that the Lord's name be known to all peoples.

One senses that Second Isaiah, after protracted disputations with the exiles and polemics against foreign idols, in these closing words finds rest in the sublime beauty of God's presence. The image in verses 10-11 is suffused with quiet confidence in the triumph of God's righteousness and the trustworthinesss of God's promises. Human beings do not produce the rain and snow. It descends upon the earth apart from human effort, producing grain and food: 'So shall my word be that goes out from my mouth; it shall not return to me empty, but it shall accomplish that which I purpose, and succeed in the thing for which I sent it' (Isaiah 55:11).

The sense that the prophet is arriving at a point of repose, task accomplished and day finished, is reinforced by the inclusio completed here by reference to the word going forth from the mouth of God. For in the call narrative at the beginning of Second Isaiah, the prophet moved from despairing over the grasslike inconstancy of human beings to the dependability of the one central reality that endures: 'The grass withers, the flower fades; but the word of our God will stand for ever' (Isaiah 40:8).

Faithfully, Second Isaiah has delivered that awesome word to despairing human beings, motivated by the belief that upon God's word alone could their personal and corporate lives be reconstructed. At the end of his labours he, like the Servant receiving his reward (53:12), delights in the truth of the word of God: 'It shall not return to me empty, but it shall accomplish that which I purpose, and succeed in the thing for which I sent it.' (Isaiah 55:11)

The Servant and the Word play closely related roles in relation to God's will in Second Isaiah: 'Through him [i.e. the Servant] the will of the Lord shall prosper' . . .

The description of the word of God in the call narrative was followed by an announcement of God's coming to the people: 'Here is your God.' Drama also rounds off Second Isaiah's message, as in verses 12-13 the prophet announces the festive procession of the freed exiles as they return home in joy and peace. It is a fitting conclusion, for ultimately salvation is God's accomplishment, to which human beings need only to open their hearts with rejoicing and their voices with song. In the festive celebration, humanity is joined by nature, for everything in creation is brought to wholeness by the Redeemer. The transformation into glory of all that the Lord has created provides the proper milieu for the abiding presence of the God of glory. Perhaps the most sublime commentary on the biblical theme of God's return to the renewed creation is the one written by John of Patmos: 'See, the home of God is among mortals. He will dwell with them as their God; they will be his peoples, and God himself will be with them; he will wipe every tear from their eyes. Death will be no more; mourning and crying and pain will be no more; for the first things have passed away' (Revelation 21:3-4).

In Second Isaiah's depiction of the procession to Zion (see also Isaiah 35:8-10), as well as in John's vision of the New Jerusalem, we see the completion of the work assigned by God to the heavenly assembly: 'Comfort, O comfort my people, says your God. Speak tenderly to Jerusalem, and cry to her that she has served her term, that her penalty is paid, that she has received from the Lord's hand double for all her sins' (Isaiah 40:1-2).

Once the new creation has been brought to its God-intended fullness, 'It shall be to the Lord for a memorial,' Second Isaiah adds (55:13b). Then it is that not only the prophet but reality in its totality will be gathered to the purpose for which all was created, giving glory to the only one worthy of praise, the Holy One of Israel.

Paul D. Hanson
Isaiah 40-66

On a warm sunny morning during May last year, I walked around the Castle Hill area of Budapest. From there I had a spectacular view of the city along with the river Danube. I had made this visit as a kind of pilgrimage to remember the life and times of a remarkable young Jewess called Betty Schimmel, who loved to spend time in the Castle Hill area with her boyfriend, the great love of her life, Ritchie Kovacs. I looked carefully for their names carved somewhere, but as the whole area was being refurbished, it proved an impossible task.

Betty and Ritchie had a wonderful time together at first, then the Nazis came and they were tragically separated, with Betty and her close family being force marched in the depths of winter, to a concentration camp in Austria. There she suffered intense misery and pain until, half-dead from typhoid fever, she was liberated by American forces. Prior to being liberated Betty prayed to God for the miracle of liberation, but never believed her prayers would be answered. Here now is an extract taken from her story as she recorded it in her book 'To See You Again':

Every night, before we fell into an exhausted sleep, my mother would pray to God for a miracle. Dutifully, we would echo her prayers, but we never believed he would answer them.

There were others who were more optimistic. In fact, one group of women in the camp began collecting scraps of material which they painstakingly sewed into a quilt designed to look like the American flag. I would look at those bright stars and stripes, and the country they represented seemed as remote as the moon.

'The Americans will come, you'll see,' one of these women said to me as I stood looking on as they worked. 'The rumours are everywhere that this can't last much longer.'

I would nod politely, thinking to myself that she was mad. The women were careful to hide their work. They knew they would have paid with their lives if the guards had found this symbol of their perfidy.

Somewhere out there, beyond those grim barbed wire fences, spring was beginning to come to Austria. But inside the camp's boundaries, there was only the winter of death and despair . . . But then:

A woman came running back into the tent, her thin, lined face radiant. 'The Americans are here,' she shouted. 'They've come to save us. The Germans are gone – they've run away. We're free, we're free.'

My sister and brother awake now, we struggled, fighting back tears, trying to take it all in. My mother came over to me and wrapped her arm around my shoulders. 'I told you we would survive this horror.'

Betty Schimmel
To See You Again: The Betty Schimmel Story

Ninth Sunday of Epiphany

1 Kings 8:22-23, 41-43

*We have this
treasure – in
earthen jars – in
order that the
glory may belong
to God.*

First Kings 8, as the account of Solomon's dedication of the temple in Jerusalem, lies at the heart of what later generations considered most important about Solomon. Foremost among his many building projects was the magnificent temple. The verses assigned for reading on this day come from the king's dedicatory prayer. The prayer had been preceded by the account of the assembly and installation of the ark of the covenant in the new building (verses 1-13), and Solomon's address to the assembly (verses 14-21). After the prayer (verses 22-53), the king addresses the people again with a sermon (verses 54-61) and then concludes the ceremony with sacrifices and a feast (verses 62-66).

Virtually all of the chapter bears the marks of the theology and style of the Book of Deuteronomy and thus stems from the Deuteronomistic Historians who were responsible for collecting and editing the account of Israel's history from the time of Moses to the Babylonian Exile (Deuteronomy through 2 Kings). Although there are numerous older and written sources in the work, and there probaby was a pre-exilic edition of it, the work as a whole was completed shortly after the last event it reports (2 Kings 25:27-30), during the Babylonian Exile (circa 560 BC). Consequently the report of the dedication of the temple was composed for a people who had lost their land and Holy City, and knew that the magnificent temple of Solomon lay in ruins.

Solomon's prayer of dedication is a series of four prayers of petition. The first (verses 23-26) is a prayer that God confirm the promise to David that one of his sons would always sit on the throne in Jerusalem. The second (verses 27-30) and fourth (52-53) are general requests that God hear and respond, and the third (verses 31-51) contains a series of petitions concerning seven possible future situations.

Our assigned verses contain the narrative beginning and the initial lines of the first prayer (verses 22-23), and the fifth of the petitions concerning future circumstances (verses 41-43), the one that expects 'foreigners' to come to the temple.

The first verse (verse 22) of the reading, as well as its larger context, invites reflection on prayer, particularly public prayer. Some of the liturgical features are obvious here, and others are not. It is assumed that Israel's kings performed important priestly functions and were a special link between the Lord and the people. As the temple is dedicated, Solomon is said to be standing before the altar and in the presence of the assembled people, but the precise location is difficult to identify. (The parallel account in 2 Chronicles 6:13 has him in the courtyard of the temple on an elevated platform.) The posture of prayer is standing with hands outstretched 'to heaven' (cf. Exodus 9:29; Isaiah 1:15). In view of the fact that gods, like kings, in the ancient Near East generally are pictured as sitting on thrones, the posture of supplication is to stand with outstretched arms. Note, however, that when the prayers are concluded, Solomon is said to have been kneeling before the altar (8:54).

The initial lines of the prayer itself (verse 23) invite reflection on several matters central to the biblical faith. First, the Lord, God of Israel, is addressed as incomparable ('no God like you'). This is not an assertion of monotheism, although it comes close. Rather, it parallels the view of the First commandment ('You shall have no other gods before me,' Exodus 20:3). Devotion to their God, rather than the abstract question of the number of gods, is the central concern for ancient Israel. Second, Israel's God is trust-worthy and loyal, 'keeping covenant' and 'steadfast love' to those who are faithful. These two expressions are virtually synonymous, emphasising the stability of God's relationship with the covenant people.

The petition in verses 41-43 indicates that ancient Israel's concerns reach beyond boundaries of nation and culture. It is an intercessory prayer on behalf of any 'foreigner' who comes to pray in the temple.

If the Lord is incomparable, other peoples will hear and come to worship him. Solomon asks that their prayers be heard. Although stressing the importance of the temple, the petition acknowledges that God's true dwelling place is 'in heaven' (verse 43). The goal is that the Lord's 'name' – who he is and what he has done – be known to all peoples (verse 43). The Lord does not actually dwell in the temple, but it is called by his name, and is the place where he chooses to 'put his name' (Deuteronomy 12:5).

Gene M. Tucker
Preaching Through the Christian Year: Year C

John Killinger, an American minister and formerly Professor of Preaching and Literature at the divinity school, Vanderbilt University, tells how he was once invited to preach to a large congregation at Chautauqua Institute. He was nervous, but comforted by thoughts of some of the great men who had stood in the same pulpit in bygone days. People like Talmage of Brooklyn, Dwight L. Moody, Harry Emmerson Fosdick and George Buttrick among many others. Memories of them made him realise that he was part of a great cloud of witnesses. He then goes on to mention G. A. Johnston Ross who, when invited to be one of the first preachers in the restored abbey at Iona, the ancient Christian community founded by St Columba in the sixth century, said:

As I took my place at the little temporary pulpit beside the ancient altar base, and looked first at my congregation (composed in part of scientific men from England, in part of the aged fishermen whom I had known as stalwart lads) and then through the glassless windows at the burial place of sixty-six of our Scottish and Norwegian kings and earls, whose bodies a thousand years ago had been brought there because of the sanctity of the holy isle, there swept over me (need you wonder?) an awe of the Eternal who had laboured so long within the aspirations of men. What I preached that day is long ago forgotten, as is most meet; but I shall never forget what I was that day – consciously the child of the centuries and of the variegated grace of God which they carried. All petty provincialism was impossible: the broken altar base, the stern lift of the walls, the presence of the august dead forbade. And this elevation of soul and broadening of view do come to the men who appreciate the presence of God in the community of faith.

Community is, after all, what it's about. We are part of a great community. We do not stand on our own platform when we preach, but on the community's. We do not invite people to join ourselves, but the community which is initiated by God, called by God, sustained by God, served by God.

Recognising this makes a great difference in what we preach and in how we approach the task of preaching. It banishes our fears. It identifies our audience. It determines our message. It guarantees our success.

We have this treasure, said Paul – this *inestimable treasure* – in earthen jars – *fragile pottery, not very good for the ages* – in order that the glory may belong to God – *who is not fragile and is building his community for ever.*

John Killinger
Fundamentals of Preaching

Last Sunday of Epiphany
Transfiguration Sunday

Exodus 34:29-35

*The word has
to do with light
and brightness,
not with darkness
and dullness.
The word has
to do with warmth
and passion,
not coldness
and apathy.*

Word and Body

Verses 29-35 report Moses' return from the mountain to the encamped people of Israel. What receives special attention is not Moses' instruction of the people, as important as that is, but the shining appearance of his face (the verb can also be translated 'horned,' leading to many renderings of a horned Moses, e.g. Michelangelo; Chagall). It had its origins in the context of God's speaking with him (verse 29), of which Moses was initially unaware (and hence not of his own doing). Moses wore a veil to conceal this shining, except on two occasions: when God was speaking to him in the sanctuary (see 33:7-11) and when he spoke God's words to the people.

In other words, the face of Moses is *visibly* shining (i.e. unveiled) whenever there is a communicating of the word of God. No reason is given for Moses' wearing a veil when a communication of the word of God is not involved; it may entail a recognition that Moses was not always functioning in this capacity (no doubt to the relief of both Moses and people!). Verses 34-35 show that this is a continuing reality for Israel, beyond this time and place. This suggests that we have to do with a concrete theological symbol, not a historical reality.

While the significance of this shining is much debated, it likely is concerned with two matters:

1. It gives a prominence to the mediator of the word of God in the community of faith. There is a reflection of the effulgence of the glory of God himself in the face of Moses. As such, it is made clearer that Moses is speaking for God. Once again (see 19:9) God sees to an external means by which the mediator of the word of God can be shown to be authentic to the larger community. Appearance does make a difference to words, commanding greater attention and respect. Even more, it shows that Moses is not simply a speaker for the word of God; in some sense he *embodies* that word. The people thus do not only hear that word being spoken, they see it standing before them. There is conveyed in *Moses' own*

body something of the nature of divine communication to the community.

There are affinities here with the appearance of the messenger of God in theophanies (see especially Judges 13:6; Exodus 3:2). In effect, Moses now functions as a divine messenger. In this connection, the reference to Moses' face ties this narrative back to chapter 33 and the issue of the face of God. We are told in 33:11 that God speaks to Moses face-to-face. Yet it is twice stated that God's face cannot be seen in all its fullness, even by Moses (33:20, 23). One might then say that *Moses' shining face is the vision of the face of God which is available to the community of faith* (see the comparable language for Jesus in 2 Corinthians 3:18; 4:6 in a context that works with this Exodus passage; see also the story of Jesus' transfiguration in Matthew 17:1-8). Finally, it might be noted that the use of 'horn' language may be intended as a deliberate correlation of Moses and the golden calf. As such, this may convey to the people (especially in view of 32:1) that their need for a mediator of the word is sufficiently present in Moses; there is no need for a non-living image.

2. The shining conveys something of the nature and significance of the word of God being communicated. The embodiment of the word conveys that which is concrete, tangible, with distinct implications for the life of those who hear that word. The human response can never only be to believe or speak; it must also mean to do, to re-embody the word in the world. Moreover, the word is imaged in a shining, a radiance, a brilliance, an incandescence, a fieriness. As such, it evokes freshness, vividness, intensity, and splendour. The word has to do with light and brightness, not with darkness and dullness. Because it is Moses' skin that is affected, the image may also be one of ruddiness. As such, it evokes ardour, zeal, vigour, and vitality. The word has to do with warmth and passion, not coldness and apathy. All in all, the shining evokes an understanding of the word of God that is living and active, munificently present among the people for their good. The reference to God's face shining on the people in the Aaronic benediction (Numbers 6:25; see Psalm 80) places this understanding into the ongoing worship life of the people. There they are assured of the constancy of the shining face of God.

Moses' shining face anticipates the filling of the tabernacle with the divine glory (Exodus 40:34-38),

81

fore-shadowing that glory in both its radiance and its
veiledness.

Terence E. Fretheim
Exodus

Shekinah

Much of what has been said of glory is true also of the
rabbinical term *shekinah*. Underlying the use of the term 'glory'
is the belief in the Lord's personal presence on earth. He dwelt
among men or caused his name to dwell in the Temple. The
Hebrew root for dwell is *sh-k-n*, from which the post-biblical
word *shekinah* is derived. The use of the term naturally carries
with it the idea of God's presence among men. 'A heathen
asked R. Joshua b. Karha: Why did God speak to Moses from
the thorn bush? R. Joshua replied: If he had spoken from a
carob tree or from a sycamore, you would have asked me the
same question. But so as not to dismiss you without an answer,
God spoke from the thorn bush to teach you that there is no
place where the shekinah is not, not even a thorn bush'
(quoted in Montefiore and Loewe, *Rabbinic Anthology* (1938),
page 13).

Those who live a devout life are worthy to see the face of
the shekinah; but there are four classes of men who do not see
it – mockers, hypocrites, slanderers, liars. The phraseology
sometimes suggests that it is thought of as something distinct
and distinguishable from God: 'I have caused my shekinah to
descend because of Israel.' Alongside the dominant idea of
presence there remains also that of brightness. It is explained
that the brightness on Moses' face as he descended the mount
was because he had shared in the brightness of the glory of the
shekinah whilst on the mount. Its light is said to be more
intense than that of the midsummer sun. But although in these
ways it continued to express the apprehended presence of
God, like the term glory, it was also used as a circumlocution
for God himself; it was simply a reverent equivalent for God,
and is frequently so used in rabbinic literature.

L. H. Brockington
Quoted in *A Theological Word Book of the Bible*

First Sunday of Lent

Deuteronomy 26:1-11

When a people forgets its past, it loses both its present and its future.

It is interesting to scan the index of a standard book of quotations and to notice how differently various writers have responded to the idea of history. (The examples that follow are from *The Oxford Dictionary of Quotations*, 2nd edition; Oxford University Press, 1953.) Some believe that only by understanding the human past can a nation or a society come to terms with its own identity and its own future. Francis Bacon, for example, was of the opinion that 'histories make men wise.' While Samuel Taylor Coleridge appeared to agree, he seemed somewhat less optimistic about the matter, musing that 'if men could learn from history, what lessons it might teach us!' On the other hand, the Victorian writer Charles Kingsley believed that 'history is a pack of lies', at least if we are to believe what his contemporary William Stubbs says about him. And the celebrated philosopher Georg Wilhelm Hegel laid down this pessimistic axiom:

> What experience and history teach is this – that people and governments never have learned anything from history, or acted on principles deduced from it.

The Old Testament is rather clear-headed on this issue. That is especially true with respect to the book of Deuteronomy and that great history which Deuteronomy inspired, the books of Joshua through Second Kings (excluding Ruth). The basic assumption here is that the memory of the community of faith not only allows each generation of God's people to re-live God's great deeds of redemption of the past, but opens them up to God's continuing activity in their own lives. What is more, it is through their common memory that the integrity, the wholeness, of the community is retained across the generations.

> Recite [the traditions of Israel] to your children and talk about them when you are at home and when you are away, when you lie down and when you rise. (Deuteronomy 6:7)

Deuteronomy knows that when a people forgets its past, it loses both its present and its future. It is no accident that Deuteronomy and the Deuteronomistic History contain three important passages that many scholars believe to have been credal statements originally spoken in a context of public worship. As such, these texts provide the ancient Israelite with an opportunity to re-impress on himself or herself and on his or her family an awareness of the presence of God in their lives and an awareness of who they were as people. One of these important texts is the Old Testament lection for this day (notice also Deuteronomy 6:20-25 and Joshua 24:1-28).

It is clear that the setting for Deuteronomy 26:1-11 is a harvest festival, an occasion for celebrating God's gift of the fruitfulness of the earth. Although there were two major festivals of this kind in ancient Israel (not including Passover), the focus here seems to be upon the Festival of Weeks in the spring, also known from the New Testament as Pentecost (Acts 2:1). Occurring seven weeks after Passover, this feast was held to observe the conclusion of the harvest of grains and cereal produce. (The Festival of Booths in the autumn celebrated the harvest of vines and fruit trees.) According to the instructions at the beginning of the passage, the worshipper is to come to the sanctuary bringing as a gift to God a basket containing a portion of the actual harvest, in effect returning to God a small part of that which God's grace has bestowed on the worshipper.

The heart of the passage is the confession that is to come from the lips of the worshipping Israelite (verses 5-9). It is a recital of Israel's history, beginning from the time of Israel's earliest ancestors (Jacob is probably the 'wandering Aramean' of verse 5) and continuing until the settlement in the Land of Promise. Throughout this brief but revealing text, emphasis is placed on the grace of God, who in response to the cries of the people, saved them when they were unable to save themselves. From a situation of danger and oppression in an alien land, God brought them to safety in their own home. The basket of produce in the hands of the worshipper is itself evidence of God's continuing care of the people in their land.

Thus the moment celebrates the past. It also rejoices in the people's future under the benevolent rule of their God. Beyond that, however, the history that is recited here, and thus re-impressed on the memory, is the means by which the community of faith understands its own identity.

The Christian faith is also based on the collective memory of the people of Christ (1 Corinthians 11:24), and it goes without saying that the church's memory – its creeds, if you will – celebrates God's saving deeds of the past and God's continuing promise to redeem now and in the future. The church's story is also the means by which Christian people identify themselves both individually and corporately. All of this is so axiomatic and self-evident that it would seem to need no repetition. Yet the matter is so foundational and crucial to the life and identity of the Christian community that it needs to be repeated over and again, especially in an age that, in some respects, has so little regard for history of any kind.

Yet a caveat is in order. A people's memory is a beneficial force in their lives and in the lives of others only to the extent that it reminds the owners of the memory that there are other stories and other memories. One of the challenges facing the twenty-first century is how humankind's many-splendoured ethnic and religious memories may be used in the service of the whole human family. If the ancient hatreds are ever to be laid to rest, some selective forgetfulness must take place or humans will continue to fight the old battles over and over. So George Santayana was only partly right. It may be true, as he wrote, that those who 'cannot remember their past are doomed to repeat it', but it is also true that those who remember history too vividly are doomed to be enslaved by it.

James D. Newsome
Texts for Preaching: Year C

The Affluent Society

The old man
sat alone in the sun;
thinking of Arthur his
friend drowned in the mud
at Flanders, his only son lost
at sea in '42, and watching
the village youths spraying
obscenities on the wall
of the church.
Who is left to die
for freedom? he
thought.

The Death Touch

When a daughter went
away to college, she reluctantly
left her plants and her
goldfish in her mother's care.
Once the daughter telephoned
and her mother confessed
that the plants and
the goldfish had died.
There was a prolonged silence.
Finally, in a small voice,
the daughter asked,
'How's Dad?'

H. O. Phillips and Dawn Hunt respectively
Taken from *The Book of Mini Sagas*
Ed. Brian Aldiss

Second Sunday of Lent

Genesis 15:1-12, 17-18

. . . this letting go is itself the heart of prayer: the cry of the heart that has emptied itself of everything that is most precious to it . . . so that it may be filled with the fire of the living God.

The Covenant with Abram

The covenant with Noah had consisted in an open covenant for the whole human race, but now God makes a special covenant with Abram, making Abram and his family specially chosen. In one sense this is only a repetition of the call in chapter 12; in another it is an important new stage in which God formally binds himself by ritual. In this sense it already looks forward to the definitive covenant on Sinai which embraces the whole people of Israel.

The incident begins with an assurance by God, which is little more than a repetition of the promise given in chapter 12. But this time Abram demurs and questions God's earnestness, since he is childless.

The horror of childlessness appears on two levels: firstly, the primitive state of belief in a future after death makes continuance of the line by means of children all the more important; the dead person simply returns to the fathers, and an heir carries on his personality.

Secondly, in a primitive desert nomadic experience, old people, unsupported by the vigour of youth, are in a truly sorry state. It is common enough today in Palestine that when a father has a son he deserts his own name and renames himself the father of his son: Abu Dahud, the father of David. So important is an heir. If Abram has no heir of his family, he will have to adopt a member of his household as his heir, a process well attested in ancient Mesopotamian legislation.

The Faith of Abram

After the repetition of the promise, however, comes the first crucial reference to Abram's faith, which 'was reckoned to him as uprightness' (NRSV and many modern translations use the word 'righteousness'). For Christians this statement is irrevocably marked by the use made of it by Paul in his letters to the Galatians and Romans. There he uses it in a particular theological context, controversy over the value and function of the Mosaic Law. Paul insists that no observance of the Law can merit uprightness: God's original promise, long before the Law was given, was not to those who observed the Law, but to those who had faith in him, a faith which is now fulfilled in Christ, his Son.

The sense of two words, 'faith' and 'uprightness', to the Hebrew mind is clearly crucial. The latter concept is straightforward enough: there is no lack or deficiency in something 'upright'. An upright weight is the true, correct weight, not one which defrauds. Someone who rightly wins, in a battle or controversy as well as a law court, is vindicated and is considered upright. People who are true to themselves and their promises are upright. It is perhaps, as much as anything, a conception of wholeness. So for Abram this made him all he should be, this was all that was necessary, he was complete and pleasing to God.

The idea behind 'faith' here is nothing to do with intellectual belief. The basic idea here expressed by 'put his faith' is finding reliability, firmness and stability. The root word is 'Amen'. 'Amen' is a response and an acceptance. You say a prayer and I add 'Amen' to express that it is my prayer too. You challenge me to an oath and I say 'Amen' to show that I bind myself to that oath. I make that prayer or that oath firm. So when Paul calls Christ the 'Amen' of the Father (2 Corinthians 1:19-20), he means that in Christ the promises of the Father are realised and fulfilled. So in this case of Abram it means he placed all his confidence in God and ceased to worry.

The Ritual

The scene of the covenant is mysterious and awesome, in the darkness after sunset, when a trance or a deep, dark dread has come upon Abram. Is it a dream or a waking reality? The ritual of cleaving the victims in two has a magical origin: may the two halves come together again if I break my oath. Normally the two parties making the pact or contract take the path between the halves of the victims. In this case only God, under the awesome image of the smoking torch, takes the path, for the pact is one-sided: God is binding himself, and Abram is only the recipient of the promise.

Henry Wansbrough
Genesis: The People's Bible Commentary

The Wilderness of Faith

Today in our uneasy culture of casual brutality, nuclear intimidation, and the cheapness of life, we are constantly faced with outward and visible signs of an immense inward and spiritual grace, a gift of the Holy Spirit, which is to *let go*. The various processes of letting go can be thought of as a holocaust, of letting go of the familiar and therefore safe concepts of self, of how things ought to be and never will, of how they have been – so we can bring about the genuinely new order which is the only means by which the earth will survive; of going out, like Abram, from all that is familiar, from the illusion of security into the desert where fire falls from heaven.

For all the world has become this desert. Here, in our wanderings, we are called to make each place, like Little Gidding, a place where prayer can be valid. And then to let it go; to make each step, each moment, a holocaust of prayer, praise, and thanksgiving, and then let it go. And this letting go is itself the heart of prayer: the cry of the heart that has emptied itself of everything that is most precious to it – even its own idea of itself – so that it may be filled with the fire of the living God.

We are all journeying into the wilderness of faith, and we are all, though it may remain completely hidden, given one of the greatest gifts God gives of himself: the gift of Abraham – to go into the Promise, into the vows we have made by our baptism, knowing that we are called out of all that is familiar, to bless God for it, to bless the unknown, to bless, finally, even our own death.

The future is always unknown, but in these latter days there are no longer even any inklings of what will be asked of us, whether city dweller or woodland hermit. Only one thing is sure: that we will be asked to accept, thank, offer and repent in the midst of constant flux.

Maggie Ross
The Fire of Your Life: A Solitude Shared

Third Sunday of Lent

Isaiah 55:1-9; 1 Corinthians 10:1-13; Luke 13:1-9

Amid stormy temptations Christians are to cling to the faithfulness of God, who will enable them to come through.

Just in case anyone thought the Old Testament was all gloomy and the New cheerful, here are two passages of dire warning from the New Testament preceded by a warm, redeeming invitation from the Old. Underlying both is God's summons to accept his mercy and his way now, while there is time: 'Seek the Lord while he may be found, call on him while he is near.' Unstated, but powerfully implied, is the message which Isaiah had in common with Luke's Jesus. 'The time may come when you wish you had.'

Jesus' warnings about coming judgement should not be mistaken for old fashioned hell-fire preaching. Focus on the 'likewise' in verses 3 and 5: 'Unless you repent, you will perish as they did.' Who are 'they'? The Galileans cut down by Roman swords in the Temple; the Jerusalemites crushed when the tower of Siloam fell. What does 'repent' mean in this context, then? Not simply 'give up your private sins'; rather 'turn from your headlong flight way from God's mercy, from your quest for your own national salvation by rebellion against Rome.' Unless you give it up, Roman swords and falling stonework will be your lot, not as an arbitrary punishment from a vengeful God but as a direct result of the way you have freely chosen, following your own thoughts rather than God's thoughts. Jesus' tough little parable, then, relates directly to his own work; he has been coming to Israel, seeking fruit and finding none, and now is offering one last chance. As he says at the end of the chapter, he has longed to gather Jerusalem as a hen gathers her chicks for safety under her wings, but the offer has been refused.

Worryingly, Paul confronts Christians with more or less the same challenge. Don't think that baptism and Eucharist will magically save you; they put you in the same position as the Israelites in the wilderness, and look what happened to them. Gospel symbols invoke God's presence, but doing that while misbehaving is thumbing one's nose at divine mercy. 1 Corinthians 10 joins strong sacramental and pastoral theology. When faced with idolatry or immorality, Paul doesn't pretend that baptism and Eucharist don't mean anything; nor does he suggest that they exempt one from moral obligation. Nor, however, does he suppose that Christians have to meet this challenge unaided. Amid stormy temptations they are to cling to the faithfulness of God, who will enable them to come through.

Back, then, to Isaiah. Why does he explain the invitation to return (verses 6-7) by saying that God thinks differently from how we do (verses 8-9)? Presumably because no human being would have been faithful and merciful when faced with Israel's rebellion. Isaiah appeals to the transcendence of God, not to frighten, but to explain just how much more generous and merciful God is than we could ever have imagined. Not for nothing is he called, in the old sense, the evangelical prophet.

N. T. Wright
Twelve Months of Sundays: Reflections on Bible Readings: Year C

Fourth Sunday of Lent

Joshua 5:9-12

And the people
praise the Lord!

The words from an old spiritual might serve as a summary of this brief lectionary text: 'There's a new day dawnin', yes, my Lord.' These verses from Joshua 5 relate in terse, almost telegraphic language the story of Israel's first Passover celebration in the Land of Promise. Unlike the accounts of some later Passover celebrations (compare 2 Chronicles 30), we are given so little detail in this passage that it is easy for the reader who is working through the book of Joshua in systematic fashion almost not to notice. However, one should not be misled by the understated character of the narrative, for this is a signal moment in the history of Israel's life in the land.

A few pages earlier, at the beginning of the book, we are reminded of Moses' death (Joshua 1:1; compare Deuteronomy 34) and are informed that the nation is now under the leadership of his divinely appointed successor, Joshua. Immediately Joshua begins preparations for entering the land, directing the people to be ready (Joshua 1:11) and despatching scouts to reconnoitre (chapter 2). Then as the people cross, led by the priests carrying the Ark of the Covenant, the waters of the Jordan are turned back so that the people cross over on dry land (chapter 3). At this point the text goes out of its way to emphasise the miraculous nature of the crossing, calling attention to the oversized condition of the river, swollen by spring floods (3:15). What is more, the geographical location, 'opposite Jericho' (3:16), is near the mouth of the river, and thus the people confront the river at a spot where, under any circumstances, its expanse is the widest.

Thus, the crossing is clearly carried out under the direct intervention of the Lord, a miracle of God. A passing reference by the writer(s) to the earlier crossing of the Red Sea is reserved for somewhat later in the narrative (4:23), but it would be abundantly evident to any devout reader of this text that the authority of Israel's God, previously exercised so decisively over the sea, is now on display again as the power of the surging Jordan is tamed for the benefit of the people. This would not be the last time that an ancient Hebrew writer would subtly invoke the images of the exodus as a model of God's saving activity in Israel's present (compare Isaiah 43:16-21, the lection for the Fifth Sunday in Lent, this year).

A stone memorial is then erected on the spot of the crossing in order that all future generations might remember the greatness of the Lord (Joshua 4; note especially verses 21-24). Also, because the practice of circumcision had been discontinued in the wilderness, thus permitting an entire generation of Hebrew males to grow up without this ritual reminder of the Lord's covenant (see Genesis 17:1-14), there is a mass circumcision (Joshua 5:2-9) – as with the about-to-be-celebrated Passover, the first observance of this important rite in the Land of Promise.

The text appointed by the lectionary begins at verse 9, but because this verse forms the conclusion to the narrative of the circumcision of the nation, it does not make much sense unless verse 8 is included in the lectionary reading. The meaning of the phrase 'the disgrace of Egypt' is not quite clear, but it almost certainly refers to the conditions of oppression forced upon the Israelites by their Pharonic masters. On one level, verse 9 is an attempt to provide a logical explanation for the name Gilgal, a word akin the Hebrew verb meaning to roll. (Incidentally, this is one of our best clues to the location of the settlement of Gilgal, that is, that it is near Jericho. The exact site of this important town – see 1 Samuel 11:14-15; Amos 5:5 – has never been identified.) But on a deeper level, Josua 5:9 is a declaration of freedom, a manner of asserting that the old has passed away (the slavery of Egypt, the nomads' wandering in the wilderness) and that the new is at hand (life in the Land of Promise). Perhaps this association between the new freedom of the people and the city of Gilgal accounts for the reference to this site in connection with the establishment of Israel's monarchy (1 Samuel 11:14-15).

The first-ever-in-the-land Passover is celebrated, just when it should be, that is, on the 14th of Abib (Joshua 5:10; compare Leviticus 23:5; Deuteronomy 16:1). This most important meal in the liturgical year of ancient Israel is on this occasion made up of foodstuffs produced in the land. (The text does not address the moral question of how the tribes obtained produce sown and raised by other people.) And immediately the manna ceases: 'The Israelites no longer had manna; they ate the crops of the land of Canaan that year' (Joshua 5:12).

Thus an essential promise of the Lord has been kept. To be sure, the nation will undergo many adventures before the land is their possession in anything approaching a complete sense. But they are here – now! The Land of Promise is not some distant goal, but is beneath their feet. And the tribes greet 'this new day dawnin' in the most appropriate manner possible: they give thanks to God for this present grace by recalling the grace of God of old. Red Sea and Jordan co-mingle. And the people praise the Lord!

James D. Newsome
Texts for Preaching: Year C

Having worked as a stage hand in one of the last surviving old time Music Halls I have grieved over the demise of such theatres, but enjoyed many visits to other theatres to see a wide variety of plays. However, as the years have passed, I have come to enjoy the cinema even more because of the amazing spectacular visual treats in such films as *Lord of the Rings* and any thriller in the James Bond mode.

One film I did enjoy some years ago was called *Driving Miss Daisy*. It starred Jessica Tandy in her 80th year who won an Oscar for her performance as a wealthy, aristocratic lady living in Atlanta, Georgia. Her social life included many a whist drive, meeting friends for social chit-chat and regular visits to the shopping mall.

Now because Miss Daisy has an accident in driving out of her garage, her son insists that she has a chauffeur and promptly employs a local black resident for the job. At first Miss Daisy refuses to be driven to the shopping mall, but slowly comes round to accept the idea and eventually there blossoms a deep and loving friendship between Miss Daisy and her driver. As the years swiftly fly, Miss Daisy is forced to give up her own home and moves into residential care and it is in that home that some of the closing scenes are shot. One of the most memorable is the sight of the old chauffeur feeding Miss Daisy with a spoon because she is helpless. The scene reveals a loving intimacy that is very moving.

It occurred to me after pondering the film, that Miss Daisy slowly recognised that her old way of life was finished. No more whist parties, no more visits to her friends' homes, no more shopping; and with her family home being sold, no more place that she could call home. As I thought of all this it occurred to me that in a sense her chauffeur's old way of life had finished also. He was now retired and spent time visiting Miss Daisy and driving her old car as he had bought it from her.

Our lection today is I believe an illustration of an old way of life ending and a new one opening up for the Israelites. They were no longer nomads in the wilderness and as soon as they had entered the Land of Promise, the manna, the food that had sustained them in their desert wanderings, ceased instantly. For now they were in the land that God had promised, a land 'flowing with milk and honey'. Now the living in tents and much travelling was a thing of the past. For now they would experience a settled way of living and growing and harvesting their own crops. But not everything from the past way of life had gone, because the ritual of Passover, their worship of their God continued to influence and shape their lifestyle and they were to discover that the God who had led them out of slavery in Egypt with a Pillar of Cloud by day and a Pillar of Fire by night continued to be with them in the Land of Promise. They were to learn that though the past way of life was gone for ever, the God who shaped them in the past would send prophets and wise men, leaders and sages to inform the present and point to an even brighter future when their Messiah would come and make all things new.

Ron Dale

Fifth Sunday of Lent

Isaiah 43:16-21

*Only those who
have experienced
the creating and
saving love of God
can adequately
declare that God
to others.*

This part of Isaiah has as its overall theme the gracious salvation of God and the way he will use his servant Israel to bring this about. Here, this is related to his nature shown both in creation and history. Two aspects of God in particular are woven together: one is his constant faithfulness and the other is his constant bringing about of change.

The exodus, so prominent in this section of Isaiah, is celebrated in verses 16-17. Yet the main verbs, in fact obscured by most of the translations, are present tense and thus the exodus is not merely an event of the distant past. Israel's faith must not be in past events but in the living God.

Thus God says, 'Forget the past (verse 18) – not, of course, to forget the great saving events themselves but rather to avoid using them as a straight-jacket, as if God was committed always to work in the way he once did. God here is speaking of a new exodus, indeed a new creation. God who dried up the sea can irrigate the desert, he provides for every living thing. He is not a prisoner in the world he has created.

The reason for all this is given in verse 21. The people he formed (an echo of 43:1) have been created to praise him – not only so but to 'proclaim' his praise. His people are to tell to the nations of the world what God has done. Doxology is the basis for mission. Only those who have experienced the creating and saving love of God can adequately declare that God to others.

Revd Dr Robert Fyall
The Ministry of the Word

Palm / Passion Sunday

Isaiah 50:4-9a

*God never seems
weary of trying to
get himself across.*

The Servant Songs of Second Isaiah take us from Passion Sunday to Good Friday. This is the third of the songs. The first (Isaiah 42:1-9) and second (Isaiah 49:1-7) are read on Monday and Tuesday of Holy Week. This one is repeated on Wednesday, and the fourth (Isaiah 52:13-53:12), the song of the suffering Servant, is the Old Testament reading for Good Friday. Read in the context of Christian worship on these occasions, the texts help interpret the life and death of Jesus for us, just as they did for the early church.

The text, of course, did not arise in the church, but in ancient Israel. Although there has been some debate on the point, it is generally accepted that the Servant Songs come from the same figure responsible for their literary context, Isaiah 40-55. That dates this as well as the other poems to a time immediately before the end of the Babylonian Exile in 538 BC. Second Isaiah, who almost certainly was one of the exiles, announced the good news of release and return to Jerusalem. The prophet's understanding of suffering as part of the servant's role must be indebted in important ways to the experience of Israel in exile.

Who was Second Isaiah's servant of the Lord? No convincing concensus has emerged on the question, and answers vary, to a great extent depending upon which of the songs one emphasises. If Isaiah 50:4-9 is viewed alone, then an individual rather than a corporate interpretation suggests itself. The text is in the first person singular, as if the prophet were speaking, and the images are personal and physical. Notice the references to the parts of the body: 'tongue' and 'ear' (verses 4-5); 'back', 'cheeks', 'beard', and 'face' (verses 6-7). But a specific individual social role is indicated by the references to hearing and speaking, that of the prophet. This is not to conclude that the servant was necessarily a particular prophet – either Second Isaiah himself, one of his contemporaries, or a prophet from the past such as Jeremiah. It indicates, however, that among the roles of the servant was that of the prophet, namely, the hearing and communication of the word of God.

There are two main parts to the song, verses 4-6 and 7-9. In both of them an individual speaks, at first reflecting the language of the individual lament psalm, such as the

97

responsorial psalm for this text (Psalm 31:9-16). Verses 4-5 allude to the prophetic vocation and reception of revelation. There are close parallels to the so-called confessions of Jeremiah, which also reflect the individual lament psalms. Both the servant and Jeremiah have suffered because of faithfulness to their callings (Jeremiah 20:7-16). The second part of the song becomes an affirmation of confidence that borrows language and ideas from the Israelite law court.

Several expressions in the poem call for some explanation. The Hebrew word translated 'those who are taught' (verse 4) is rare and is best understood as 'disciples' (see Isaiah 8:16), indicating faithfulness to the teacher and that which is taught. The imagery of verse 6 suggests violent and hostile opposition to the servant, endured without complaint or reaction. Pulling out the beard was a particularly humiliating action (2 Samuel 10:4; Nehemiah 13:25). In verse 8, the speaker issues a formal summons of an adversary to a lawsuit, in which he expects the Lord to be a trustworthy judge who will not find him guilty.

The passage has a distinctly autobiographical tone and content. It moves from allusions to the vocation of the servant as a disciple (verse 4), through his faithful execution of his duty (verse 5); it gives an account of his patient endurance of suffering (verse 6) and then affirms his confidence that God will in the end vindicate him (verses 7-8). The Lord God is with him to help, making him resolute (verse 7) and enabling him to contend against his adversaries. His confidence is not in his own strength, but in the Lord who helps.

Gene M. Tucker
Preaching Through the Christian Year: Year C

Because Isaiah 50:4 speaks of the servant 'knowing how to sustain the weary with a word' I include this quotation on the power of words:

In Hebrew the term *dabar* means both 'word' and 'deed'. Thus to say something is to do something. 'I love you.' 'I hate you.' 'I forgive you.' 'I am afraid.' Who knows what such words do, but whatever it is, it can never be undone. Something that lay hidden in the heart is irrevocably released through speech into me, is given substance and tossed like a stone into the pool of history, where the concentric rings lap out endlessly.

Words are power, essentially the power of creation. By my words I elicit a word from you. Through our conversation we create one another . . .

God never seems weary of trying to get himself across. Word after word he tries in search of the right word. When the creation itself doesn't seem to say it right – sun, moon, stars, all of it – he tries flesh and blood . . . Jesus as the *mot juste* of God.

Frederick Buechner
Wishful Thinking: A Theological ABC

Easter Day

Isaiah 65:17-25; 1 Corinthians 15:19-26;
Luke 24:1-12

God the Father sees our need long before we do and meets that need, sometimes without any asking at all on our part!

The passage begins with a connection to the preceding passage which ends with: 'for the former tribulations should be forgotten' (Isaiah 65:16b). Isaiah 65:17-25 describes why such a forgetting is possible: the answer is the new creation. The key verb-form that sets the pace for this passage occurs only in Second Isaiah (Isaiah 40:28, 42:5, 43:15, 18; 57:19, 65:17, 18). The verb *bara*, which we encounter for the first time in Genesis 1, is connected to God's unique work of creation. The form here is a participle, whose predominant use is to connote a continuing action. So the JPS translates this, 'I am creating'. However, the same form can indicate immediate action. Hence the NRSV uses the phrase, 'I am about to create'. . .

The object of creation once again sends the reader back to Genesis 1, to the new heaven and earth. The language of new heaven and earth has no parallel in the Hebrew Bible; but the New Testament parallel is well known (Revelation 21:1): Then I saw a new heaven and a new earth; for the first heaven and the first earth had passed away, and the sea was no more.

This text invites us to pay attention to those times when the *no* can be the most profound *yes*. The rest of the passage is dominated by no fewer than ten negatives. The first is *do not remember*. This not-to-be-remembered language has interesting parallels in Ezekiel (18:24, 33:13, 16), where the forms are the subjects of the verb actions. This indicates that the former things refer to, as they say in the legal profession, previous bad acts.

It shall never again come to mind. The process of remembering is more than an abstract detachment; on the contrary, it is an expression of wholeness. The language 'come to mind' in the NRSV, which could also be translated 'come upon [the] heart', reminds the reader of Jeremiah 3:16, which describes the fruit of repentance. The remaining question is how to translate *leb*: some interpreters translate it 'closer to mind', whilst others prefer 'heart'. In either case, *leb* should indicate the heart as the seat of the will.

Revelation 21 points to the complete transformation of everything; it is right that we call this process of envisioning a new church transformation. The passage points not only to the new creation but also to the end of chaos. From Genesis to Revelation, the sea is consistently used as a metaphor for chaos and evil. In an earlier passage, Isaiah 57 suggests that idolatry will be no more; thus the negative is taken away. Here Isaiah 65 invites us to pay attention to those times when the *no* can be the most profound *yes*.

The yeses connect God and the people of God. For the people there is delight; for God there is rejoicing in Jerusalem. If these yeses of the passage are the yeses of God, then what are the corresponding noes?

Never again shall there be heard weeping and wailing. It would be worthwhile to tarry a moment to allow the congregation to experience what we mean by the term weeping. Weeping is a full-bodied cry that leaves us exhausted; many humans know this level of grief. It shall be no more.

No longer will it be that people live out less than their full time on earth. Full days is more than simply a length of time; it is a quality of life. The theologian Paul Tillich suggested that we rethink our notions of eternal: we should not think of it only as infinite in length (the person who dies at 100 years of age shall be reckoned as a youth) but as infinite in quality. This means meaningful work and restful and stimulating retirement.

The yeses continue the theme of meaningful and productive work: the people get to live in the houses they've built; they plant gardens and eat and enjoy their fruits. Today, as we note the disparity of wealth in North America, it is not unusual for those who keep the lawns cut to lack the money to buy the houses that rest on those lawns. Those who build and repair homes often cannot afford to buy those homes. This text assures us of a time when there will be a correspondence between work and reward.

The yeses have their corresponding noes. They shall not build for others to live in, nor will they plant for others to enjoy. They shall not work without purpose. Work does not go away; rather, it is transformed. The generativity of the people, that is to say, their work and their offspring, will come to fruition.

One of the most compelling noes for us is the end of terror: No longer will they bear children in terror. Fear predominates in North American culture; the statistics on violent crime may go down, but the sense of safety in cities still remains tenuous. Thus purposeful work has a parallel in the definition of the good life: the safety of the children. Across the continent today there are parents who fear for their children. Some parents fear because of random violence against minority groups, others because of the random violence between persons, and others because of domestic violence. This passage echoes Micah 2 (And none shall make them afraid).

The yeses of God continue. The text describes a world of God's attentiveness and of peace among the nations. Prayer will be answered, which refers us to one of the recurring themes in Hebrew laments, the inattentiveness of God. This passage makes the bold claim that God will answer every prayer. Peace will replace the world of predators. The new heaven and earth is a place where the lion and the lamb will lie down together. Truly a new era!

These texts remind us that God is optimistic, and in God we are optimistic about what we can be and what the Church can be. But it just doesn't happen by itself. Rather, we are called to start working on this wonderful project of God: building the Church and the people of God.

Stephen Breck Reid
The Lectionary Commentary: Old Testament and Acts

There have been occasions in my past life and ministry when Isaiah 65:24 has suddenly been made real for me: 'Before they call I will answer, while they are yet speaking I will hear.' The very first instance I recall is when I was in charge of a small group of students from my theological college, sent out to preach for a six-week period. So during the long hot summer of 1959 we preached every day, sometimes at two or three very different venues, moving on after a few days in each place. Because the weather was so warm and humid we were very, very thirsty on one occasion, having left some soft drinks behind at the previous village.

When we finally arrived at our new host church, unpacked our belongings and prepared for the next worship service we were all saying how nice it would be if we could each have a long, cold soft drink; it would be heavenly. Just as we were discussing all this, the door opened and a young girl of about twelve entered carrying a large and heavy bag.

After enquiring if we were the long awaited preachers and receiving our assurance, she opened her bag and produced two or three bottles of orange and lemon squash along with some fresh fruit and sandwiches. In the process of emptying the bag, the girl said, 'My mum sent this, she thought you might need it.' After expressing our sincere thanks, the girl went home and we all looked at one another. What timing! Because we had no money to buy anything, we believed that God had more than met our needs, BEFORE we had a chance to tell him. 'Before they call, I will answer', we felt came true that day, and for me personally those words were particularly appropriate on a number of subsequent occasions. I like to believe that all were part of God's providential care, and I discovered recently that the word 'providence' comes from 'pro' and 'video', meaning 'to see before'. God the Father sees our need long before we do and meets that need, sometimes without any asking at all on our part!

Ron Dale

'It seemed to them an idle tale.' In Jesus' world, nobody thought of 'resurrection' as happening to one person within ongoing history. It would happen at the very end, when God would raise all his people to share in the new heavens and new earth of prophetic promise. Nothing there about a dead-and-buried person being transformed or re-embodied.

This makes it hard to imagine that the Easter stories resulted from wishful thinking, or from what is sometimes called 'cognitive dissonance', in which people restate their hopes rather than face disappointment. Plenty of people in first-century Judaism had hopes (nationalistic, messianic, libertarian) dashed again and again. None of them went around saying that the dream had in fact come true, though not in a way they had expected. Except the Christians.

What they did say was not what you might have expected. An empty tomb; a rumour of angels; disbelief and puzzlement. No heroics, no great faith, no instant sense of everything clicking into place. Rather, a new tune, starting so quietly that by the time you hear it it's already well under way, growing and swelling into music so rich, so powerful as to make you want to dance and cry at the same time. The resurrection had already happened, had come forward to meet them, God's future rushing like an express train into the present, into the middle of history, the middle of the world's pain, of Israel's broken kingdom dreams. The kingdom had arrived in an unready world, like grand guests stepping out of the Rolls-Royce to find the family having breakfast in pyjamas.

The women rushing around in the early morning, Peter scratching his head staring at empty grave-clothes, might well be puzzled: this was not part of the plan. They had thought Jesus' language about his own dying, and rising again, to be a dark metaphor indicating perhaps a great struggle against paganism or Israel's current leaders, followed by a great victory. They had not reckoned with it being literal, or with the battle being waged against the last enemy, death itself. They were going to have to get used to living in a present which was shot through with God's future, a world in which the continuing disjointedness of creation was to be seen as out of date, waiting to be brought into line with the future which had already begun to happen. Paul wrestles with the implications of an 'end' that has already happened and an 'end' which is yet to happen, but he did not invent the idea. It came with the message of the first Easter morning. The world was now to be seen, neither as a tired old system going round and round without hope or meaning, not as a sick joke in which intimations of immortality always ran into the brick wall of death and cynicism, but in terms of new grass and spring flowers growing through a fresh crack in a concrete slab.

N. T. Wright
Twelve Months of Sundays

Second Sunday of Easter

Psalm 118:14-29

The stone which the builders refused is become the headstone of the corner. This is the Lord's doing; it is marvellous in our eyes.

Verses 1-4 form an introductory call to the whole assembly to offer thanksgiving to the Lord for his love which never fails (cf. Psalm 115:9-11 and Psalm 136).

The king then describes how, when he was almost crushed by his foes, the Lord came to his help and showed himself to be his strong support (verses 5-14). Especially we notice his utter reliance upon the Lord. Like Isaiah he declares the futility of human aid (cf. Psalm 20:7; Isaiah 30:15; 31:1-3). Faith in the Lord gives complete security.

Amid cheers of victory, the king approaches the doors of the temple (verses 15-21). He reaffirms that the Lord has delivered him from the forces of 'Death' and has restored him to full life and prosperity. As in Psalm 24, the procession, led here by the king instead of the ark, pauses at the doors of the temple and seeks admittance. A priest responds by asserting that only the *righteous* may enter the gate of the Lord (cf. Psalm 15 and Psalm 24:3-6). But the king's righteousness has been vindicated. He trusted in God and God delivered him. Now king and people know that the Lord has acknowledged the righteousness which is the only firm basis of their welfare.

There follows a hymn of welcome (verses 22-27b). This is the day of the Lord's decisive intervention. He has saved the one who seemed helpless and whom men had cast aside. Hence this is a day of great rejoicing. National prosperity in the coming year is assured.

The last three verses contain a summons to dance in festal procession round the altar and renew the thanksgiving to the Lord for his constant and unwavering love.

Apart from verse 6 (see Hebrews 13:6), two sections of this psalm are quoted in the New Testament (see Matthew 23:39; Mark 11:9, 12:10-11; Acts 4:11; 1 Peter 2:4, 7). The cry in verse 25 is Hosanna – Save, we beseech thee – the shout of the crowds as Jesus entered Jerusalem in triumph. It is uncertain whether the psalm was interpreted messianically in the time of our Lord, and Mark may have thought of the word simply as a shout of homage and jubilation. Yet the significance of the quotation, if our interpretation of the psalm is correct, is greater than the crowds or the evangelist realised. For Jesus came as a suffering messianic King, who did not drive out his enemies by the force of his own power, but allowed them to humiliate him. He was 'righteous' as the Israelite kings could never be, for not only was he the sinless Son of God, but his whole life expressed the faith seen in his words 'Not what I will, but what thou wilt' (Mark 14:36). And God's salvation was the vindication of Easter Day. The ritual of the pre-exilic temple reflected the working of God in a strange way. Like the Davidic king, Jesus became the *stone which the builders rejected*', which God made the chief cornerstone and upon which the Church is built (cf. Ephesians 2:20; in the Early Church the 'Stone' was a title given to Jesus). Through him 'Life' and salvation come to his disciples, and from him they derive that righteousness without which no man may enter into God's presence.

Note: Psalm 118:24 – *'which the Lord has made'* – or rather 'on which the Lord has acted'. For the Christian, Sunday is the day on which God 'acted' in the resurrection of Christ.

Cyril S. Rodd
Psalms 73-150

God Vindicates

The picture is that of a great building – such as a university, a cathedral, a library or a court of justice – rising from its foundations. The contractor inspects a load of quarried stone which has just been delivered. Some stones he approves, a few he rejects. Later in the day the architect arrives on the scene to survey the growing structure and sees a small heap of discarded stones piled on the edge of the site. One stone catches his attention, and he examines it closely. He has never seen anything so flawless. It will make the perfect corner-stone. Calling the contractor, he asks, 'Why have you rejected this one?' The builder replies, 'It doesn't fit in with the others.' 'Then the others must be chiselled to fit in with this one,' says the architect. So the stone which the builders refused is polished, inscribed and set in the place of honour; it becomes the headstone of the corner.

That could be a parable of Jesus. Actually it was the figure of speech used by an Old Testament Psalmist to describe the activity of God in his life and which caused him to cry out of a full heart, *'O give thanks unto the Lord; for he is good: because his mercy endureth for ever.'* We don't know who wrote the 118th Psalm or what were his exact circumstances but we can quickly infer from the Psalm itself that the author had been tossed aside like an unwanted stone, alone and rejected. As a king or a military leader he had been betrayed by his allies and smothered by his enemies. *'They compassed me about like bees,'* he writes. With every man's hand against him he nevertheless stood his ground, believing it *'better to trust in the Lord than to put confidence in princes'*. His trust was not ill-founded, because in the end God came to his rescue. *'I called upon the Lord in distress: the Lord answered me, and set me in a large place.'* God vindicated his faithful servant, championed his cause, gave him victory over his enemies and proved him right in the eyes of all his people. Thus he describes his personal triumph: *'The stone which the builders refused is become the headstone of the corner. This is the Lord's doing; it is marvellous in our eyes.'*

Leonard Griffith
God in Man's Experience; the Activity of God in the Psalms

Third Sunday of Easter

Psalm 30

*God's silence
is stunning,
especially for
those of us who
talk a lot.*

Thanksgiving for Recovery from Sickness

A man who has been ill comes to the temple to express his thankfulness to God. He remembers his suffering and his prayers (verses 6-10) and calls on all who serve God with loyal devotion to join him in his praises (verses 4-5) . . . The ideas of this psalm are similar to Psalm 6. Sickness is regarded as punishment sent by an angry God, and the psalmist's enemies point to it as proof of his guilt. Illness is described as in part the weakness of death, and the psalmist feels that he has already entered some way into Sheol, where there is no fellowship with the Lord and no opportunity to praise him.

As he recalls his sickness, he realises that when all had gone well with him he had fallen into a self-sufficient confidence which could not imagine that any trouble would ever come to him. If verse 7a speaks of God's loving care which had sustained him, this may slightly ease the sinfulness of his self-confidence but he had come very near to the thoughts of the wicked in Psalm 10:6. Even his prayer in distress was concerned more with himself than with God. He reminded the Lord that those in Sheol cannot praise him and that he would lose a worshipper if he did not heal him.

The singers of Israel can speak to our heart because they are so human. We, like this psalmist, act most of the time as if we were immortal, and through that strange quirk of the human mind which makes us think that though distress and sickness come to others they will never afflict us, we always have to face trouble with spiritual resources that have been drained dangerously low. If we smile at the naivete of the psalmist's prayer, we should remember that most of our prayers are as childish. Indeed, in times of trouble no prayer can really go beyond his final plea, 'Hear, O Lord, and be gracious to me! O Lord, be thou my helper!' (verse 10, RSV).

But the grief and the illness are now past. God has healed him. His sorrow has been turned into dancing. His inner being ('*my glory*', see 16:9) pours out its praises. He can never cease to express his thanksgiving.

Despite his forgetfulness of God and his reliance upon his own resources, God's anger had only lasted for a moment and sorrow was a lodger who left at dawn.

While we cannot accept that God vents his anger by sending disease and pain, the whole gospel is the proclamation of the immensity of God's love. Though we are heedless of his presence and will not credit that without him we can do nothing (John 15:5), he still maintains us in prosperity and gives more joy than sadness. We should give thanks to him unceasingly; yet he still blesses us, as Christ healed the ten lepers though only one returned to give thanks (Luke 17:11-19).

Some textual notes:

30:4 – 'saints', i.e. those who are devoted to God. The word does not necessarily include moral goodness, though those who are dedicated to God and loyal to the covenant will seek to obey his law and to respond to his love by imitating it in their own lives.

30:5b – The Hebrew is very terse, but the sense is probably as the Revised Version. God's anger brings suffering, but lasts only a short time. His favour brings life in all its fullness. The Revised Version margin takes the verse in the sense of Isaiah

54:7-8 – With either meaning the stress is on the greatness of God's goodness and the blessing this brings to man.

C. S. Rodd
Psalms 1-72

I had at last become a true child of the modern world, completely tangled up in petty and useless concerns with myself, and almost incapable of even considering or understanding anything that was really important to my own true interests.

Here I was, scarcely four years after I had left Oakham and walked out into the world that I thought I was going to ransack and rob of all its pleasures and satisfactions. I had done what I intended, and now I found that it was I who was emptied and robbed and gutted. What a strange thing! *In filling myself,* I had emptied myself. In grasping things, I had lost everything. In devouring pleasures and joys, I had found distress and anguish and fear.

Thomas Merton
The Seven Story Mountain

'Why do we fast, but you do not see?' God's people ask in the fifty-eighth chapter of Isaiah . . . 'Why do we worship, but you do not reveal yourself to us? Why do we pray, Sunday after Sunday, for peace, for health, for safety, but you do not give us those things? Why is the world so far from our desires for it, and why don't you speak – loudly and clearly – so the whole world can hear?'

God's silence is stunning, especially for those of us who talk a lot. We think, perhaps, that we can solve the problem by making more noise ourselves, but it is only when we stop, and hush, that the silence can teach us anything: namely, that our disillusionment is not a bad thing. Take the word apart and you can begin to hear what it really means. Dis-illusion-ment. The loss of illusion. The end of make-believe. Is that a bad thing? Or a good thing? To learn that God's presence is not something we can demand, that God's job is not to reward our devotion, that God's agenda may in fact be quite different from our own. Is that a bad thing or a good thing to know?

Barbara Brown Taylor
Gospel Medicine

Fourth Sunday of Easter

Psalm 23

God is the only real necessity of life!

A friend told me recently that when Psalm 23 was read aloud during morning worship, she could see in people's faces the powerful effect of the psalm. Another friend, a hospital chaplain, once remarked concerning the use of Psalm 23 in pastoral situations: 'I mean there is *power* in the twenty-third Psalm!' Indeed there is – a power matched only, perhaps, by the simple beauty of the psalm.

The psalm begins with a simple profession, 'The LORD is my shepherd,' which has radical implications: 'I shall not want.' The sense of this statement is probably best captured by the translation, 'I shall lack nothing' (see Deuteronomy 2:7). I prefer to retain the NRSV, however, because we live in a culture that teaches us to want everything. It is particularly radical in our setting today, 'I shall not want'; that is, God is the only real necessity of life! The rest of the psalm explicates this fundamental profession of trust.

In the ancient world, kings were known as the shepherds of their people. Their job was to provide for and protect the people, but they often failed to do so (see Jeremiah 23:1-4; Ezekiel 34:1-10). In contrast to the failure of earthly kings, God will be what a shepherd/ruler is supposed to be (see Ezekiel 34:11-16). God will provide for every need, and the rest of Psalm 23 tells how.

Verses 2 and 3 are usually understood to offer images of peace and tranquility, suggesting security and rest. They do, but they also relate how God provides all the basic necessities of life. For a sheep, 'green pastures' mean food, and 'still waters' mean drink (verse 2). In short, God 'keeps me alive', as verse 3a could be translated (see Psalms 30:3, 116:8). For a sheep, to be led in 'right paths' means that danger is averted and proper shelter is attained (see Psalms 5:8, 27:11). Thus, the shepherd provides food, drink, shelter – the basic necessities of life. The psalmist professes that life depends solely on God, and that God makes provision for the psalmist 'for his name's sake' (Psalm 23:3b) – that is in keeping with God's fundamental character.

By alluding to God's character, verse 3b anticipates the mention of 'goodness' and 'mercy' (verse 6), two fundamental attributes of God. Not surprisingly, the vocabulary of verses 2-3 occurs elsewhere in relation to key events that reveal God's character. For instance, the two Hebrew verbs, translated 'leads', in verses 2 and 3 occur together in Exodus 15:13 in a song that celebrates the exodus. The verb in Psalm 23:2 also occurs in Isaiah 40:11, where God is also portrayed as a shepherd who leads the people home from exile (see also Isaiah 49:10-11, and the following texts where God's role is shepherd: Genesis 49:24; Psalms 28:9, 74:1, 95:7, 100:3; Jeremiah 31:10; Micah 7:14). God keeps the people alive.

Verse 4 of Psalm 23 is the structural and theological centre of the psalm. At the moment of greatest threat, God still provides. Thus, the psalmist can 'fear no evil.' This affirmation recalls the prophetic salvation oracle, 'Do not fear', which occurs frequently in Isaiah 40-55 (see 41:11-13, 14-16; 43:1-7, 44:6-8, 54:4-8). The word 'comfort' is also a key theme in Isaiah 40-55 (see 40:1-2, 49:13, 51:3, 12, 19; 52:9), in which the prophet proclaims deliverance from exile, Israel's 'darkest valley'. The echoes of exodus and deliverance from exile in Psalm 23:2-4 provide a corporate dimension to what is usually and legitimately understood as individual assurance.

The shift to the second person as the psalmist addresses God reinforces the closeness of God and God's help: 'You are with me', an affirmation that again belongs to the salvation oracle (see Isaiah 41:10, 13; 43:5; Genesis 15:1, 26:24; compare Psalm 118:6). The 'rod' may be understood as a shepherd's tool of trade, but the word more often means 'sceptre' and connotes royal authority (Genesis 49:10; Judges 5:14; Psalm 45:6; Isaiah 14:5). God's provision is reliable, because God is sovereign. Not even the darkest, most deadly threat can separate the psalmist from God (see Romans 8:31-39).

It appears that the metaphor shifts in Psalm 23:5 and 6, from God as shepherd to God as a gracious host who welcomes the psalmist into 'the house of the Lord'. Verse 6b may refer to the Temple and suggests an original cultic setting for the psalm, perhaps as part of a thank-offering ritual; however, it is more likely that the 'stay in the sanctuary is . . . metaphorical for keeping close contact with the personal God' (Erhard Gerstenberger: *Psalms, Part 1*, with an introduction to cultic poetry, *Forms of the OT Literature 14*). In this case, verse 6b reinforces the central affirmation, 'You are with me' (see Psalms 27:4-6, 36:7-9, 52:8-9, 61:4). Indeed, the psalmist cannot get away from God, for God's 'goodness and steadfast love will *pursue* me all the days of my life' (Psalm 23:6a; author's translation). God's active pursuit of the psalmist is striking in relation to the mention of 'enemies' in verse 5. Usually it is the enemies who pursue the psalmist (see 7:5, 69:26, 71:11, 109:16, for example), but they are harmless.

In Psalm 23:5-6, the gracious host does for the guest what the shepherd does for the sheep – that is, provide the necessities of food ('a table'), drink ('my cup'), and shelter or protection ('in the presence of my enemies'/'the house of the Lord'). Both metaphors proclaim the same radical message – life depends solely upon God (see Matthew 6:25-34). This message is reinforced by Isaac Watts's beautiful paraphrase of Psalm 23:6:

> The sure provisions of my God attend me all my days; O may your House be my abode, and all my work be praise. There would I find a settled rest, while others go and come; no more a stranger, or a guest, but like a child at home.

The childlike trust articulated in Psalm 23 recalls Jesus' words about entering the realm of God 'as a little child' (Mark 10:15). It is appropriate finally that Christians hear Psalm 23 in relation to Jesus, who said, 'I am the good shepherd' (John 10:11, 14); who as gracious host invites persons to eat and drink at his table (1 Corinthians 11:23-26); and whose name Emmanuel means 'God is with us' (Matthew 1:23).

Walter Brueggemann
Texts for Preaching: Year C

Most of the time we tend to think of life as a neutral kind of thing, I suppose. We are born into it one fine day, given life, and life itself is neither good nor bad except as we make it so by the way that we live it. We may make a full life for ourselves or an empty life, but no matter what we make of it, the common view is that life itself, whatever life is, does not care one way or another any more than the ocean cares whether we swim in it or drown in it. In honesty one has to admit that a great deal of the evidence supports such a view. But rightly or wrongly, the Christian faith flatly contradicts it. To say that God is spirit is to say that life does care, that the life-giving power that life itself comes from is not indifferent as to whether we sink or swim. It wants us to swim. It is to say that whether you call this life-giving power the Spirit of God or reality or the life force or anything else, its most basic characteristic is that it wishes us well and is at work toward that end.

Heaven knows that terrible things happen to people in this world. The good die young, and the wicked prosper, and in any one town, anywhere, there is grief enough to freeze the blood. But from deep within, whatever the hidden spring is that life wells up from, there wells up into our lives, even at their darkest and maybe especially then, a power to heal, to breathe new life into us. And in this regard, I think, every person is a mystic because everyone at one time or another experiences in the thick of joy or pain the power out of the depths of life to bless. I do not believe that it matters greatly what name you call this power – the Spirit of God is only one of its names – but what I think does matter, vastly, is that we open ourselves to receive it; that we address it and let ourselves be addressed by it; that we move in the direction that it seeks to move us, the direction of fuller communion with itself and with one another. Indeed, I believe that for our sakes this Spirit beneath our spirits will make Christs of us before we are done, or, for our sakes, it will destroy us.

Frederick Buechner
The Magnificent Defeat

Fifth Sunday of Easter

Psalm 148

*There are times
when an
unbounded
jubilation should
reign and carry us
to the limits of
celebration, to
the borders of
insanity, and to
the heights of
self-transcendence.*

Psalms 146-150 constitute a small collection of hymns of praise. All begin and conclude with the cultic shout 'Hallelujah' that calls upon the community to 'praise the Lord'. Psalm 148 consists of two types of genres: two extended calls to praise (verses 1-4, 7-12) and two statements giving the reason or rationale for praise (verses 5-6, 13-14).

The psalm is an exuberant summons for the whole of creation to join in shouting out and celebrating the name and glory of the Lord. Practically no aspect of creation is omitted in the call to praise: angels, heavenly hosts, sun and moon, shining stars, snow and frost, stormy wind, mountains and hills, fruit trees and all cedars, wild animals and all cattle, creeping things and flying birds, kings, princes, rulers, young men and women, old and young. What a chorus!

In spite of its tone, Psalm 148 should not be faulted for a Pollyanna perspective on life. There are times when an unbounded jubilation should reign and carry us to the limits of celebration, to the borders of insanity, and to the heights of self-transcendence. Few are the times when the whole world is a chorus and the music of the spheres invades every nook and cranny of existence. Their scarcity should only endear their occurrence. It is only in such moments that we can spiritually and sensually realise the truth that modern ecology has taught us. We are all – from shining star to slithering snake – in this together, and we need to sing, at least occasionally, the same song and join in a common medley.

The psalm offers two reasons undergirding such praise. The first (in verses 5-6) declares that the Lord is the creator of all, who has established everything and set a law that cannot pass away (NRSV margin). The created order is divine handiwork in which every part serves its function within a created natural order (see Jeremiah 5:22-24; 31:35-36). The second (in verses 13-14) alludes to the rule of the Davidic monarch, the horn raised up for the people of Israel. (On the horn as the symbol of strength and royalty, see 1 Samuel 2:10; Psalms 75:4-5, 89:17, 24; 92:10, 112:9, 132:17; Lamentations 2:3, 17.) The psalm thus anchors praise in the divine rule in the universe and the messianic rule over the chosen people.

John H. Hayes
Preaching Through the Christian Year: C

Praising God

Let not any of you say, this employment is not for me: for it is the duty of 'every thing that hath breath'. There is no creature in the universe so afflicted, but he has encouragement to pray, and scope for praise – some have an idea that nothing but sighing and mourning are suited to their condition; and that the voice of praise and thanksgiving is for those only who have attained a fuller assurance of their acceptance with God. But they might as well say that gratitude was not their duty, as, that they were not called upon to express their gratitude in the language of praise. Know, brethren, that 'whosoever offereth God praise, glorifieth him'; and, his desire is, that every mourning soul should 'put off his sackcloth, and gird him with gladness'. I would not discourage humiliation; for I well know that it should ever be an associate of our sublimest joys; but this I would say to all: that Christ came to 'give unto them the oil of joy for mourning, and the garment of praise for the spirit of heaviness'; and that, in the experience of this, they shall approve themselves 'trees of righteousness, the planting of the Lord, in whom he will be glorified'. To every creature then, without exception, whether high or low, rich or poor, old or young, I would say with David in a foregoing psalm, 'Praise the name of the Lord'; yea, begin and close your every service with 'Hallelujah, hallelujah'.

Charles Simeon
The Duty of Praising God (Psalm 150:6): Discourses on the Old and New Testaments

Sixth Sunday of Easter

Psalm 67

The circle of blessing is completed when man blesses God.

That Your Way May Be Known

Numbers 6:24-26 records the blessing to be used by Aaron and his sons, the priests, when they bless the congregation of Israel. The first verse of Psalm 67 is the creative re-use of the first two sentences of the priestly blessing: 'The Lord bless you and keep you; the Lord make his face to shine upon you and be gracious to you.' In the psalm, the priestly blessing is used to introduce a congregational prayer for a blessing that will make the Lord's way known among all the peoples of the earth.

1. The theme of the psalm is stated in its first two lines, a blessing for the people of the Lord. The literary structure of the psalm develops the theme. The psalm begins with a focus on the blessing of the congregation (verse 1), moves to the praise of the Lord by the nations (verses 2-5), returns to the topic of blessing for the Lord's people (verse 6), and concludes with a line that combines the two (verse 7). The style of the psalm is predominantly that of a bidding prayer with an alternation between indirect and direct address. The form of the Hebrew verbs allows for a different decision about their function, whether they express statements or requests . . .

2. In its theme of a blessing that will make the nations know the Lord, the psalm can be related to two great theological traditions of the Old Testament. The first is the Lord's promise to Abraham of a blessing by which all the families of the earth shall be blessed (Genesis 12:1-4). The psalm sees God's favour to Israel as that which will bring the nations to fear the Lord. Notice how the motif 'earth' is used in verses 6-7; the earth gives a harvest as a blessing of the Lord, and all ends of the earth come to fear the Lord. The second tradition is the prophecy of Isaiah 40-55 and its proclamation that the Lord's salvation of Israel will be a revelation to the nations that the Lord reigns and leads the ends of the earth to praise the Lord (e.g. Isaiah 40:1-5, 45:20-25, 49:22-26). In the psalm, what the nations are to come to know is the Lord's way as saviour (verse 2). His salvation of Israel will reveal his identity as judge and shepherd of the nations (verse 4). The blessing of Israel will gain the

attention of the nations, and they will see in Israel's story the revelation of the reign of the Lord. The blessing of the church is for the salvation of the nations.

James L. Mays
Psalms

Bless, Blessed, Blessing

In the Bible blessing means primarily the active outgoing of the divine good will or grace which results in prosperity and happiness amongst men. In the Old Testament this prosperity or blessedness is usually measured in material things – long life, increase of family, crops and herds, peace, wealth (Genesis 1:22; Deuteronomy 33:11; 2 Samuel 6:11, etc); but for the wisdom writers wisdom itself is the chief result of the divine blessing; righteousness and peace are held to be the marks of the coming Messianic blessedness on the part of the later apocalyptic writers. Jesus gives a much more profound and spiritual connotation to the idea of blessedness in the Beatitudes (Matthew 5:2-12) and elsewhere. Even when the blessing is pronounced by men it is to be understood that it is a divine blessing that is imparted, because such men stand near to God, as in the case of the priestly orders (Leviticus 9:22, Aaron) or in that of saintly individuals (Genesis 48:14ff, Jacob). Two outstanding instances of this latter type are to be seen in Genesis 27 (Isaac's blessing of Jacob) and Numbers 23 (Balaam's blessing of Israel); here the word spoken is prophetic in character and has a self-fulfilling efficacy and cannot be recalled. The action symbolic of blessing was often that of laying on of hands, an action used by Jesus himself (Matthew 19:15); sometimes it was that of uplifting the hands (Leviticus 9:22). Finally, the circle of blessing is completed when man blesses God; God's blessing does not return to him void; it is reciprocated by the Church's response: 'Blessed be the God and Father of our Lord Jesus Christ' (2 Corinthians 1:3; cf. Revelation 7:12 etc.) – a response which Christianises ancient Jewish usage found frequently in the Psalms and elsewhere (cf. especially also 'the Benedictus', Luke 1:68).

Alan Richardson
A Theological Word Book of the Bible

Ascension Day

Psalm 47

The kingdom of the world has become the kingdom of our Lord and of his Christ, and he shall reign for ever and ever.

The Kingdom of God

Psalm 47 is one of the hymns of the Psalter which exult in the kingship of God. Sometimes these Psalms are called 'enthrone-ment Psalms'; that is, it is claimed that they were used on the occasion of the Jewish New Year Festival to celebrate God's re-enthronement over creation and history in a ceremony com-parable to that used on the occasion of installing an earthly monarch. Certainly God is thought of as King of Israel and of the universe. And this Psalm has been recited on New Year's Day in the synagogue through many centuries. But the language of the Psalm may be metaphorical rather than literal. In no sense is God thought to be enthroned by man through magical ritual. His sovereignty is acknowledged and pro-claimed, not created. In the so-called enthronement Psalms the accent is upon the coming reign of God, and the thought may be compared to the phrase of the Lord's Prayer, 'Thy kingdom come.' New Year's Day suggested the creation of the world and the end of the created world, which was not to be a dead end but a new beginning, a manifestation of the kingship of God. Through worship at the sanctuary, God's people as a corporate unity were caught up by faith into that future consummation.

Although it is possible to divide the Psalm into three major divisions (1-4, 5-7, 8-10), two are more in keeping with the literary form and thought content (1-5, 6-10). As in the case of Psalm 100 there are two calls to worship (1 and 6) and two sets of reasons for worship (2-5 and 7-10). In other words, this structure gives the effect of a double hymn.

The Nationalistic Outlook (47:1-5). Clapping the hands and shouting were a part of the ceremony of the installation of an Israelite king (2 Kings 11:12, 9-13; 2 Samuel 15:10). All people are called upon to join in these expressions of praise to God as King of all the earth, who is 'terrible' in the sense that he inspires fear or reverence. In times past God showed his sovereign power by subduing the nations of Canaan and giving their land to Israel. Israel was both a Church and a state, which means that a nationalistic outlook was inevitable until church and state should be separated. As the earthly king was installed with 'shout' and the sound of the 'trumpet' (1 Kings 1:38-40), so at the Festival, God is acknowledged as King.

The Missionary Perspective (47:6-10). The second call to praise refers to God as 'our King'. Yet the reasons for praise by the Covenant people include the fact that God is King over all the earth. His reign, though real in every generation, will one day be consummated when the rulers of all peoples gather 'as the people of the God of Abraham' – the fulfilment of the promise made in Genesis 12:3, 'in you all the families of the earth will be blessed' (margin).

According to Paul, men become sons of Abraham by faith in Jesus Christ (Galatians 3:6-29). Verse 10 finds the Christian counterpart in Revelation 11:15, 'The kingdom of the world has become the kingdom of our Lord and of his Christ, and he shall reign for ever and ever.'

A. B. Rhodes
Psalms

The kingship of God is stressed in Psalm 47 and we need to remember that kingship also meant 'shepherd'. As Walter Brueggemann puts it: 'The term shepherd is political in the Bible. It means king, sovereign, lord, authority, the one who directs, to whom I am answerable, whom I trust and serve.' (See his book 'The Threat of Life', page 91: Fortress Press, 1996.) So now a passage on the nature of God as Shepherd/King:

There is . . . throughout the Bible a deep unity underlying all its various insights into the character and purpose of God. These various insights represent partial truths, and the differences between them must not be minimised. There is development, or perhaps we should rather say *deepening*, in the varying conceptions of God at different stages of Hebrew history . . . But the recognition of differences in viewpoint in the various strata of the biblical revelation should not be allowed to obscure from our eyes the essential unity of the biblical conception of God. Throughout the biblical records it is the same God to whom the testimony points, even though in places the testimony may be expressed in primitive and (in the light of later insight) distorted ways; this God is the God whose final and clearest revelation is seen in Jesus Christ. The same recognisable conception of God appears throughout the Bible, though under many forms and expressed in terms of widely different social, political and ideological conditions. In the far-off nomadic days, God is the shepherd/King of his flock, ruling with severity but with goodness. If later he appears under the guise of a monarch of the 'oriental' type, he still nevertheless leads and feeds his chosen people. When, later still, he comes to be known as the Lord of the whole earth, he yet remains the faithful Keeper of the Covenant with Israel. When he manifests himself as the Judge of the nations – of Babylon or of Judea – he is still the loving God whose mercy is being exercised and revealed in the fulfilment of his purpose of salvation by means of his chosen instrument, the Old Israel or the New. There was in being a knowledge of God and a religious view of the world, when 3000 years ago, a slave-tribe came out of Egypt: that faith and that religious view remain today, vastly deepened and enlarged, as the faith of a world-wide Church throughout which the message of the Bible is proclaimed.

Alan Richardson
A Theological Word Book of the Bible

Seventh Sunday of Easter

Psalm 97

But all shall be well, and all manner of thing shall be well.

An enthronement psalm, Psalm 97 (see also Christmas, Second Proper) celebrates the exaltation/ascension of the Lord and the consequences of this for the world and human existence. The psalm is fundamentally a hymn about the Lord. The single exception is verse 9, which is prayer or speech addressed to God.

The psalm opens with a central affirmation: 'The Lord has become king.' (This appears a better translation than the NRSV's 'The Lord is king.') Everything else in the psalm tends to radiate outward from this point. Joy and gladness are the responsive tones that should greet such an affirmation.

Verses 2-8 are a cantata describing the universe's reaction to divine kingship; they reach a crescendo in the assertion that Zion hears and the daughters (cities) of Judah rejoice.

The metaphorical descriptions in verses 1-5 borrow from the imagery of thunder-storms – clouds, darkness, fire, lightning – which assault the earth and devour the divine enemies (see Psalm 29). Tucked away amid this assortment of meteorological metaphors is a calming voice among the thundering sounds – 'righteousness and justice are the foundation of his throne' (verse 2b). In spite of the violence and apparent irrationality of the characteristics of God, the Divine is consistent, just, and righteous.

God's voice and presence, heard and seen throughout the cosmos (verse 6), are bad news and a destroying presence to those who worship any deity other than the Lord; even the other gods worshipped with idols bow down to (i.e. 'worship') the God of Israel (verse 7).

What others hear in fear and trembling, Zion and Judah, Jerusalem and the Judean towns, hear with rejoicing (verse 8). The two responses of the world (the worshippers of idols) and Zion manifest three reactions to the Divine: being awestruck at the divine might, being humiliated and shamed by discovering the silliness of other worship, and being gladdened by the judgements that come as affirmations.

The psalm concludes with what might be called a moral lesson or a theological homily (verses 10-11) and then an altar call (verse 12). If we take the marginal reading of the NRSV in verse 10, which provides a literal translation of the Hebrew 'You who love the Lord hate evil,' the 'altar call' begins earlier.

Probably the regular reading in the NRSV is correct, because it merely presupposes that the same Hebrew letter was wrongly repeated. This then gives three affirmations about God, in verse 10, which produces two qualities for humans – light and joy (verse 11).

Psalm 97, with its assurances of divine rule and of the value of righteousness, even righteous hatred, leaves the reader with a sense of calmness that all is well with the world after all, because the Lord reigns.

John H. Hayes
Preaching Through the Christian Year: Year C

The closing words of the last quotation from John H. Hayes raised a few questions for me, but also reminded me of some words of Julian of Norwich. John Hayes says that reading Psalm 97 'leaves the reader with a sense of calmness **that all is well with the world after all**, *because the Lord reigns.* [author's emphasis]

The words of Mother Julian, the great fourteenth-century mystic are on the theme of all being well with the world:

Because of our good Lord's tender love to all those who shall be saved, he quickly comforts them, saying, 'The cause of all this pain is sin. But all shall be well, and all manner of thing shall be well.' These words were said so kindly and without a hint of blame to me or to any who shall be saved. So how unjust it would be for me to blame God for allowing my sin when he does not blame me for falling into it.

In these words I saw the deep, high mystery of God which he will show to us in heaven. Then we shall understand why he allowed sin to be. And in knowing this we shall have endless joy in God.

However, it seems to me that we shall never appreciate the beauty and power and relevance of Mother Julian's words, unless we know also something of the historical setting of her time. So here is Kenneth Leech on that very theme:

The fourteenth century in England was a period of great social upheaval and of intense interior striving, an age of militancy and of mysticism, of upheaval in soil and soul. Externally it was a time of distress among agricultural labourers, of exploitation of the rural peasants and of the urban poor, of sickness, disease and social violence. It was the age of the Black Death and of the Peasants' Revolt. Among the peasants and others who rose up in 1381, there was a thirst for social justice and for equality, a desire to see the end of serfdom and bondage . . .

At the interior level, the fourteenth century marked the climax of a process which had begun several centuries earlier, often referred to as 'the feminisation of language', the rebirth of an effective sensitised piety. There was a profound quest for the inner way, combined with a fundamental optimism about the universe, features which are clearly seen in the writings of Julian as of other mystics before her. The flowering of an effective spirituality in the period after the twelfth century has been described by Caroline Bynum in her *Jesus as Mother*.

The affective piety of the high Middle Ages is based on an increasing sense of, first, humankind's creation in the image and likeness of God, and, second, the humanity of Christ as guarantee that we are inextricably joined with divinity. Creation and incarnation are stressed more than atonement and judgement. (See Caroline Walker Bynum, *Jesus as Mother: Studies in the Spirituality of the High Middle Ages*, 1982, page 130.

Kenneth Leech
Julian: Woman of Our Day

Pentecost

Genesis 11:1-9 (Alternative)

Pride is certainly the deadliest of the sins because it will neither yield itself nor receive love from anyone else.

The Tower of Babel

The final story of the primitive history of humanity seems in some ways to double as another story of the origins of evil. Again the fault is pride and attempting to do by personal efforts what should have been left to God.

Alternatively it may be regarded as a different account of the diversification of the peoples, corresponding to the list of chapter 10, but concentrating on how they split up, rather than on the end result.

This would be an excellent example of the different approaches of the Priestly and Yahwistic traditions: the former gives a detailed or even exhaustive list; the latter offers a lively, suggestive narrative, with plenty of character but not much detail of the peoples.

It is amusing that the writer needs to explain the building-materials; his audience is clearly unfamiliar with Babylonian materials, brick and bitumen, explaining them as the equivalent to the stone and mortar commonly used in the rocky Israelite hill-country. The point of the story is already suggested by the seemingly unmotivated fear of the tower-builders that they may get scattered all over the world.

The whole is nicely topped off by the pun, 'Babel', the name of the town, being associated with the verb 'balel', which means 'to confuse, confound'. Such puns on names are much beloved of biblical authors. With this the English word 'babble' is associated, though in fact from the inarticulate sounds of baby talk.

The tower-builders wish to reach up to heaven by their own initiative; do they wish to become gods, or to have direct communication with the deity, or simply to build an outstandingly tall tower? It is certainly some manifestation of pride.

Isaiah's satire on the fallen king of Babylon describes the same phenomenon, 'How did you come to be thrown to the ground, conqueror of nations? You who used to think to yourself, I shall scale the heavens; higher than the stars of God I shall set my throne' (Isaiah 14:12-13). Similarly Ezekiel's satire on the fall of Tyre mocks the city, 'Because your heart has grown proud you thought, I am a god. I am divinely enthroned far out to sea' (Ezekiel 28:2). To build a high tower was to make a proud claim to divine power.

Ziggurats

The complex of ideas, of idolatrous claims to divine power, was no doubt related to the ziggurats of Mesopotamia. These were towering temples, built solid in receding steps, and reaching up some sixty to seventy metres. The act of worship took place on top.

Over two centuries ago the ziggurat of Borsippa, a few kilometres south of Babylon, was hailed as the original tower of Babel. It still stands thirty-five metres high, and shows clear traces on the top of a vertical cleft and mud-bricks vitrified by the heat of a lightning-strike. In the excitement of the discovery, this evidence of a lightning-strike was taken as the manifestation of God's vengeance.

Pentecost

In the Christian tradition the miracle of languages at Pentecost is understood as a reversal of the scattering of the peoples at Babel. The ability of the people of so many nations to understand the same language is a sign of the beginning of the restored unity of the world. It overcomes the disunity and hostility of the scattered nations, making them again into one united community. It therefore presages the coming of peace and harmony which is to be brought into being by the outpouring of the Spirit.

Henry Wansbrough
Genesis: The People's Bible Commentary

Pride: The Deadliest of Sins

Jealousy is probably the most important factor leading us to give false evidence against a neighbour. What we ourselves have failed to achieve we begrudge in the life of someone more favoured than we are. That we may in fact be less worthy than the other person is too intolerable to consider, and instead we conjure up fantasies of intrigue and subversion to explain how others always fare better than we do. That underhand manipulations do sometimes allow us less worthy contenders to win the accolade of public esteem is well known. That secret cabals may play a part in misdirecting justice is no idle thought, but in the end those who work subversively earn their reward of exposure and humiliation. People attaining spiritual mastery do not patronise these circles. The false accusations levelled at Christ were an amalgam of jealousy and fear. His opponents could not bear his effortless spiritual superiority and they were afraid that he would expose their weakness to the crowds. In fact, had they trusted Jesus, he would have supported their frailty and given them strength to face the darkness within them. But pride prevented them from either opening themselves to him or permitting his healing love to suffuse their distorted personalities with new life. Pride is certainly the deadliest of the sins because it will neither yield itself nor receive love from anyone else. Therefore it leads to absolute stagnation, until its proverbial departure before the inevitable fall: only a major calamity can force it to be relinquished, and then at last the power of love can penetrate the bereft personality. Rancour, jealousy and the fear of being exposed in one's naked impotence all feed pride, which in turn will plot to put an end to anyone who may threaten its tenuous security.

Martin Israel
The Discipline of Love: The Ten Commandments for Today

Trinity Sunday

Proverbs 8:1-4, 22-31

While evil and chance must be dealt with day by day, beyond the apparent randomness of things is the compassion of a rational God.

The sum of our passage, then, would appear to go like this: the Lord has fashioned an ordered and good world, a reasoned shape that is evident for all to see. When women and men allow this Wisdom to govern their lives, the result is wealth, (verse 18), justice (verse 20), happiness (verse 32), and life itself (verses 4, 35-36). The experience of a truly wise person begins with a fear of the Lord (verse 13; compare Proverbs 1:7) and is consummated in joy and prosperity.

The strength of such a proposition lies in its obvious appeal, not just to the human mind, but to the emotions as well. Life is under control. Given the presuppositions of Wisdom, truth may be known and one's day-to-day living adjusted accordingly. Evil is banished; randomness and chance are kept at a safe distance. 'God's in his heaven: All's right with the world,' as Robert Browning put it.

Yet those who live in the 'real' world know that this declaration, while genuine, is only partial. Evil is not so easily dispelled. Chance and chaos lurk on every hand. Job knew that well, and complains against all tidy rationality, such as that expressed in Proverbs 8:

> The earth is given into the hand of the wicked; [God] covers the eyes of its judges . . . if it is not he, who then is it? (Job 9:24)

Yet while evil and chance must be dealt with day by day, beyond the apparent randomness of things is the compassion of a rational God. Perhaps when all has been said, that is the real value of Proverbs 8.

James D. Newsome
Texts for Preaching: Year C

Believers throughout the centuries have tried to describe God, but very few have been satisfied with their descriptions. Their words turn out to be too frail to do the job. They cannot paint a true portrait of God, because creatures cannot capture their creator any better than a bed of oysters can dance *Swan Lake*. The best any of us has ever been able to do is to describe what the experience of God is like – how it sounds, how it feels, what it reminds us of. Whether the experience originates in the pages of scripture or in the events of our own lives, the best any of us has ever been able to do is simply to confess what it is like when we are in the presence of God.

The problem is that it is rarely the same experience twice in a row. Some days God comes as a judge, walking through our lives wearing white gloves and exposing all the messes we have made. Other days God comes as a shepherd, fending off our enemies and feeding us by hand. Some days God comes as a whirlwind who blows all our certainties away. Other days God comes as a brooding hen who hides us in the shelter of her wings. Some days God comes as a dazzling monarch and other days as a silent servant. If we were to name all the ways God comes to us, the list would go on for ever: God the teacher, the challenger, the helper, the stranger; God the lover, the adversary, the yes, the no.

God is many, which is at least one of the mysteries behind the doctrine of the Trinity. That faith statement is our confession that God comes to us in all kinds of ways, as different from one another as they can be. The other mystery is that God is one. There cannot be a fierce God and a loving one, a God of the Old Testament and another of the New. When we experience God in contradictory ways, that is our problem, not God's. We cannot solve it by driving wedges into the divine self. All we can do is decide whether or not to open ourselves up to a God whose freedom and imagination boggle our minds.

Barbara Brown Taylor
Home by Another Way

Proper 4/Ordinary Time 9

1 Kings 18:20-21, (22-29), 30-39

*When it comes
time to rest, or
pray, or wait on
the Lord, what
gets in the way?
Whatever it is,
it is a golden calf
for sure.*

By making explicit the connection between the drought and apostasy (verse 18) Elijah transforms the conflict between Ahab and Elijah into a contest on a higher level. Ahab is accused of following the local baals. Whether the contest to follow is with the Canaanite high god Baal (Hadad), the local baal of Carmel, or the foreign god imported by Jezebel (Melqart or Baal Shamen) is totally immaterial in this context. Apostasy is apostasy no matter what the details. Indeed, the narrative's refusal to be precise is itself testimony to the worthlessness of all other gods. They are lumped together and dismissed. To specify precisely which Baal failed at Carmel would dilute the sweeping condemnation of them all. Israel is gathered to witness the contest (verses 19-20), for it is their exclusive loyalty to the Lord that is at stake (verse 21).

The Contest (verses 21-40)

The Carmel ordeal moves from preparation (verses 21-24) through the contest itself (Baal, verses 25-29; the Lord, verses 39-40). A time scheme structures the flow of events from noon (verses 26-29) until the time of oblation (about 3pm; verse 29) to the time of oblation itself (verse 36).

Another way of looking at the structure of verses 21-40 is to consider the five proposals made by Elijah. The proposal of verse 21 to the people is aborted when they do not answer. The second (verses 23-24) is accepted, and the contest to determine which God will 'answer' (verse 24) begins. Verse 25 is a proposal to the prophets of Baal which goes nowhere because there is no answer (verse 37) which proves the Lord is God. The prophet's last proposal to the people is accepted, as demonstrated by their actions (verse 40).

The exact translation of Elijah's accusation (verse 21) remains unclear, but the meaning is clear. The people must choose. To limp along undecided is in effect to choose to dance with Baal's prophets (verse 26). The refusal on the part of the people to answer pushes the narrative into conflict. In verse 24, Elijah assumes that the people are on the side of Baal ('your god'), as in fact they are. By refusing to choose, they have chosen Baal by default. The altar of the Lord inevitably falls into ruin (verse 30b) in a syncretistic environment.

The contrast between the Baal prophets and Elijah could hardly be sharper. Their preparations are sketchy, their prayer abrupt, their liturgical action frantic. Nothing happens. Elijah's preparations are methodical and correct. His prayer is impressive and dignified. He does nothing; God alone acts. Things are made as hard for the Lord as possible. Elijah is one prophet against four hundred and fifty (verse 22). Baal's people get first choice of a bull and get the chance of a pre-emptive victory by going first. Water poured all over Elijah's altar loads the dice against the Lord. As a storm god, Baal ought to be able to produce lightning if he can do anything.

The narrative uses bitter, mocking humour to diminish Baal in the reader's opinion, although the details of Elijah's insults are no longer understood. Probably 'he is musing, or he has gone aside' (verse 27) ought to be combined into synonyms, into simply 'he is busy'. . . although the common suggestion that 'he has gone aside' refers to Baal's being preoccupied with a bowel movement certainly captures Elijah's insulting tone! Although the idea of a busy or sleeping god would not be shocking to an ancient reader (cf. Psalm 44:23), Elijah is probably making sly references to Baal's mythological adventures and his annual death sleep during the dry season, preserved for us in the Ugaritic texts. Whatever the details, Elijah is emphasising the emptiness of Baal. He is no god; he is a joke!

The prophets of Baal unconsciously join in the joke by taking Elijah's mocking advice and crying all the louder. In what was probably a funeral rite for the temporarily dead Baal, they gash themselves to demonstrate their commitment and to attract their god's attention (cf. Jeremiah 41:5). Nothing happens.

The time notices (verses 27, 29) emphasise how long the Baal prophets are at their fruitless orgy and hint proleptically that the Lord will emerge victorious. The Lord's liturgy (Exodus 29:39; Numbers 28:3-4, 8) sets the chronology, and the time for the oblation has arrived!

The description of Elijah's preparations and prayer slows the narrative and prevents the climax from coming too quickly. The excitement builds slowly; every detail is savoured. There is a decided contrast between the excesses of the Baal devotees and the measured preparations and dignified prayer of Elijah. The building (or rebuilding) of the altar is described twice (verses 30b, 31-32a). The prayer goes over the same ground twice (verses 36b, 37). Elijah pulls out all the patriotic stops: twelve stones, twelve jars of water (four jars poured out three times), reference to the change in Jacob's name (Genesis 35:10), and the patriarchs. The nation as a whole is being recalled to its national God. Although we no longer understand the references to seed (verse 32), it may have something to do with fertility. In any case, the trench holds twelve jars of water to increase the impressiveness of the upcoming miracle.

Elijah's prayer clarifies the stakes: The people must come to know that the Lord is God (verse 37). It is only at verse 36 that Elijah is termed a prophet (cf. verse 22), emphasising his authority at this moment and underscoring the emptiness of the claim of the Baal prophets to that title. Verse 37b is both intriguing and ambiguous. The people will learn that it is the Lord who has turned them around in an about face. While the natural assumption is that this means God will have turned the people back to fidelity, it could also be taken as an assertion that God had previously caused their apostasy to Baal.

The dramatic descent of fire from heaven raises the narrative to its climax (verse 38). This is no ordinary lightning, for the sky is still clear. It is the weapon of the Lord the divine warrior (Leviticus 9:24, 10:2; Numbers 16:35; cf. Judges 6:21, 13:20), consuming not only the sacrifice and the wood, but even the stones, the dust, and the water which had soaked it all. This is not just a miracle but a perfect whole burnt offering. The destruction of the altar solves the problem any Deuteronomistically inclined reader may have had with this non-central sacrifice.

The consequences of this climax are twofold. As the fire fell (verse 38), the people fall (verse 39) and confess that the Lord is God. They respond with a repeated acclamation formula from the liturgical tradition (Psalm 95:7, 100:3, 105:7) which is in perfect harmony with Deuteronomistic ideals (8:60; Deuteronomy 4:35, 39; 7:9). The prophets of Baal are slaughtered in accordance with Deuteronomistic principles (verse 40; Deuteronomy 13:13-15) and to offset Jezebel's murder of the Lord's prophets. The plot line will carry on into chapter 19, where Jezebel's reaction is described (19:1-2).

Richard Nelson
First and Second Kings

The above passage from 1 Kings 18 is one of the classic texts in the Old Testament dealing with the problem of worshipping foreign gods or idols. The other classic text is found in Exodus 32 where the Israelites made a golden calf whilst tired of waiting for Moses to come down a mountain where he had been communing with God. So here is Barbara Brown Taylor expounding the story for us:

Finally, there was Moses himself. A very stern guy, as trip leaders went – entirely humourless, pious beyond words. They were grateful to him, make no mistake, but his expectations of them were too high. He expected them to be as single-minded as he was, to walk and walk without complaint, to believe that God was guiding them on their tortuous path. That was all right for him, maybe, but they were just ordinary human beings. They needed a break, some way to unwind.

So when Moses went up Mount Sinai and did not come back down for weeks and weeks, they got creative. They collected all their gold jewelry, melted it down, and made a little golden calf to worship. They thought they might have better luck getting what they wanted from a small, portable god – something they could carry around with them, something they had made all by themselves. The God who had made them turned out to be too hard to deal with, so they switched over to a god they had made instead. It should have killed them, only Moses intervened. He ground the calf to gold dust and soon they were on their way to the promised land again. But it was a remission and not a cure, and to this day the people of God show a marked weakness for golden calves. Our reasons have not changed all that much through the years. The God who made us is still hard to deal with, God's ways are still not our ways, and our comfort still does not seem to be very high on his list of priorities.

So we are always fooling around in our spiritual basements, cooking up alternative gods that promise to be more responsive to our needs. If you think you do not have any, I can suggest several golden-calf detectors. Your cheque-book, for instance. What is it you invest in most heavily? What do your cheque-stubs teach you about what you worship? Or your calendar. What gets the lion's share of your time – which, after all, is more precious than your money? When it comes time to rest, or pray, or wait on the Lord, what gets in the way? Whatever it is, it is a golden calf for sure. A job that promises security. A house that promises comfort. A portfolio that promises protection. A relationship that promises safety. A position in the community that promises power. A car that promises prestige. All the little golden calves lined up on our mantelpieces – none of them bad things, by the way, did you notice?

The raw material of a golden calf is almost never a bad thing. It is usually a good thing – like gold – made into an ultimate thing – like God. Only that is where the trouble starts, because things are not God. They never have been, and they never will be. Things may produce results for a while; they may even produce results for a long while, but talk to someone whose job has just evaporated, or whose marriage has just ended, or whose health has just failed, and let that person tell you what a golden calf is worth. Remember that you are dust, and to dust you shall return.

God, on the other hand – the one, true, and living God – does not seem very interested in producing results, or at least not the ones that interest us. God seems more interested in producing life – not mere pulse and respiration life, but abundant life, extravagant life, my-cup-runneth-over life, which has very little to do with comfort, security, power, or prestige.

Barbara Brown Taylor
Gospel Medicine

Proper 5/Ordinary Time 10

1 Kings 17:8-16 (17-24)

Elijah at prayer, however, is determined, powerful, and filled with authority.

The full Old Testament reading includes two episodes in the stories of the prophet Elijah, found in 1 Kings 17:1-19:21; 2 Kings 1. The setting of the stories is the Northern Kingdom during the reign of Ahab (874-852 BC) of the dynasty of Omri. The Elijah stories are an old collection doubtless handed down in prophetic circles before they were incorporated by the Deuteronomistic historians into their account of Israel's past. Such stories were particularly important to the Deuteronomistic writers because of their conviction that history was set on its course by the word of God through prophets.

Elijah appeared on the scene abruptly and without introduction, announcing to Ahab that there would be 'neither dew nor rain these years, except by my word' (1 Kings 17:1). The word of the Lord then led him first to a brook east of the Jordan to be fed by ravens (1 Kings 17:2-7) and then to Zarephath to be fed by a widow.

In the background of the stories in 1 Kings 17:8-24, then, is the conflict between prophet and king, but that is set aside for the moment. More immediately there is the drought. Although they are linked thematically, these two stories are complete and self-contained: first the tale of the prophet and the widow of Zarephath, and then the account of Elijah's miraculous raising of the widow's dead son.

In the first story (verses 2-7) the drought provides the narrative tension, the uncertainty that creates suspense. That suspense is heightened by the Lord's command that a widow will feed him, and even more by the revelation that she is so poor that her life and that of her son are threatened (verse 12). It is not the greatness of the man of God that will save them all, but the power of the word of the Lord through him. 'Do not be afraid,' he says, and not as simple reassurance but as an oracle of salvation. Then in typically prophetic form he announces the word of God concerning the future: 'The jar of meal will not be emptied and the jug of oil will not fail until the day that the Lord sends rain upon the earth' (verse 14). And that is the way it turned out. It is a story of life and death that ends with the promise of continued life.

In the second story (verses 17-24), the issue of life and death is even more explicit. Illness and accusations provide the narrative tension. The widow's son becomes so ill that he is as

135

good as dead: 'There was no breath left in him' (verse 17). That initial diagnosis might leave doubt, but as the narrative moves on it becomes quite explicit that the boy is dead. The woman's reaction is to blame the prophet: 'You have come to me to bring my sin to remembrance, and to cause the death of my son!' (verse 18). After taking the boy to his room and placing him on his own bed, Elijah in turn blames the Lord: 'O Lord my God, have you brought calamity even upon the widow with whom I am staying, by killing her son?' (verse 20). After stretching himself upon the child three times, Elijah prays that the Lord revive him. The result is a foregone conclusion: the Lord heeds the prophet's prayer and revives the child (verses 21-22). Then Elijah brings the boy to his mother, who affirms that Elijah is indeed a 'man of God' who speaks the true word of the Lord (verses 23-24).

Both the episodes are miracle stories with legendary and folkloristic features. One of their goals is stated in the concluding verse – to validate Elijah as a true prophet. They are told, however, not to glorify Elijah, but to show how the power of God, in the form of the prophetic word, was made manifest through him. Although the Bible contains more dramatic miracle stories than this one, we are still meant to be astonished. To provide a rationalistic explanation – for example, the generosity of the widow moved her neighbours to bring meal and oil, or the prophet revived the boy with a primitive form of artificial respiration – may serve only to reduce the astonishment that the divine word could solve such problems.

Especially when this story is considered in connection with Luke 7:11-17, the role of the widow becomes crucial. That the widow was poor is not surprising. In ancient Israelite society, economic well-being generally required a male head of the household. Even all the Old Testament texts that express God's concern for the widow and the fatherless indicate that there was need for such concern. She is not only poor; she is a foreigner. All the more dramatic then is her willingness to be generous with what little she had, trusting that the prophet's word was indeed the word of God.

Gene M. Tucker
Preaching Through the Christian Year: Year C

The trouble in Israel was structural and systemic. There was no rain. The drought brought with it death. Drought is an ancient form of energy crisis. The energy crisis means that the government has failed. The king could not cause rain, could not give life. The king was impotent, the government was discredited. The world had failed. The situation was right for despair and dismay.

Such an energy crisis affected everyone, rich and poor. As usual, however, the crisis impinged upon the poor first, and most decisively. Our attention is focused on a nameless woman. She had nothing, neither name nor food nor hope. Actually, she had one thing, her beloved son. He was her only hope, her welfare system, her lean link to life.

The story begins in the failed royal system with this nameless, forlorn widow. Elijah enters the story. He is another kind of character. He is uncredentialed, uncontaminated by the system, uncompromised by government plans for rain. He is also untested, because nobody knows what he can do. He works through no royal arrangements. He is simply despatched by the Lord, an abrupt, unexplained command: 'Go to the widow' (verse 9). He goes to meet the widow. Oddly, he gives her an unending supply of food (verse 16). He does for her what the king cannot do.

The plot now thickens and we pick up the story. Elijah did the wondrous miracle of food, solving the hunger crisis. Now, however, the stakes are much higher. The boy, the widow's only hope in this age or in the age to come, dies (verse 17). She loses her son. She loses her grip on reality. She loses her cool. She blames Elijah for his death: 'Why have you come against me – to cause the death of my son!' (verse 18). She is frightened, perhaps embarrassed that she trusted such an odd man. She panics, because she has lost her life support and now entered her personal energy crisis. Probably she is a little guilty that she mistrusted the royal system. There is a death. Someone must be blamed. She draws the conclusion that if you deal with this man, trouble will come. (That is the same conclusion drawn by the king, 18:17.)

The death of the boy looms more severe than drought or hunger. We watch to see what this odd man will do now. Nobody would expect a king to deal with death, as kings never claim power for such ultimate matters. Elijah, however, has hinted at much more than any king would undertake. Could Elijah now do what kings won't try to do?

He is abrupt, magisterial, not caught in the woman's terror. He acts decisively: 'Give me your son' (verse 19). He takes the boy into his care and into his power. He gives the impression to the widow that he is prepared to take on even the reality of death. He is prepared to take on the deep problem the king will not address. He is prepared to do what the king cannot do.

Elijah acts in a remarkable way. He prays. He turns the problem of death over to the reality of God. He speaks to make death be a concern for God. His words open the power of death to the power and care of God. The woman is not now in the scene. There is only Elijah. He dominates the action and the drama. Elijah prays twice. His prayer asserts that the reality of death is a larger issue than this woman ever suspected. The limits and edges of life concern the reality, power, and faithfulness of God. Elijah knew that.

Elijah's first prayer is an accusation against God (verse 20). Elijah knows that God deals in matters of life and death. Elijah asks God if God has caused this death, for Elijah knows that he himself is not responsible. There is of course no firm answer from God, as God will not take such bait. Elijah at prayer, however, is determined, powerful, and filled with authority. He prays again. This time he prays an imperative to God. His is a voice of deep, demanding faith. Elijah speaks to God in an imperative: 'Return the life of this child' (verse 21). God holds the power for life. Some may have thought the king was in charge of life, but the king does not figure in the world of Elijah. Elijah has recast the human issue and there is only death, God and prayer.

God yields to Elijah. Elijah has compelled God to act. God heard! (verse 22) . . . God gives life back to the boy at the behest of Elijah. The boy lives! (verse 22). The prayer, faith, courage, and daring of Elijah have changed the world. Elijah takes the new-birthed boy back to his mother, who is frantic, confused, and upset. Elijah says simply, 'Your son lives' (verse 23). Elijah does not celebrate himself. He does not even mention God nor bear witness to God. He only describes the new reality wrought out of intense, demanding faith.

The woman is as changed as the boy. The last time she had spoken, she accused Elijah (verse 18). But now she celebrates Elijah without reservation: 'I know you are a man of God. The word of God is in your mouth' (verse 24) The woman knows that where new life comes, the unexpected power of God is visible. She celebrates Elijah, but she confesses much more: I know God has not quit. I know the power for life is at work. I know the rule of God is not contained in the pitiful little regime of the pitiful, dysfunctional king. Indeed, the king is completely absent from this drama. Why would anyone call on him? He can do nothing. Life has broken loose; the king cannot enact life; the king cannot block life from coming. 'My son was dead and is alive!' God has done what the king cannot do.

This is a story about the oddness of Elijah. Elijah is shown to have the power for life. That power is not explained; it is only witnessed to. It is linked to faith and to prayer, to a refusal to accept the woman's little faith or the king's little power. The world enacted by Elijah breaks all such conventions, routines, and stereotypes: New news has come. The boy lives! The news given us in this story is that the power for life is offered. It is carried by a human agent.

Walter Brueggemann
The Threat of Life: Sermons on Pain, Power, and Weakness

Proper 6/Ordinary Time 11

1 Kings 21:1-10 (11-14), 15-21a

*Judgement will
come in the end.*

The story of Naboth's vineyard illustrates the disobedience of the people of God throughout the Old Testament. Ahab is both a member of that people, with an individual responsibility to keep the covenant made at Sinai, and at the same time a leader with responsibility to ensure that his subjects as a whole keep the covenant.

He has already broken the first and second commandment by his idolatry, and the third and fourth in consequence. He has broken the fifth by not honouring his kingly forebears and the throne he has inherited. In this story he begins by coveting and moves on, through his wife, to bearing false testimony, murder and theft.

As a king, he allows himself, sullen and angry, to be guided by his Phoenician wife, who aggressively seeks to impose her pagan views and convinces him that being king puts him above the law. He subverts and betrays his subordinates, forcing them to sin for him. With echoes of Macbeth and Lady Macbeth, and with many examples of lawless warlords in our world today, this appalling behaviour of those with power happens all the time. The challenge is to be like Elijah and to confront with the truth: 'You will not get away with it. Judgement will come in the end.'

Mrs Margaret Killingray
The Ministry of the Word: Year C

Proper 7/Ordinary Time 12

1 Kings 19:1-4 (5-7), 8-15a

It is hard to live with broken symbols, hard indeed to accept that the breaking of such hallowed symbols may be a necessary element in continuing faith.

Faced with this angry queen, threatening to cut short his life – and with ample power to make her threat effective – Elijah flees despairingly south into the safety of the distant desert, and on to Horeb the traditional mountain birthplace of Israel's covenant faith: he went on for forty days and forty nights to Horeb, the mountain of God. He entered a cave and there he spent the night (1 Kings 19:2).

The parallelism with Mosaic tradition is explicit and intentional – Moses who spent forty days and forty nights on the mountain (Exodus 24:18), who experienced his strange theophany as he sheltered in the crevice of a rock (Exodus 33:2). But if the parallelism is intentional, its effect is to heighten the contrast between Moses and Elijah. In response to Elijah's self-pitying explanation as to why he had fled far from the scene of action to this southern mountain of God. The answer came:

> Go and stand on the mount before the Lord. For the Lord was passing by: a great and strong wind came, rending mountains and shattering the rocks before him, but the Lord was not in the wind; and after the wind there was an earthquake, but the Lord was not in the earthquake; and after the earthquake fire, but the Lord was not in the fire. (1 Kings 19:11-12)

The Lord was not in the wind . . . not in the earthquake . . . not in the fire . . . *but he ought to have been.* Wind, earthquake and fire are recurring symbols of God's mysterious presence in many early narrative and poetic traditions in the Old Testament, not least in the Exodus traditions. The Lord had been in the wind, 'the strong east wind' that turned the sea-bed into dry land to enable the Hebrew slaves to escape the pursuing Egyptian forces (cf. Exodus 14:21-23 and its poetic parallel in 15:8). The Lord had been in the earthquake. The Song of Deborah, one of the earliest poems in the Old Testament, describes the Lord coming to the aid of his people:

> O Lord, at thy setting forth from Seir,
> When thou camest marching out of the plains of Edom,
> Earth trembled; the heavens quaked:

141

Mountains shook in fear before the Lord, the Lord of Sinai,
Before the Lord, the God of Israel. (Judges 5:4-5)

The Lord had been in the fire: in that bush, strangely on fire,
yet not burned up, when Moses received his call (Exodus 3:2-3,
cf. the symbolism of the 'smoking brazier and the flaming
torch' in the narrative of the covenant with Abraham in
Genesis 15:17). All accounts of what happened at Mount
Sinai/Horeb speak in terms of fire: 'Mount Sinai was all
smoking because the Lord had come down upon it in fire'
(Exodus 19:18, cf. 24:17).

The mountain was ablaze with fire to the very skies: there
was darkness, cloud and thick mist. When the Lord spoke to
you from the fire you heard a voice speaking, but you saw no
form: there was only a voice (Deuteronomy 4:11-12, cf. 5:24).

And who better than Elijah to know from personal
experience that the Lord was powerfully present in fire. In
response to his prayer on Mount Carmel:

> . . . the fire of the Lord fell. It consumed the whole
> offering, the wood, the stones and the earth, and licked
> up the water in the trench. When all the people saw it
> they fell prostrate and cried, 'The Lord is God, the Lord
> is God'. (1 Kings 18:38-39)

But now the Lord was *not* in the wind . . . *not* in the earthquake
. . . not in the fire. If a voice had once spoken to the people from
the fire, the fire was now dumb. It was as if the traditional
symbols, which had once conveyed the reality of God's
presence, had been emptied, left meaningless, no longer able
to bear the burden of the reality of God's presence, no longer
able to speak. But the Lord was not absent: he was there, his
presence indicated by a phrase which most traditional English
translations, including the RSV render 'a still small voice': the
NEB has 'a low murmuring sound', the Good News Bible 'the
soft whisper of a voice'. Behind these different renderings lies
a strange Hebrew expression. The adjective differently
rendered 'still', 'low', 'soft', (Hebrew *dqh*) is nowhere else in
the Old Testament used of sound. Usually it refers to a very
fine material or cloth. The other key word in the phrase, the
noun which it qualifies, (Hebrew *dmmh*) is related to verbal
forms which can either mean to be silent or to whisper. In
Psalm 107:29 the word is used in the context of the stilling of a
storm; in Job 4:16 it occurs as part of a description of a night
vision which strikes dread into Job; an apparition looms before
him and he hears 'the sound of a low voice' (NEB) or 'a voice
out of the silence' (Good News Bible). In 1 Kings 19:12 the

phrase seems to be pointing to a kind of silence so intense that you can hear it; what S. Terrien has called 'the sound of utmost silence . . . the stillness which, by dramatic antithesis, may indeed be heard'. It is in this intense silence that there comes a voice, the challenging, demanding voice of the Lord. We are not dealing here with the inner voice of conscience. This is not the description of a man turning away from the external God of nature to the God of his own inner soul. The intense silence is as much a part of nature as wind, earthquake and fire. Nor is this, as has been claimed, the whispered word of the personal and spiritual God of the prophet replacing the nature mythology he has destroyed. Prophetic experience is never so described anywhere else in the Old Testament. Terrien argues that Elijah at Horeb marks a turning point in Israel's spiritual pilgrimage and perception; 'it closed the era of theophany and relegated it to the realm of the unrepeatable past. At the same time it opened the era of prophetic vision when miracles of nature became miracles of character.'

This draws far too sharp a contrast between theophany and prophetic vision, nature and character. Rather than seeing the incident as a turning point in Israel's religious history, it is better to keep it firmly within its given context, the prophetic experience of Elijah . . . On the one hand there is noise, turbulence, the power of wind, earthquake and fire; on the other what appears to be the exact antithesis, total silence. According to the narrative Elijah had reached a crisis point in his life. He had played his ace against what he believed to be paganism, only to find it trumped by Queen Jezebel. The fire of the Lord had fallen, but on the other side of momentary triumph, Elijah is gripped by despair. 'It is enough,' he said 'now, Lord, take my life for I am no better than my fathers before me' (1 Kings 19:4).

The traditional symbols of the Lord's presence and activity no longer seemed to carry power or conviction. Where he had been taught to believe that the Lord was present, in wind, earthquake and fire, there he found him to be disturbingly absent. Yet the Lord was there in something that appeared to be totally different in character from what had hitherto been comfortingly familiar. The unexpected replaced the expected. The Lord's puzzling absence was the prelude to his surprising presence. Elijah does not stand alone at this point in the Old Testament tradition. Some of the most hallowed symbols of God's presence with his people, whether verbal (e.g. a particular interpretation of God's relationship with his people) or visual (e.g. the temple of Jerusalem) had to be broken so that the people might find God anew. But it is hard to live with broken symbols, hard indeed to accept that the breaking of such hallowed symbols may be a necessary element in continuing faith.

Robert Davidson
The Courage to Doubt

The Wise Counsellor:
A Meditation on 1 Kings 19:11-13

Persons come to the minister of God in seasons of despondency; they pervert with marvellous ingenuity all the consolation which is given them: turning wholesome food into poison. Then we begin to see the wisdom of God's simple homely treatment of Elijah, and discover that there are spiritual cases which are cases for the physician rather than the divine.

God calmed his stormy mind by the healing influences of nature. He commanded the hurricane to sweep the sky, and the earthquake to shake the ground. He lighted up the heavens till they were one mass of fire. All this expressed and reflected Elijah's feelings. The mode in which nature soothes us is by finding meeter and nobler utterance for our feelings than we can find in words – by expressing and exalting them. In expression there is relief. Elijah's spirit rose with the spirit of the storm. Stern wild defiance – strange joy – all by turns were imaged there. Observe, '*God* was not in the wind', nor in the fire, nor in the earthquake. It was Elijah's stormy self reflected in the moods of the tempest, and giving them their character.

Then came a calmer hour. Elijah rose in reverence – felt tenderer sensations in his bosom. He opened his heart to gentler influences, till at last out of the manifold voices of nature there seemed to speak, not the stormy passions of the man, but the 'still small voice' of the harmony and the peace of God.

Frederick W. Robertson
Sermons on Bible Subjects

Proper 8/Ordinary Time 13

2 Kings 2:1-2, 6-14

By the power of the Spirit, these early prophets could speak the words of the Lord that gave meaning and hope to the present and the future.

This reading is a tale of two prophets – the end of one's career and the beginning of the other's. The atmosphere is heavy with the mysterious and miraculous power of God manifest through these two and worked upon them. Elijah was taken up into heaven in a whirlwind, having used his mantle to divide the waters of the Jordan. That places the emphasis upon the older prophet. But the younger prophet loyally followed his master, actually saw him taken up, and also divided the waters of the Jordan with the same mantle. That places the emphasis on Elijah. In the broader literary context in the Book of Kings, the chapter makes the transition from one prophet to the next, but it emphasises the latter, confirming Elisha as Elijah's successor. Binding the story together is the account of the journey, the itinerary of the prophets from Gilgal to Bethel to Jericho, across the Jordan and then – for one of them – back again. Elijah had been a remarkably peripatetic prophet all along. These movements heighten the tension and turn what would otherwise be a brief anecdote into a story with a plot, that is, the creation of tension, its resolution, and its results.

The plot does not turn on the question of what will happen to Elijah. From the very beginning we know Elijah's fate, that the old prophet will be taken 'up to heaven by a whirlwind' (verse 1). Left in doubt is Elisha's future. The ground is laid for an answer in the account of the journey. At each stopping place, Elijah asks Elisha, 'Stay here' (verses 2, 4, 6), and in every instance the younger prophet vows not to leave him. Were these requests Elijah's way of testing his successor's stamina and devotion? Their effect is to underscore both Elisha's persistence and his unqualified loyalty to his master.

In the background is the 'company of prophets' (verse 7; 'sons of the prophets' in the RSV), here fifty in number. These were members of the prophetic guild, probably under the leadership of a 'father' such as Elijah. The allusion to this group is a clue to the institution that would have been most interested in perpetuating the stories of the miraculous exploits of the great prophets.

But Elisha stands out from all the others. Thematically, there is a link with Elijah's commission on Mount Horeb and his designation of Elisha as his successsor, the one to carry out God's will for the house of Ahab (1 Kings 19:15-21).

145

There, too, Elijah's mantle had played a role. But our text for the day makes no explicit reference to that original encounter between Elijah and his successor. One might think that Elijah had forgotten altogether the Lord's instructions to commission Elisha.

Once the two prophets have crossed the Jordan, a dialogue transpires that is the key to the story (verses 9-10). Elijah, aware that the end is near, invites Elisha to make a final request of him. The request for 'a double share' of Elijah's spirit asks a great deal, as he points out. (Although according to Deuteronomy 21:17 a double inheritance is the rule for the eldest son.) So Elijah sets a condition: 'If you see me as I am being taken from you, it will be granted you; if not, it will not' (verse 10). The climax is thus not the description of the manner of Elijah's departure in verse 11 – at the same time graphic and elusive – but the affirmation in verse 12 that Elisha did, indeed, see it. In its resolution we see the story's question clearly: Will Elisha be the successor of Elijah, and one fully endowed with 'a double share' of his spirit? The presence of that spirit is confirmed when Elisha divides the Jordan with the mantle, just as Elijah had.

Several specific points in the story call for comment. When Elisha cries out to Elijah, 'Father, father! The chariots of Israel and its horsemen!' (verse 12), he is using two titles. The first, 'father,' indicating respect and affection, stems from his role in relation to the prophetic groups. The second, with its reference to military might, also is applied to Elisha when he is about to die (2 Kings 13:14). The phenomena that attend the prophet's ascension suggest both disruptions in nature (whirlwind, fire) and military imagery. They recall the theophany to the prophet on Mount Horeb (1 Kings 19). Some aspects of the story parallel the Moses traditions: the parting of the waters, and the fact that both Moses and Elijah meet their ends beyond the Jordan and leave to their successors the completion of their tasks. As there is continuity of authority and power between Elijah and Elisha, so there are contrasts. The former is a solitary individual, always at odds with the royal household. The latter will always seem to have others – prophets, kings, soldiers – around him. He will intervene directly in the political arena, bringing the destruction of the house of Ahab that Elijah prophesied. Finally, Elisha, even with a double share of his master's spirit, will die an ordinary death.

Gene M. Tucker
Preaching Through the Christian Year: Year C

Plumbing the Text

These verses begin what is known as the cycle of Elisha stories that are gathered together in 1 Kings 2:1-13:21. Actually, our text forms one unit with the whole of 1 Kings 2, but the meaning can become clear from the first twelve verses.

We know from verse 1 in the text that Elijah's ministry is about to end with his 'translation' or ascent into heaven in a whirlwind. He will not undergo death, but will be transported immediately to the heavenly realm, reminding us of the notice about Enoch in Genesis 5:24 and of the ascension of our Lord.

With this first verse we have entered into the realm of mystery, having to do with events that are not of this earth, as the transfiguration of Christ was not of this earth (Mark 9:2-8). So the two texts go well together.

Elijah, and Elisha go on their way together in a rather pointless journey from Gilgal to Bethel to Jericho (which is only a few miles from Gilgal) to the Jordan. All of the towns named are located in the hill country of Benjamin, and there is no notice given as to why Elijah leads his apprentice from one place to the next. At each site mentioned, Elijah tries to rid himself of the company of Elisha, but the latter shows his absolute loyalty to his master by refusing to stay behind, sealing his determination with the phrase, 'As the Lord lives.' Nothing stronger can be said, because the Lord is the supremely living One.

At each place, the two are also met by 'sons of the prophets'. That is a designation for the early, non-writing prophets, who usually lived together as bands of prophets in closed colonies at the various sanctuaries. They had two characteristics that distinguished them from the later writing prophets. First, revelation was given to them through the Spirit, whereas the emphasis in the prophetic writings is on revelation by the word of the Lord. Second, most of them were ecstatic prophets, who by the gift of the Spirit were given heightened physical and mental powers in a state of ecstasy (cf. 1 Samuel 10:11-12). For example, in the spirit, Elijah was able to run ahead of the chariot of Ahab the seventeen miles from the top of Mount Carmel to the plain of Jezreel (1 Kings 18:46).

Similarly, by the power of the Spirit, these early prophets could speak the words of the Lord that gave meaning and hope to the present and the future. It was only later when they corrupted their prophetic office, by pridefully speaking their own words and not God's, that they were condemned by many of the writing prophets.

147

The fact that these sons of the prophets are true prophets is confirmed in our text by their foreknowledge of Elijah's departure. They are, however, forbidden to speak further of the matter.

Elijah's power as a prophet is attested in this particular story by his parting of the waters of the Jordan, reminiscent of Moses, the greatest of the prophets, at the Red Sea (Exodus 14:21, 27) and of God's act for Joshua at the entrance into the promised land (Joshua 3:14-17).

Before his translation into heaven, Elijah grants Elisha one request, and Elisha asks for a double share of Elijah's prophetic spirit. Elisha is not trying to be greater than his master. Rather, he is asking for the inheritance that was given a first-born son by his father (Deuteronomy 21:17). Thus, we are enabled to know that Elisha is Elijah's successor, inheriting Elijah's prophetic spirit, in an intimate relation likened to that of a father with his son (cf. verse 12). Elisha will be confirmed as the successor, however, only if he witnesses that which ordinary sight cannot see – the translation of Elijah into heaven by the whirlwind (verse 10).

Further, as Elijah's successor, Elisha is called to complete Elijah's task of toppling the great Omri dynasty in the northern kingdom and of putting Jehu on the throne of Israel and Hazael on the throne of Syria. In short, Elisha is called to complete the work of the prophetic revolution, which God had foretold (1 Kings 19:15-18).

As the two men talk and walk on together, they are separated by a chariot of fire and horses of fire, and at that moment, Elijah is taken up, not in the chariot, as artists and tradition have long portrayed, but by the whirlwind. Overcome by the vision, Elisha cries out to his father-master that he sees the chariots and horsemen of Israel.

Who are these strange chariots and horses or horsemen? In other passages of the Old Testament, similar images represent the power and presence of God. Fire is frequently associated with the theophany or appearance of God or the Lord (Exodus 3:2, 24:17, numerous passages), and the horses and chariots are symbols of his unseen power (2 Kings 6:15-18, 7:6-7). Connected with Elijah, therefore, are the power and presence of God, and both are concentrated in the Word of God that the prophet speaks. That word is Israel's defence. Elijah, in the power of the Spirit, spoke the word that overcame Israel's enemies, and that word and Spirit are now to be passed on to Elisha.

The real point of the passage and of the chapter as a whole is contained in the following verse 15: 'The spirit of Elijah rests on Elisha', and the miracles of Elisha that follow in the Elisha cycle are intended as testimony to that gift.

Elizabeth Achtemeier
Preaching Hard Texts of the Old Testament

Proper 9/Ordinary Time 14

2 Kings 5:1-14

THE CHEAP CURE
Independence Day
2 Kings 5:1-15a

God created him all over again, and he was made new.

I have never spent the Fourth of July in New York City before, but after the fireworks over the East River last night I believe there is no better place to be. While I watched them, I thought about the Statue of Liberty out there, and Ellis Island, and the hovering spirits of so many immigrants whose children and grandchildren have turned this little spit of land into a hologram of the world.

'Sweet land of Liberty.' That is what all the fireworks are about. We call it Independence Day but sometimes I wish we would call it Freedom Day, so we could spend a little more time wondering what that word means. What are we free from? What are we free for? How do I know I am really free? Is my sweet liberty strictly a political thing – my freedom to speak, my freedom to vote – or is it a larger concept, one that includes having enough money to do what I want to do, or being able to choose how I will spend my time?

One of the most peculiar things about America, it seems to me, is that we have so much freedom and are still so unwell. As a nation we are strong, but we are not particularly healthy. Our families, our schools, our cities, and our political systems are all showing signs of disease. Beefed up on steroids of wealth and power, we look pretty good from the outside, but the truth is that inside we are feeling a little shaky.

A few minutes ago we heard the story of Naaman the Syrian, whose main claim to fame is that Jesus mentioned him in a sermon once (Luke 4:27). His story is found in the book of Kings, which is just what it sounds like – a history of the kings of Israel, from David to Zedekiah. Naaman shows up about halfway through, in the ninth century before Christ, when Jeroboam was king of Israel. Although Israel and her neighbour Aram (which we know as Syria) were frequently at war, they were momentarily at peace. Aram had the better army, however, and Israel knew it. Israel even knew the name of the commander of the Aramean army, since he had beaten them up more than once. His name was Naaman, which means 'pleasant' – an unlikely name for a warrior, perhaps – but even his enemies admitted that Naaman was a great man, whom God had favoured in battle. Think Colin Powell, only with one important difference. Naaman did not photograph well. He had leprosy, which was not as big a problem for a Syrian as it might have been for a Jew, but which ate away at Naaman in more ways than one.

He was a national hero, for goodness' sake. He had an office with a view at the Aramean Pentagon. He hobnobbed with heads of state, but there was always that awkward moment when he met people for the first time. Some handled their surprise well, but others stared at him or looked quickly away. He had learned the hard way about shaking hands. It was better to offer a slight bow, he found, with both hands clasped behind his back. That way he did not have to watch the other person decide whether or not to be brave when he held out his scabby hand. He was so tired of seeing questions register on their faces. *Good Lord, is that stuff contagious? Poor guy. It must be awful to have to deal with that. Why doesn't he just stay at home and spare himself the grief?* But their questions were nothing compared to his own. If God favoured him, then why was he sick? And why couldn't anyone in Aram make him well?

Naaman's help came from a source he never expected – a young Jewish girl who had been taken captive during one of his military raids on Israel. She was the least of the least in Aram – a slave, a child, a girl. The book of Kings does not even give her a name, but she was the one who led Naaman to his cure. She did not speak directly to him – he was far too scary for that – but she spoke to his wife, whom she served. 'If only my Lord were with the prophet who is in Samaria!' she said to her mistress one day. 'He would cure him of his leprosy!'

It was a preposterous suggestion. When the king's own physicians had failed to do Naaman any good, he was supposed to go hunting for a faith healer in Israel on the advice of a pre-adolescent serving girl? It was preposterous, but Naaman jumped right on it. If you have ever been that sick yourself then you understand why. Once you run out of respectable doctors, having done everything they said – once you have taken the pills, applied the poultices, practiced the twenty minutes of positive imaging a day and nothing has changed – well, if someone tells you about a clinic in Mexico where a doctor with a degree in veterinary medicine has discovered a substance that works wonders on humans, there is a good chance you will get in your car and go there. It may sound preposterous, but if you really, really want to get well, then you cannot afford to leave any stone unturned – even if the stone turns out to be a holy man in Israel.

As soon as Naaman's wife told him what the serving girl had said, he went to see the king of Aram, who was happy to oblige his star general. 'Go then,' the king said to him, 'and I will send along a letter to the king of Israel.' Naaman took the letter and went home to pack. Since he had no idea what a cure for leprosy cost, he emptied his bank account, loading his chariots with 750 pounds of silver and 150 pounds of gold, plus ten sets of fine clothes. Then he kissed his wife goodbye and set off for Israel, where he presented his letter to the king.

'When this letter reaches you,' it said, 'know that I have sent to you my servant Naaman, that you may cure him of his leprosy.' It was a nice gesture, however misguided. The problem was that Naaman's boss, the king of Aram, did not understand about real power. He thought the king of Israel was the man to see – that if there was a cure available in Israel then the king would surely know about it. Only the king did not know about it, because the only kinds of power he had were political power and military power. He did not know one thing about healing power – the power of God – which was why he got so upset when he read the letter.

The first thing he did, before he told anyone what it said, was to grab his royal robe and tear it right down the middle. Then he howled out loud, 'Am I God, to give death or life,' he said, 'that this man sends word to me to cure a man of his leprosy?' It sounded like a trap to him. The king of Aram had asked him to do something he could not do so that Aram would have an excuse to declare war on Israel. It was all politics to him. Politics was all he knew.

Word of the king's distress got around town pretty quickly. When Elisha – the prophet whom the little Jewish serving girl knew about, even though the king of her country did not – when Elisha heard about it, he sent a message to the king. 'Why have you torn your clothes?' he asked. 'Let him come to me, that he may learn that there is a prophet in Israel.'

That may not have been a strange message at the time, but it sounds pretty strange now. Who would think of going to a prophet for a cure? For a prediction about the future, maybe, or for a hair-raising sermon on the righteousness of God, but for help with a skin disease? What a strange idea.

But as I said before, when you really, really want to get well, you will try anything. So Naaman got directions to Elisha's house and went there. Then he lined up all his horses and chariots in the front yard and waited for the prophet to come out. What was the protocol, exactly? Should he approach

Elisha or let Elisha approach him? Was he supposed to kneel or something? He hoped not. Kneeling was really out of the question. He would offer a slight bow, with his hands clasped behind his back. 'Good sir,' he would say, 'I am General Naaman, commander of the army of the king of Aram.' That should set the proper tone. Then he could soften up a little. 'I have heard so much about you. I come with high hopes, and quite a lot of money besides. I am prepared to pay anything you ask for your services.'

While Naaman was still rehearsing his speech, the door to Elisha's house opened and a messenger came out. 'Go, wash in the Jordan seven times,' the man said to Naaman, 'and your flesh will be restored and you shall be clean.' Naaman was so surprised that he hardly heard what the man said. What kind of shabby welcome was this? Where was Elisha, the man of God? At the very least, he owed his visitor a seat in the shade and a cup of cool water. Couldn't he even come out of his house and say hello?

Naaman was furious. He had fully expected Elisha to come out to him – there in the yard – to say some grand words, to make some grand gesture, so that Naaman was cured in a spectacle that no one watching would ever forget. Instead, he was being sent away by a messenger, to go splash in the shallow, muddy Jordan River like a five-year old boy – he! General Naaman, commander of the army of the king of Aram, with nine hundred pounds of gold and silver in his luggage!

It was too much. It was too, too much. 'Are not Arbana and Pharpar, the rivers of Damascus, better than all the waters of Israel?' he spat out. 'Could I not wash in them, and be clean?' Then he turned and went away in a rage.

His servants must have known him pretty well – well enough to know that he was more hurt than mad – because they tiptoed up to him and convinced him to give it a try. *If he had given you something hard to do, you would have done it*, they reasoned with him. *So he gave you something simple.* So?

It was the beginning of Naaman's cure. He was completely emptied out. His royal connections had gotten him nowhere. His bags full of money had gotten him nowhere. Elisha would not even come out of the house to meet him, and now he had been given this supremely stupid thing to do – to strip down in front of all his men and take the world's longest bath in a river that barely came up to his knees.

But because he really, really wanted to get well, he did it. He left his clothes and shoes on the bank. He picked his way through the rocks to the deepest part of the river, where the current bumped against his body like soft pillows. The water was greenish and smelled of fish. There was nothing remotely sacred about it. Naaman found a place to kneel and sank down for the first time. It was cold under the water but not on top of it. He did not dare to look at his skin. Seven times he made the passage from cold to hot, from river to sun. Each time he rose he sucked air like a newborn. Then he went down again with his eyes wide open so that the sky wrinkled and turned green as the water. He tried not to think of anything but the numbers. By the seventh time, he was winded. He was also very clean. When he looked down at his skin, he saw the flesh of a five-year-old. It was smooth. It was fresh. He was well.

Later on he tried to pay Elisha, but Elisha would not hear of it. *Your money's no good here*, he told Naaman. *God works for free.* So it was a cheap cure. All Naaman had to do was follow directions. All he had to do was empty himself out, abandoning the pretence that who he was or what he was worth could get him what he needed. All he had to do was strip himself down until his hurt flesh was exposed for everyone to see and go play in the water like a little boy. Then God did for him what military victories and kings' bags of money could never do. God restored his flesh. God created him all over again, and he was made new.

I could explain this story to death, but I don't think I will. You may never hear it again on a Fourth of July weekend, but maybe the next time you are saying your prayers for this great, shaky nation of ours, you will remember that great, leprous man Naaman, whose wealth and power turned out to be useless to him in his search for health, and who was ready to trade it all in when God surprised him with a cheap cure that made him truly free.

Barabara Brown Taylor
Home By Another Way

Proper 10/Ordinary Time 15

Amos 7:7-17

God demands fair play, accurate weights and measures, no cheating and therefore love, respect, from traders and buyers.

With this text from Amos the lectionary begins a series of readings from the prophetic books (in the sense of books associated with individual prophetic figures), which continues for the balance of the liturgical year, the only quasi-exception being Proper 22 (Lamentations is associated with Jeremiah, but is no longer believed to have been written by him). The order is chronological, the first six texts (Proper 10 through Proper 15) being from pre-exilic prophets.

The passages appointed for this day and for Proper 11 both come from a section of the book of Amos in which four, or possibly five (depending on how one classifies them) visions are recorded. The sequence of these visions is important, and helps to set the theological outlook of the lectionary passages. The first two visions (7:1-3 and 7:4-6) are identical in form. The prophet see images of destruction (locusts, fire) which indicate God's impending judgement on the people.

In each case the prophet successfully intervenes, and the Lord decides not to pursue the divine purpose. The second set of visions (7:7-9; 8:1-3) is similar in structure to the first pair, in that each begins with a vision of destruction. (The plumb line is obviously the Lord's standard by which the people's justice and faithfulness are determined . . .) But the second set of visions takes an ominous turn in that, following each vision, there is no attempt by the prophet to intervene on the people's behalf. What is more, there is no change in the Lord's intentions: judgement appears inevitable; the people will be destroyed.

(A fifth vision is found in 9:1-4, but its form is considerably different from any of the visions in chapters 7 and 8.)

Amos 7:7-9, which constitutes the beginning of the present lection, is thus a sharp turning point in the series of visions. One suggestion is that the prophet has become so discouraged about the possibility that the people will ever pull back from their sinful ways that he makes no effort to dissuade the Lord from the Lord's purpose, as he had in 7:2, 5. Amos' complaint is twofold: the people have turned their worship into a meaningless exercise (4:4-5) and they have replaced compassion with cruelty and greed in their dealings with one another (2:6-7). Those who possess power and wealth are especially condemned (6:4-7), and they and the nation will be forced into exile (note 3:2, Amos' message in a nutshell). The prophet's memorable appeal in 5:21-24, perhaps the most often quoted passage from Amos, seems to imply that he still has hope that the nation can be saved. But it lies beside another text, 5:18-20, which suggests that even Amos has lost hope for a reconciliation between the people and their God. Perhaps, then, 7:7-9 marks that moment in time when the prophet surrenders in anger and disgust over the people's ways. It appears to be Amos' way of saying, 'You have been patient long enough, O Lord. I can no longer ask you to delay the inevitable consequences of the nation's sinfulness.'

The balance of our passage, 7:10-17, contains one of the few biographical references to the prophet. (The book of Amos, it will be remembered, is a watershed in the writing of the Bible. Whereas earlier prophets had been remembered anecdotally – the stories about Elijah and Elisha are examples – Israel now begins to collect anthologies of what its prophets have said. The book of Amos thus helps give shape to the books of Hosea, Isaiah, Jeremiah, and the like.)

Amos' preaching (see 1:3-2:16, where we may have an entire sermon by the prophet) had reached the ears of those in high places, and the results were predictable. The prophet's attacks on social predators and on false worship threatened the political-religious establishment, because their interests were vested in precisely those abuses which Amos exposed. Because the temple at Bethel, like the Temple at Jerusalem, was under the protection of the king, the priest Amaziah had no trouble receiving royal sanction for his order to Amos to leave the land. This is a pattern that would be repeated again and again, involving such persons as Jeremiah, John the Baptist, and – of course – Jesus himself. (Also note 1 Kings 22:1-28, which records a similar incident a century before Amos.)

At first glance, Amos' reply in Amos 7:14-15 seems puzzling. How is it that this man could claim to be 'no prophet . . . '? When one remembers, however, that much early Israelite prophetic activity was carried on by groups like 'the company of prophets' of Elijah and Elisha (see 2 Kings 2:7; note also 1 Samuel 10:5), it becomes evident that Amos is saying that he belongs to no prophetic band, but has been designated by the Lord to be a solitary bearer of the divine word. How much lonelier this would have made Amos' task! Amos had obeyed the command of God to assume the prophetic role, not because he cherished it, but because, like Jeremiah (Jeremiah 20:7-9), he had no alternative. He could not be the Lord's person and say no to the terrible task to which the Lord called him. And so he answers

Amaziah's demand with a further promise of judgement to come (verses 16-17). Whether he was punished for his faithfulness we can only guess.

James D. Newsome
Texts for Preaching: Year C

Verses 7-9 of the above reading speak of God setting up a plumb line and reminded me of a visit I once made to – the then – newly opened Coventry Cathedral.

At the time I was doing my theological training for the Methodist ministry at Handsworth College in Birmingham. As part of that training I spent a month working in Coventry, being based at the Central Hall. This meant that I was ideally placed for frequent visits to the cathedral both for the pleasure of looking around the building and also participating occasionally in worship.

On one visit I noticed an addition to the symbolism of the cathedral. I was familiar with the symbolic stained glass windows, the tablets of the word, the wonderful tapestry of Christ in glory and the Gethsemane Chapel; but here was something very different.

On one wall of the cathedral I saw a kind of plaque which, on inspection, pictured a city (it might have been Jerusalem) and dangling from top to bottom was a weight on a piece of string. It was a plumb line, the kind of thing a builder uses to see if his brick-laying is upright and true.

At first I wondered what it was meant to say, and then I remembered this passage from Amos, and it made sense. For God was reminding his people that he had laid down moral standards of behaviour enshrined in the Ten Commandments. Those standards had eroded or were ignored in the time of Amos. More than that, the people were dabbling in idolatry by worshipping foreign gods such as Baal. Therefore God says he will make the 'high places' (places of idol worship) desolate and lay waste all the idolatrous sanctuaries.

I believe that the old crosses in many of our country market towns functioned at first to do the same kind of thing that the plumb line did for Amos. They remind us that God demands fair play, accurate weights and measures, no cheating and therefore love, respect, from traders and buyers.

Maybe the standard of judgement for the Jew is the Ten Commandments; for the atheist, the Parable of sheep and goats that Jesus told; and for the Christian the Beatitudes of Jesus lived out by taking up the Cross and following in the same self-sacrificial way of he who is the Christ.

Ron Dale

Proper 11/Ordinary Time 16

Amos 8:1-12; Colossians 1:15-28

In the absence of moral purpose we become smaller.

Put Paul alongside Mary and Martha, and which one does he remind you of? 'For this I toil,' he writes, 'and struggle with all the energy that Christ powerfully inspires within me.' More like Martha? Yes and no. It has been customary to play the two sisters off, passive spirituality versus aggressive fussiness. Mary wins, but at a cost: as feminists point out, the model keeps both in the neat boxes devised by a male world, the one sedate and devout, the other making the tea and sandwiches.

The reality is more complex. People sat at a teacher's feet in that world, not to gaze languidly with drooping eyelids, but in order to become teachers themselves. Paul, after all, had 'sat at the feet of Gamaliel', and that hadn't made him exactly passive. Mary had crossed a boundary, entering the man's world of discipleship; Jesus had affirmed her right to be there, indeed the desirability of her being there rather than simply staying in the kitchen. Once Mary had drunk in the rich teaching of Jesus, she too would be on her feet, but not simply in the background.

Paul's energy was not simply a character trait. It was the surging new life of one who had worshipped at the feet of Jesus. Colossians, steeped in the adoration of Jesus the image, the first-born, the head, the reconciler, the fullness of God, is also a practical, down-to-earth letter, energetically getting on with the job.

Paul was commissioned 'to make the word of God fully known' (1:25). When Amos inveighs against social injustice, economic trickery and exploitation in Israel, the most terrible of his threats (8:11-12) is that there is to be a famine, not of bread, but of the word of YHWH. A vivid picture of panic: people wandering to and fro, running this way and that, longing for the word of YHWH and not finding it. Those who turn their back on the written word that commands justice, sabbath-keeping, and care for the poor, will find the spoken word gone silent on them as well. Paul's gospel, against this background, is the answer to the secret but desperate longing of the heart: the image of the invisible God, the sound of the inaudible God, the touch of the untouchable God.

Which is why, we may presume, this gospel is proclaimed in the midst of, and indeed acted out in and through suffering. When the world has gone its own way, trampling on the needy, cheating on weights and measures, casting God's wise ordering of life out of the way so that it can make another quick buck, the word of grace is bound to cause a different sort of panic. If that stuff were to get around, profits would drop. Not for nothing else does Paul celebrate the fact that Christ is Lord of the principalities and powers. Sit at the feet of this teacher, and you will find work soon enough.

N. T. Wright
Twelve Months of Sundays: Year C

Mammoth productive facilities with computer minds, cities that engulf the landscape and pierce the clouds, planes that almost outrace time – these are awesome, but they cannot be spiritually inspiring.

Nothing in our glittering technology can raise us to new heights, because material growth has been made an end in itself, and, in the absence of moral purpose, we ourselves become smaller as our works become bigger. Gargantuan industry and government, woven into an intricate, computerised mechanism, leave the person outside. The sense of participation is lost, the feeling that ordinary individuals influence important decisions vanishes, and we become separated and diminished.

When an individual is no longer a true participant, when they no longer feel a sense of responsibility to their society, the content of democracy is emptied. When culture is degraded and vulgarity enthroned, when the social system does not build security but induces peril, inexorably the individual is impelled to pull away from a soulless society. This process produces alienation – perhaps the most pervasive and insidious development in contemporary society.

Martin Luther King
The Words of Martin Luther King
Selected by Coretta Scott King

Proper 12/Ordinary Time 17

Hosea 1:2-10

This is a God whose very nature demands justice and fidelity, and who cannot tolerate a relationship from which these qualities are absent.

Sin, judgement, restoration. The full panoply of the divine-human drama is etched out in the lines of this brief passage, which continues the cycle of Old Testament readings from the pre-exilic prophets.

The sin of the nation is characterised in verses 2-3, a celebrated text which, although it presents formidable problems for the interpreter, is clear in its larger import. The reader feels an urge to protest God's command to the prophet that he marry a prostitute, even if – as is commonly assumed – Gomer is no common 'lady of the night' but a cultic prostitute attached to a local Baal shrine. How could God order so repulsive a thing? How could any self-respecting worshipper of the Lord comply?

Some have suggested that Hosea married Gomer only *later* to discover that she was engaged in sacral or some other kind of prostitution. Another possibility is that 'whoredom' is not a literal description of Gomer's activities but is, rather, a metaphor for idolatrous worship, as in 2 Kings 9:22. (Second Kings 9-10 contain another important parallel to Hosea 1; see below.)

But the likely interpretation is that it was the very reprehensible nature of Hosea's action that caused it to be such an object lesson to the prophet's contemporaries. Hosea seems to have married Gomer knowing the full measure of her character, and this union is then transformed into a paradigm of God's relationship with Israel, a relationship that the nation has corrupted almost beyond recognition (compare Hosea 2:1-15).

The relationship between 1:2-3 and 3:1-3 raises intriguing questions. Are Gomer and the unnamed woman of chapter 3 the same person? Some interpreters have understood that these are the same woman and that 3:1-3 is an autobiographical account of the same events that were described by a third party (a follower of Hosea?) in 1:2-3. But if that is so, how can the sexual absence of 3:3 be reconciled with the three children born, according to 1:4-9, to Hosea and Gomer?

God's word of judgement on the nation (verses 2-9) is vested in the names of the three children who are born to this scarred marriage: Jezreel (God Sows), Lo-ruhamah (Not

Pitied), and Lo-ammi (Not My People). Of these three, Jezreel is the most intriguing, as it recalls the bloody events recounted in 2 Kings 9:1-10:11. A curious thing is that the prophet Elisha is portrayed in this latter text as condoning, in the Lord's name, the massacre at Jezreel of the royal house of Israel (note 10:10), but Hosea cites these same events as evidence of the nation's sin (Hosea 1:4-5). Not only so, but the carnage inflicted by Jehu on Ahab's family will soon be imposed by the Lord on the nation itself, a kingdom presently ruled by Jehu's descendant, Jeroboam the Second.

Not Pitied (verse 6) and Not My People (verse 9) are names of a different order from Jezreel in that, instead of pointing to the past, they indicate the Lord's present activity: 'I will no longer have pity . . . '; 'You are not my people and I am not your God.' The Lord's patience is at an end and – not because the Lord wishes it to be that way, but because there is now no alternative – the special ties binding this people to their God are about to be broken once and for ever.

And yet . . . And yet . . .

Hosea understands as few do the essential nature of the God of Israel. This is a God whose very nature demands justice and fidelity, and who cannot tolerate a relationship from which these qualities are absent.

And yet . . . And yet . . .

These sinful people are the Lord's people. They are persons of the Lord's own choosing, connected by ties that can never be totally dissolved. Elsewhere (11:8; see Proper 13) Hosea expresses the anguish of a God who cannot ultimately let go even of those who repudiate God:

How can I give you up, Ephraim?
How can I hand you over, O Israel? . . .
My heart recoils within me;
my compassion grows warm and tender.

And so, even when it appears that the final word of God's judgement has been spoken, there is still a further word of restoration (1:10): 'In the place where it was said to them, "You are not my people," it shall be said to them, "Children of the living God." '

Now the full power of the family metaphor is felt. Like a spouse whose life has been turned to shambles by an unfaithful partner, the Lord has grieved. Like a parent who cannot love his or her children into being the kind of persons they are capable of being, the Lord recognises a relationship of brokenness. But in the end, the Lord – loving spouse, loving parent – will never turn loose. In the end, the Lord – loving Creator, loving God – will finally redeem.

James D. Newsome
Texts for Preaching: Year C

Then Moses said to God, 'If I come to the people of Israel and say to them, "The God of your fathers has sent me to you," and they ask me, "What is his name?" What shall I say to them?' (Exodus 3:13).

. . . And now – we wait in breathless suspense – what is God going to answer to this most urgent of all human questions in the field of religion? 'I will be that which I will be.' The form of expression in Hebrew makes it plain that this mysterious phrase is intended to paraphrase and to explain the hidden name of God JHVH. But is this really an explanation? Is it not rather an evasion than an answer? Yes, this is the first impression that is bound to be left upon our minds – God is withdrawing himself from the importunity of human beings. He does not allow anyone to lay claim to him, as we would so gladly do; he preserves his own freedom and the mystery of his being. But we have only gone half-way to expounding this utterance, if we see in it no more than God's refusal to answer our questions. The Hebrew word which we translated above 'I will be' signifies rather 'to be present', or even 'to take place'. Its reference, therefore, to being in act, in activity, than to being at rest; and therefore we can say with certainty that the reference here is not to God 'as he is in himself', but to God 'as he turns himself towards us'. That is, then, a word spoken by a God who condescends to us, who makes us aware of his willingness to help us. We might almost go so far as to translate it, 'I will manifest myself to be that which I will manifest myself to be'.

If God sends to those living in misery the message that he will show himself active according to his own free decision, from the first moment the affirmation is a word of comfort, an assurance that God is 'the One who is always there'; perhaps it is not too much to say that it is an assurance of the faithfulness of God.

Gerhard von Rad
Moses

163

Proper 13/Ordinary Time 18

Hosea 11:1-11

The radical difference between God and human beings lies not in power, but in the capacity to withhold judgement, to love even those who have been unfaithful.

This passage, for good reason one of the best-known chapters in the Old Testament, reflects in extreme form the style of the Book of Hosea and brings us to the heart of what is distinctive in the prophet's message. Like Hosea 11, most of the book is characterised by sudden shifts of speaker, addressee, mood, and content, to the point that it is often difficult to determine where units of speech or literature begin and end. Frequently, the interpretation of a saying will hinge on the answers to such questions. Moreover, the message of the prophet included both judgement and salvation. How are the two related, and what is the last word? In the final structure of the book, due in large measure to those who collected and edited the prophet's words, the relationship is chronological: first comes judgement followed by salvation. In our text for today, however, we find something different.

Hosea 11 is a divine soliloquy in which the prophet hears the Lord meditating and deliberating on his relationship to the chosen people. Although the mood frequently shifts dramatically, there is continuity of metaphors and images, and progress of thought from beginning to end. The structure consists of three parts: Verses 1-7 amount to a prophecy of punishment, first stating Israel's apostasy in the context of God's saving acts (verses 1-4), and then announcing military defeat and return to captivity (verses 5-7). Second, in verses 8-9 we overhear the Lord questioning himself and changing his heart. Finally, in verse 10-11 there is an announcement of salvation.

From the beginning we are led to expect something different. The Lord recalls the exodus from Egypt, often mentioned by Hosea (2:15, 12:9, 13:4), but here he employs the metaphor of a parent's care for a child. As a father calls a son, or a mother teaches a daughter to walk or takes her in her arms, so the Lord cared for Israel. The language of love dominates the recital. But for all of this care and concern, Israel was unfaithful, turning to worship other gods (verse 2). Prophets frequently used the history of salvation to accuse the people of their failure to act responsibly. The deeper the relationship, the more serious is its violation. Consequently, justice calls for punishment (verses 5-7), such as Hosea frequently proclaims in word and symbolic action (e.g. 1:2-9).

Once the sentence has been pronounced, the divine judge deliberates within his heart (verses 8-9). The Lord asks himself how he can 'give up' Israel – make an end to the covenant – and bring destruction. Meditating on such a fate tears at his heart – the seat of the will – and evokes his compassion, so the Lord vows not to allow his anger to work itself out in destruction. That is the dramatic high point of the passage – that the Lord's compassion overthrows his wrath, that the will to love overcomes the – to be sure, justified – will to punish. The drama is not acted out on the plane of history but in the very heart of God.

But the theological high point comes in the reason for this change of heart. The turning of the Lord's will is due to no human activity. Typically, prophetic announcements of salvation do not give human works as reason for the good news. The reason is, 'for I am God and no mortal, the Holy One in your midst, and I will not come in wrath' (verse 9). On the highest and most generous scales of human justice, the Lord was justified in executing punishment, but divine justice transcends human capacities for either justice or love. Indeed, the radical difference between God and human beings lies not in power, but in the capacity to withhold judgement, to love even those who have been unfaithful (cf. Hosea 3). After this, the announcement of salvation in verses 10-11 is anticlimactic.

Hosea simply presents this soliloquy without calling for a response. What is its effect on its hearers? Certainly it reminds them of the history of their God's care for them and confronts them with their own faithfulness. But how can one react to the divine compassion, to God's radical change of heart? That is the question the prophet leaves with all who read or hear this text.

Gene M. Tucker
Preaching Through the Christian Year: Year C

Honour Everyone

You must thank – or blame – Master Gibbens (His Honour Judge Brian Gibbens 1912-1985) for my sermon this morning. It was after service last Sunday that he said he found it difficult to 'take' that phrase that comes in the blessing I always use at the end of the service: 'Go forth into the world in peace; be of good courage; hold fast that which is good; render to no one evil for evil; strengthen the faint-hearted; support the weak –

Honour everyone'; and he cited certain of the people he had had up before him of late, and has had to sentence, and asked, understandably, 'Do you really expect me to honour such men?' It was a worthwhile question . . .

Behind those words 'honour everyone', lies the belief that, if God is our creator, nothing we can do can entirely deface his image in us. Nothing can entirely remove that in us which is worthy of honour; or, indeed, that which one day may be restored to what it was always intended to be.

When Polonius has said to Hamlet, 'I will use them according to their desert', Shakespeare makes Hamlet reply: 'God's bodkin, man, much better; use every man after his desert, and who should 'scape a whipping? Use them after your own honour and dignity: the less they deserve, the more merit is in your bounty. Take them in.'

One of my heroes is John Leonard Wilson, Bishop of Singapore during the Second World War, whom later, I got to know as a friend. Before he died, he preached in the Sunday Service of the BBC and gave an account of what it meant to him to suffer many weary hours of beatings and torture by the Japanese when he was in prison.

'I did not like to use the words, "Father, forgive them",' he said. 'It seemed blasphemous to use our Lord's words; but I felt them . . . When I muttered "forgive them", I wondered how far I was being dramatic, and if I really meant it; because I looked at their faces as they stood round, taking it in turns to flog me, and their faces were hard and cruel, and some of them were evidently enjoying their cruelty. But, by the grace of God, I saw these men not as they were, but as they had been. Once they were little children, with their brothers and sisters – happy in their parent's love, in those far-off days before they had been conditioned by their false nationalistic ideals. And it is hard to hate little children. So I saw them not as they were, but as they were capable of becoming, redeemed by the power of Christ, and I knew that I should say, "Forgive".'

When John Leonard Wilson went back to visit Singapore after the war, he told me that one of his greatest joys was to confirm a number of the Japanese who had taken part in flogging him in Changi Gaol.

Eric James
Judge Not

Proper 14/Ordinary Time 19

Isaiah 1:1, 10-20

God's holiness concerns every aspect of life.

The vision of Isaiah reveals the truth about God's people with a stinging indictment of their worship.

Bad news and good news. The people are (shockingly) compared with Sodom and Gomorrah (verse 10), a byword for both sin and judgement. Their worship is an offence to God as long as there is no reform of lifestyle. But this is because God's holiness concerns every aspect of life, in particular honesty, justice and concern for the poor (verse 17; cf. Leviticus 19:34).

Form and content. Ritual and lifestyle were equal concerns of the Torah ('teaching', verse 10b). Worship consisting of one and not the other is an affront to God who is One (Deuteronomy 6:4, a central confession of Israel's faith). Rites and wrongs (verse 13b) do not mix! The blood of bulls cannot hide murderous intent (verse 15b); washing with water is no substitute for holiness of life (verse 16). Sunday and Monday belong together.

Cleansing and worship. The people are put on trial (verse 18) – but suddenly God is not only accuser but acquitter! What God offers in cleansing precedes anything we can offer in worship ('Therefore . . . offer . . . ' Romans 12:1). Even the Law (whose blessings and curses from Deuteronomy 28-30 are echoed in verses 19-20) came as a gift, the initiative of a gracious God who rescued his people.

The Revd Dr Ian Paul
The Ministry of the Word

Proper 15/Ordinary Time 20

Isaiah 5:1-7

The Lord is our God, who brings us out of bondage and bears us on eagle's wings.

The Song of the Vineyard (5:1-7)

An important debate has taken place about the genre of the song. If the song is a 'love song' in the formal sense, one would expect the singer to be the bride or husband of the beloved, on whose behalf the song is sung. Yet the prophet is clearly the singer and the Lord the beloved, and the song has more to do with the relationship between the 'beloved' and his vineyard than between the prophet and God. The singer (prophet) is therefore better understood as the friend and advocate for his companion (God); he sings a song about the love of his companion for his vineyard.

Very quickly, then, the song turns into a prophetic indictment. The singer invites his listeners to hear about the careful attention his friend showered on the vineyard and of the disappointment he experienced when the vineyard yielded nothing but rank grapes. As in the case of Nathan's parable to King David (2 Samuel 12:1-10), here too one expects the listeners to be beguiled by the straightforwardness of the tale. Moreover, the 'song' format elicits the more 'gossipy' side of their interest (Clements, *Isaiah 1-39*, page 57); everyone has a perverse interest in love gone wrong. Without warning, the prophet-singer disappears in verse 3 as the owner of the vineyard speaks on his own behalf, inviting Judah-Jerusalem to pass judgement on the guilty party. Did God not do enough for his vineyard? Did he plant the wrong species of grape, perhaps? We expect the listener to indict the vineyard when instead God himself speaks the harsh sentence of judgement (5:5). The vineyard's wall will be trampled down; it will become a waste, full of thorns and briars – an image pursued in more detail in a later chapter (7:23-25). Then the final verse includes the listeners again. They are the vineyard about to be destroyed! God looked for justice (*mispat*) but found bloodshed (*mispah*); for righteousness (*sedaqah*) but instead of righteousness found a cry (*seaqah*). A similar contrast was set forth in chapter 1, where we heard of justice turned into harlotry and of righteousness into murder (1:21).

. . . It is striking that the Song of the Vineyard is the first place in the Book of Isaiah where we see first-person speech of the prophet differentiated from divine speech, as such. In fact the success of the 'song' turns in part on the unexpected shift from prophetic persona ('Let me sing for my beloved') to divine persona, accomplished at verse 3. That is, the prophet begins by telling us he will sing a song for his best friend, but then the best friend – God – speaks on his own behalf: 'Judge between me and my vineyard' (5:3). Surely this appearance of the prophet as divine spokesman, in brief but explicit terms, has influenced the decision to designate the beginning of Isaiah's career *prior* to the death of Uzziah, as the superscription has recorded it (1:1), and not as starting for the first time in the 'call' of the prophet during the reign of Ahaz (see chapter 6). That is, the book in its present form depicts Isaiah as active as prophetic speaker in chapter 5, under the cover of God's beloved, before the death of King Uzziah and the commissioning of chapter 6 . . .

The difference between prophetic speech and divine speech cannot be overdrawn: God can only 'speak' through the words of his prophets. The point of call narratives in prophetic books is to make this absolutely clear: God puts his words in the prophet's mouth (Jeremiah 1:9). The Song of the Vineyard however, makes a similar point in the context of the Book of Isaiah. It introduces the prophet as singing a song on behalf of God (Isaiah 5:1). This having been done, the song – quite effectively – shifts to direct divine address. In sum, the Song of the Vineyard functions in part to introduce the figure of the prophet as speaker on God's behalf. It is Isaiah's first clear public act as God's prophet, even as this event has been overshadowed by the episode recorded in chapter 6.

The song also spells out the message of divine judgement (5:5-7). It is striking that the images of desolation in 5:6 resemble those uttered by the prophet to the house of David in chapter 7. Here God delivers the sentence personally to all Israel. The Lord had done all he could for his beloved vineyard: selected the best location, painstakingly cleared away the stones, planted the best variety of vines, and even built a watchtower in it. But it did not yield grapes worth eating, much less grapes worthy of all this attention (5:2). Nothing more could have been done than was done (5:4).

In the Song of the Vineyard the prophet steps forward as spokesman for his good friend. In a sense his prophetic activity 'begins' here. It would be wrong to think of the prophetic books as offering one fixed notion of the prophetic call. The Book of Jeremiah presents the most classic example of a call narrative (Jeremiah 1:4-19): it is positioned at the beginning of the book; it contains the initial address (Jeremiah 1:4-6), the prophetic objection (Jeremiah 1:6), the divine rejoinder

(Jeremiah 1:7-8), cleansing (1:9), and extended commission (1:10-12, 13-19). Yet even it presents the beginning of Jeremiah's prophetic career at a point beyond the prophet's own comprehension: before he was born or even formed in the womb (1:5). The Book of Isaiah begins with an extended vision of the future (Isaiah 1-4) in which all that is left of God's vineyard is a single booth (1:8). The prophet appears in chapter 5, only to recede from view, so that a decision for judgement might be made personally by God against a vineyard that was carefully tended but failed to bear fruit. The owner himself renders the judgement. What of the prophet's own fate in that vineyard? For the answer to that question we must wait until chapter 6 and a fuller unfolding of the prophet's call.

Christopher R. Seitz
Isaiah 1-39

The above commentary stresses, among other things, the judgement of God upon his chosen people, accusing them of thievery, rebellion and murder in chapter 1 (see verses 1:5b, 1:15b, and 1:21). God had given his people commandments to live by (see Exodus 20:1-17), which forbade stealing and murder and that called for obedience to all the commandments. Here now is Barbara Brown Taylor interpreting those commandments:

'Here', God said, setting Ten Commandments into stone, 'here are ten rules for a way of life that works':

1. You shall have no other gods before me. In the first place because I am very jealous of your affections and in the second place because other gods cannot do anything for you. I am the one who brought you out of Egypt. I am the Lord your God, and you shall not give anyone else my place in your hearts.

2. No more golden calves. You look silly bowing down to little statues that you yourselves have made, and besides, you don't need them. You have me.

3. Don't throw my name around. A name is a very personal thing, and the fact that you know mine at all is a sign of closeness. Do not abuse the privilege.

4. Keep the Sabbath, not for my sake but for yours. One day a week, stop working and remember that you are more than what you do.

5. Honour your father and mother. Whatever kind of job they did on you, they are still your roots. Lose them and you lose your place in the story.

6. Don't murder. However dubious it may seem to you, all life is precious to me, including yours. Until you can make it, don't take it.

7. Don't mess around with marriage vows, your own or anyone else's. Sticking with one person is the best chance you have got of growing up.

8. Don't take what doesn't belong to you. Life may not be fair, but that doesn't mean you can't be.

9. Don't give your word on things you know aren't true. Your word is as much a part of you as your arm or your leg. Twist it and you will limp. Why would you do that to yourself?

10. Don't fondle other people's things in your mind as if they were your own. You'll not only resent them for having things; you'll soon resent yourself for not having them too. Learn to want what you have and pretty soon you will have what you want.

The wicked still prosper and the good die young, but that does not change a thing. Keeping the commandments is its own reward. Keeping covenant with God is the way of life.

'Now, therefore, if you will obey my voice and keep my covenant, you shall be my peculiar treasure among all peoples.' We are truly both. Not only peculiar but also treasure; not only treasure but also peculiar – God's own possession from the beginning of time, the rowdiest bunch of people any God ever tried to love. But love us God does, less because of who we are than because of who God is. The Lord is our God, who brings us out of bondage and bears us on eagle's wings, who gives us the law to preserve our lives, and who, though we earn God's wrath and break God's heart, keeps covenant with us, saying, 'It's all right. I still love you. I will always love you, no matter what.'

Barbara Brown Taylor
Gospel Medicine

Proper 16/Ordinary Time 21

Jeremiah 1:4-10

*Words of hope
and assurance,
conversely,
become
messengers of
renewal and
rebirth, like seeds
planted in the
soil to await the
life-giving
spring rains.*

The account of Jeremiah's call (1:4-10) must, in company with other such prophetic-call narratives, have been composed at some interval after the event. The most likely suggestion is that it was itself composed to provide an introduction to a written collection of his prophecies. In this case almost two decades would have passed since he had first experienced this sense of a divine commissioning. The interval of time, however, makes little difference as to how it is to be understood. It reveals a sense of divine authority, compulsion, and empowering which had remained with Jeremiah throughout his prophetic ministry and upon which he must certainly have reflected many times as the years passed.

Most strikingly, the book goes on to show how this sense of divine call and empowering had been tested, almost to the breaking point at a number of crisis-points in his work. The prophet could never have known at the time when he had first responded to God's call what it would truly mean. Nor could he have known how heavy and almost unbearable would be the strains it would put upon him. It was long after the first bold words of prophetic utterance from his lips had been given that he discovered how hard the task was to be that he had undertaken and how hopelessly weak and inadequate were his own human resources to cope with its demands.

The sense of call, with all that this meant by way of reliance upon God and the stripping away of all other social and personal supports, was something that was taking shape over a long and difficult period of time. It had begun for Jeremiah at a specific moment in his personal life and had continued. The experience of inner self-discovery had not ceased since that first day. The sense of call belong too to his private inner world as a part of his personal understanding of God. Yet it had to be a public and openly declared part of his self-understanding, since it alone could explain his declarations and his perceived authority to declare them. No one could confirm or deny that he possessed this calling; it was between himself and God. Just as certainly however no one could prove or disprove the truth of his prophecies save the events themselves about which they testified. It was a supremely private event to Jeremiah, while at the same time public, national, and ultimately international in its significance and consequences (cf. 1:5, 10).

Jeremiah's readiness to criticise and oppose the politics of the royal house of David and the claims and pretensions of the Jerusalem temple would lead him to positions of an extreme and radical nature. He could never have discerned this at the moment of his call. Yet he was convinced that from the moment of his being conceived he was divinely destined to be a prophet to Israel and the nations:

> 'Before I formed you in the womb I knew you, and before you were born I consecrated you; I appointed you a prophet to the nations.' (1:5)

With such words from God to him, Jeremiah sensed that he could not be and never could have been other than a prophet to declare God's word to his entire nation. At the same time he was to be a messenger to those other nations who also found themselves caught up in the web of events which had their origin in the impress of Babylonian imperialism upon the coast-lands of the eastern Mediterranean. In a practical and relevant fashion Jeremiah's birth among the priests of Anathoth in the territory of Benjamin was to prove a significant aspect of the divine fore-ordaining to such a task.

The dialogue that embodied for Jeremiah his sense of a divine call and commissioning follows a relatively well-established pattern. Jeremiah protested to God his unreadiness and unfitness for such a high responsibility. As a youth still in his teenage years, how could he command the respect and elicit the response of kings and counsellors? Yet he ultimately and unflinchingly fulfilled these tasks through his sense that God had not only commanded him to prophesy but had empowered him to do so. Had not the prophets who had gone before Jeremiah experienced the same divine empowering? Had the same experience not been true even before them in the charismatic leadership shown by the tribal judges in the days before the monarchy? Strikingly the sense of an inner exchange of words between himself and God took on a reality so sure and certain for Jeremiah that it could almost be seen and felt. So he describes the experience in visual and tangible terms: 'Then the Lord put forth his hand and touched my mouth; and the Lord said to me . . . ' (1:9).

How far this reflects a genuine vision of God's presence and how far it expresses images and feelings hidden within his own mind has been an issue commentators have frequently discussed but it has not been resolved. In any case it is a point of psychological interest only and has no bearing on the spiritual and personal sense of a transforming gift of power from God that came to the prophet. Looking back after years of testing prophetic utterance and experienced opposition, such as Jeremiah's record of his call must undoubtedly reflect, this account of the experience has suppressed all the irrelevancies to concentrate upon the one utterly clear and totally relevant feature: God had given him the authority and strength to be a prophet.

In the concluding words of his commission the prophet reveals the two-sided nature of his task:

> 'Behold, I have put my words in your mouth. See, I have set you this day over nations and over kingdoms, to pluck up and to break down, to destroy and to overthrow, to build and to plant.' (Jeremiah 1:9-10)

With exceptional boldness such words regard the prophet's pronouncements about God's intentions as passing over inexorably into stark facts and realities. Words of judgement become messengers of doom and destruction which bring to ruin nations and kingdoms, like battering rams smashing down a city's wall of defence. Words of hope and assurance, conversely, become messengers of renewal and rebirth, like seeds planted in the soil to await the life-giving spring rains.

R. E. Clements
Jeremiah

As I reread the call of Jeremiah to the high office of a prophet of God, his calling brought very clearly to mind my own call to the Christian ministry. Jeremiah's call proved to be extremely vivid and memorable, so much so that it helped sustain him in his prophetic work all his days. And, as I look back on my own call by the risen Christ getting on for fifty years ago now, I realise not only how wonderful it was, but also how important it has proved in sustaining me through many trials and troubles, along with many so called 'mountain top' experiences in ministry.

When the risen Christ stood by my bed as I was reading the Acts of the Apostles, his words to St Paul burned on the page and spoke personally and powerfully to me: 'Do not be afraid, but speak and do not be silent; for I am with you, and no one will lay a hand on you to harm you, for there are many in this city who are my people' (Acts 18:9-10). That vision and those words made me give up my job, study for the Methodist ministry; be ordained and serve 35 years in various Methodist Circuits in this country.

As I look back, I find, just as Jeremiah found, that the words and the vision powerfully sustained me at critical times. For there were times when I felt I had nothing to say, and there appeared to be no 'word from the Lord'. Yes, I did all the study, all the diligent searching of the lectionary readings, but at times there was nothing that I felt I could say or preach. Then, the direct word from God was always spoken to my relief and joy; and once I knew of nothing to say as I sat and waited to preach. But as I rose to my feet every word, as clear as a bell, was given and spoken. It proved so wonderful that I was asked for a copy of the sermon! However, that only happened once, but every week, twice on every Sunday, a word from the Lord was given and I was strengthened to proclaim it.

However, as any preacher of the Gospel will tell you, the very act of preaching causes division. There are those who glady hear and respond, and there are those who strongly, sometimes vehemently, reject the preached word; sometimes violently. So, in my own way, I can certainly identify with Jeremiah who suffered much violence in response to his message.

Just as Jeremiah sometimes had a violent and negative response to his message, he also was promised a positive one in bringing renewal and hope to his people. That too has been my experience. It is a wonderful feeling when people tell you how your sermon has given them fresh hope and joy; forgiveness from God; even a marvellous life-changing experience of the living God. When I received my call, I was at the same time promised that these ‚positive and wonderful things would also take place. Jeremiah sometimes has a negative reputation, but for me, he will always be a hero of faith and a true servant of his Lord.

Ron Dale

Proper 17/Ordinary Time 22

Jeremiah 2:4-13

God is the great giver.

This passage has an ominous tone to it, with its resonances of a law-court accusation. God is, it appears, suing for divorce from his bride, his people. But the content of the accusation reveals God to be the great giver. He offers:

A relationship of intimacy. The words describing the Lord's relationship with his people are words of intimacy: 'devotion', 'love', 'following' (verse 2). Far from being aloof, he has journeyed with his people in bad times as well as good (verse 6).

A place of abundance (verse 7). Even if Israel's wealth could not compare with other nations for much of her national life, the promise of a land 'flowing with milk and honey' (Exodus 3:8) indicated God's abundant provision.

A source of refreshment (verse 13). One can survive weeks or even months without food, but without water death comes swiftly.

Though God's grace cannot be earned, there is a cost involved in receiving it. To receive these gifts requires:

Following his ways (verses 2-5). As in a marriage relationship, we become like the one we choose as a partner ('worthless . . . worthless', verse 5). To walk in intimacy means a life of holiness (verse 3).

Remembering his story (verses 6-7). If we forget what God has done, we will fail to understand what he has in store for us.

Depending on his provision (verse 13). Building our own cisterns is hard work, hazardous, and a poor alternative to the freshness of springs.

The Revd Dr Ian Paul
The Ministry of the Word

Proper 18/Ordinary Time 23

Jeremiah 18:1-11

The more we participate in transfiguration, the less we fear, the less we feel we have to control.

The Visit to the Potter's House

We now encounter the first of several prophetic parables and sign-actions, narrated in prose, which provide further indications of the nature and extent of Israel's sin. Surprisingly for such prophetic material, there is only a broad identification of the conduct constituting rejection of the known law of God. The disclosure of Israel's sinfulness is set out in relation to a visit made by Jeremiah to a potter's house. The action of the potter is interpreted by the prophet as a sign and an analogy for the actions of God to Israel. The incident must assuredly rest upon some authentic reminiscence of the prophet which has occasioned this interpretive elaboration. A further sign-action relating to pottery is to be found in 19:1-14, which centres upon the smashing of an earthenware pot.

The visit to the potter's house is reported in 18:1-6. To this has been appended verses 7-12, an extensive admonitory address in the first person prophetic style of divine speech, which many commentators regard as a later addition. As it stands, however, its message is inextricably bound up with the analogy provided by the work of the potter. It serves to make this demonstrably plain. The word of God connected with what Jeremiah was able to see in the potter's house is very simple: 'O house of Israel, can I not do with you as this potter has done?' says the Lord (verse 6). The potter retains complete mastery over the material he uses, and the analogy between the potter working the clay and God fashioning human lives must have been an ancient and familiar one (cf. Genesis 2:7). However, this analogy is developed in a fresh direction to demonstrate that the destruction of the kingdom of Judah can properly be understood as the work of God. The perspective that this tragedy had already occurred breathes through the present form of the narrative, although it is appropriately referred to as no more than a future possibility. In working his material there are times when the potter is compelled to abandon the pot he is working on and to begin again. In this case he simply reworks the same piece of clay. This action provides the heart of the divine message: 'Behold, like the clay in the potter's hand, so are you in my hand, O house of Israel' (verse 6). The elaboration in verses 7-12 then explains more fully what this means in terms of the divine action towards all peoples.

At first glance the primary point of the potter's action appears to be to counter the unspoken objection that it is inconceivable that God could bring about the destruction of Israel, since by their elect origin and status they are 'the people of God'. Can it be thought that God would permit, let alone ordain, the destruction of Israel when they are 'his' people? The prophetic answer is that this can be so, as shown by the analogy of the potter beginning anew by reworking the original clay (verse 4). It becomes demonstrably clear that the destruction of Israel and Jerusalem is fully within the range of the working of divine providence. There is a further hidden element in the analogy that may or may not have been intended: After the original pot had been spoiled, it was nonetheless 'reworked into another vessel'. We may discern in this feature of the analogy a positive message of hope indicating that God could begin to fashion his people Israel anew.

Elaboration of the message of the visit to the potter's house in verses 7-12 undertakes a more wide-ranging and philosophical reflection on how God deals with all peoples. In the wordy formal manner of a legal pronouncement it develops the principles by which divine providence operates for all nations and individuals. We may note especially the legal formulae: 'If at any time I declare . . . and if that nation . . . And if at any time . . . and if it does (verses 7-10). This legal terminology has been employed to fulfil a didactic prophetic function, not without a certain reminiscence of wisdom. It points to a principle of conduct deduced from the cases specified: 'Now, therefore, say to the men of Judah and the inhabitants of Jerusalem: 'Thus says the Lord . . .' (verse 11). this leads on to the conclusion: But they say, 'That is in vain!' (verse 12). In its conclusion this passage has a close relationship to the priestly legal formulation set out in Ezekiel 18, where the aim is to show the divine possibility of repentance effecting a total change in God's purposes towards Israel and towards individuals within the nation. The passage in Jeremiah serves a similar purpose in demonstrating that divine justice does not exclude the possibility of human repentance. Rather it demands and expects it! Thereby a full and effective human response to the divine will can open up a wholly changed prospect for the future. The form of address 'to the men of Judah and the inhabitants of Jerusalem' (verse 11) should also be regarded as of special interest. What we may have expected as the national dimension of reference to 'Israel' is instead narrowed down to Jerusalem and its immediate environs, almost certainly pointing to the community that survived in the land after 587 BC.

The formulation of the argument establishes two central points. First it establishes that God's purpose allows the freedom of human response through repentance to determine the shape of the future – 'Return every one from his evil way' (verse 11). The people of Judah had chosen wrongly against God and had necessarily suffered the consequences of their bad choice. They had thought: 'We will follow our own plans . . .' (verse 12). Responsibility for the ruin and destruction of Judah and Jerusalem lay fully with their citizens. Blame could not be placed on an irascible and indifferent God, but destruction and ruin were the consequences of their own self-willed folly. By the same doctrine, however, repentance and a right choice towards God on a national and individual basis could establish the ground for a wholly new beginning: 'If at any time I declare concerning a nation, or a kingdom, that I will build and plant it . . . ' (verse 9). The divine grace at work in providence was applicable to every nation and individual and was such that it both explained the past and held an open door towards a better future. By such a teaching, prophecy, which could so easily be regarded fatalistically, was shown to be opposed to all fatalistic reasonings.

R. E. Clements
Jeremiah

Repentance, renewal, redemption and providence; the ability of God to respect our freedom, pursue us when we err, redeem us and give to us a future bright with new hope and new life, are some of the themes of the above lection from Jeremiah. Here then some thoughts on repentance:

We are always in need of repentance, of the willingness to acknowledge our state of forgiveness; we are always being forgiven, transfigured and forgiving, and thus being part of God's transfiguration of creation.

Sin both matters terribly and matters not at all: matters terribly as a vehicle for evil, and matters not at all because it can be transformed in the love of God. Sin, which we cannot avoid, and the acknowledgement of sin, can be a balancing factor, not a morbid preoccupation. It is rather a knowledge that adds reality to the assessment of decisions we are about to make, and brings us to a kind of self-knowledge that surpasses gladness because of the fire in the dark, and the fire in our tears.

And because we are one organism our tears cannot stop with ourselves; our responsibility cannot stop with a narcissistic perception of where our sin leaves off and another's begins. The more we participate in transfiguration, the less we fear, the less we feel we have to control. Thus the boundaries between ourselves and others become less defined and finally disappear altogether, not because we are finding ourselves by testing ourselves against the actions and reactions of others, but precisely because we are being found in God and thus need less self-reflection.

We come to a knowledge of ourselves and, at the same time, who we are no longer matters. Thus our acknowledgement of our responsibility is not the devouring, passionate, neurotic assumption of responsibility that is false guilt, but rather a recognition of the dynamic process of being privileged to acknowledge membership in the human race, and thus be a bearer of responsibility.

Maggie Ross
The Fountain and the Furnace: The Way of Tears and Fire

Proper 19/Ordinary Time 24

Jeremiah 4:11-12, 22-28

Now . . . think of what you owe your Saviour.

Two words appear to characterise the Old Testament lection for this day: total despair. Although the text is set in a larger context that finds the prophet still believing that the people may repent and that the Lord's judgement may be averted (4:1-4; 5:1), the mood of the verses appointed for this lectionary passage seems completely negative. But are they?

The theme of the Day of the Lord is in the prophet's mind in verses 11-12, which serve as an introduction to the larger lection. As best we know, it was Amos who, among the prophets, first described this day (Amos 5:18-20), and in doing so he warned the people to prepare themselves for a terrible surprise. The implication of Amos' words is that the Day of the Lord was an occasion to which his contemporaries looked forward with great anticipation, perhaps expecting a stunning military victory or some new outpouring of the grace of Israel's God. But it would be just the opposite, said Amos, a time of unimagined terror sent by the Lord.

Jeremiah knows the lessons of Amos. 'On that day' of Jeremiah 4:9 clearly has Amos' preaching in mind, and the horror described there will be so great that even those closest to the Lord will not be prepared: 'The priests shall be appalled and the prophets astounded.' 'At that time', the words with which the present lectionary passage begins (verse 11), stands in direst reference to 'On that day' of 4:9, the Day of the Lord. The metaphor of judgement here is that of the hot east wind, which on occasions blew off the high Transjordanian plateau, searing everything in its path. The Day of the Lord will be like that terrible wind in its ferocity.

The lectionary passage now skips to verse 22, a brief statement that, as the arrangement of lines in NRSV indicates, is more closely linked to verses 13-21 than it is to verses 23-28. The prophet enters the thought-world of the wisdom philosophers and borrows their terminology and conceptualisation to make an important statement about the state of the people's relationship to the Lord. They are 'foolish', 'stupid', without 'understanding'. They are like those described in the second line of Proverbs 1:7 (compare Psalm 111:10):

The fear of the Lord is the beginning of knowledge; fools despise wisdom and instruction.

'They do not know me,' complains the Lord. '[They] do not know how to do good.' Then, in a fine use of irony, Jeremiah employs the adjectival form of the very word that means wisdom, *hakmah*, to describe the inventiveness of the people's evil. NRSV's 'They are *skilled* in doing evil' (emphasis added) does not catch this play on words as does Jerusalem Bible's 'They are *clever* enough at doing wrong' (emphasis added).

Jeremiah 4:23-26 is composed of four sentences, each of which begins with a single Hebrew word meaning 'I looked'. We are reminded again of how many of those in Israel's prophetic tradition responded to the sights and sounds of the surrounding world . . . The reader is signalled straight away that what Jeremiah is witnessing is nothing other than the undoing of the created order. 'I looked on the earth, and lo, it was waste and void' (4:23). This is the only other place in the Hebrew Bible where there occurs the phrase of Genesis 1:2 that describes the chaotic state that prevailed before God began to create the world: *tohu wabohu*. (The Septuagint renders Jeremiah 4:23 even more bluntly: 'I looked upon the earth and, behold, it was not.')

The earth before creation is the spectacle that terrorises Jeremiah's vision, as does the sight of the heavens with no light (Genesis 1:3, 14), an earth with no living creatures (Genesis 1:20, 24, 26), a desert instead of fruitful land (Genesis 1:11). All of creation must suffer because of the sinfulness of the Lord's people. (Compare similar treatments of this theme in Genesis 6:5-8; Zephaniah 1:2-3.)

Jeremiah 4:27-28 completes the passage. The desolation is to be total. There is no changing the Lord's mind! To paraphrase Ecclesiastes 1:2, 'Despair of despair, says the prophet, all is despair.'

But in the midst of this terrible clamour over the Lord's anger, there is one soft note of grace. It is so inconspicuous as to be easily unnoticed, yet it is there, crouching in Jeremiah 4:27: 'The whole land shall be a desolation; yet *I will not make a full end*' (emphasis added). So astonishing is this note of mercy, so out of character with the rest of the passage, that the editors of the standard critical edition of the Hebrew Bible, usually so insightful in their suggestions, propose that the Hebrew text is defective here and that it should read 'The whole land shall be a desolation, and I will make *of it* a full end' . . .

Perhaps they are right. Perhaps this passage does reflect a time when Jeremiah had grown so weary with the waywardness of the people and so despondent over their deafness to his message that he saw no hope that things would ever be right again (compare Jeremiah 20:14-18).

But as the record of this prophet's oracles has come down to us (through who knows how many editorial hands) the very idea of the Day of the Lord, linked so fundamentally to the Lord's coming judgement, is transformed into a message of redemption. 'The days are surely coming . . . ' says the prophet over and again (Jeremiah 31:27, 31, 38), when judgement shall be overcome by restoration.

> The days are surely coming . . . when . . . just as I have watched over them to pluck up and break down, to overthrow, destroy, and bring evil, so I will watch over them to build and to plant, says the LORD. (Jeremiah 31:27-28) (Compare Jeremiah 1:10, Proper 16)

Total despair? It is understandable that Jeremiah should sink into such desperate moods. Yet Jeremiah knew Israel's God as have few mortals, and Jeremiah knew that the Lord's final word is not judgement, but redemption.

James D. Newsome
Texts for Preaching: Year C

See, Christian soul, here is the strength of your salvation, here is the cause of your freedom, here is the price of your redemption. You were a bond-slave and by this man you are free. By him you are brought back from exile, lost, you are restored, dead, you are raised. Chew this, bite it, suck it, let your heart swallow it, when your mouth receives the body and blood of your redeemer. Make it in this life your daily bread, your food, your way-bread, for through this and not otherwise than through this will you remain in Christ and Christ in you, and your joy shall be full . . .

Now . . . think of what you owe your Saviour. Consider what he was to you, what he did for you, and think that for what he did for you he is the more worthy to be loved. Look into your need and his goodness, and see what thanks you should render him, and how much love you owe him. You were in darkness, on uncertain ground, descending into the chaos of hell that is beyond redemption . . . Remember and tremble; think and be afraid.

Consider, O my soul, and hear, all that is within me, how much my whole being owes to him! Lord, because you have made me, I owe you the whole of my love; because you have redeemed me, I owe you the whole of myself; because you have promised so much, I owe you all my being.

Anselm of Canterbury
The Prayers and Meditations of St Anselm
trans. Benedicta Ward

Proper 20/Ordinary Time 25

Jeremiah 8:18-9:1; Luke 16:1-15

The master loves the world outside and wants stewards who will seek its salvation, not merely their own.

The harvest is past, the summer has ended, and we are not saved (Jeremiah 8:20). The prophet's sense of doom and anger at the greed and injustice of the people of Judah find an echo in Luke.

The first thing to get clear about the 'parable of the wicked mammon' is that it is precisely a *parable*. It is not advice about financial management: Jesus is not telling people to cheat their bosses. It makes sense within Jesus' context on the one hand and Luke's on the other.

Rabbinic parables about a master and a steward are about God and Israel. Jesus regularly charges his contemporaries with infidelity to their commission: called to be the light of the world, they have kept the light for themselves, and have turned it into darkness. One symptom of this, evidenced in the previous chapter, is that Jesus' opponents have become so concerned in keeping what they see as their master's regulations that they cannot accept that Jesus' welcome of the poor and the outcast reflects the master's real intentions. Like the elder brother in the previous parable, or the hard-hearted miser in the next one, they risk being shut out from the master's household, being put out of their stewardship. Jesus, like Jeremiah, is warning of an awesome imminent disaster, whose approach calls all standard practice into question.

What should they do? Throw caution to the winds, and embody the generous love of the master for all and sundry. The parable may hint at some local colour: the steward was perhaps remitting interest (which the master should not have been levying) rather than capital. The master could not charge him with fraud without exposing himself as a usurer. But the thrust remains: judgement is coming upon God's steward-people, and it is time for them to make what arrangements they can with the wider world, with the outcasts and the Gentiles, forgetting the minutiae of the law and the commitment to family and property. Ancestral land, no longer 'holy' has become 'unrighteous mammon', and is best used for the God of the new community, the one which the master is paradoxically calling into being through the Gospel.

The moral teaching that follows (verses 10-13) applies this more specifically. The early Church shared property, not simply as an exercise in ancient communism, but as a symbolic act: God's people were no longer defined by sacred land. Luke's fusion of this material (what was the elder brother really cross about?) throws into sharp relief his continuing challenge to the Christian community to embody God's generous welcome to all who need the good news.

The overtones ring through into 1 Timothy. First-century Jews and Christians faced the question: Granted that, as good monotheists, we must not offer sacrifice to the Emperor, what line should we take? Call down a curse on him instead? The mainstream early Church (like many Jews) said: 'No, we must pray for him, and for all officials.' This is not just political prudence. It is based on the same covenantal monotheism that underlies Luke 16. The master loves the world outside, and wants stewards who will seek its salvation, not merely their own.

N. T. Wright
Twelve Months of Sundays

Proper 21/Ordinary Time 26

Jeremiah 32:1-3a, 6-15

When hope does awaken, an entire life awakens along with it. One comes fully to life.

Jeremiah 32 marks a dramatic change in the message and ministry of the prophet. Up to this point in his career, his message had been an almost unrelenting announcement of judgement on Judah and Jerusalem. Now that his dire prophecies are on the verge of being fulfilled in the final siege and destruction of Jerusalem by the armies of Babylon, Jeremiah comes forth with an almost puzzling proclamation of good news. And it is not just puzzling to modern readers of the Book of Jeremiah. To judge by the prayer for insight that follows our lesson (32:16-25), Jeremiah himself questioned why God's word of judgement had become a word of hope.

The historical context of the words and events reported in these verses is both clear and significant. Verses 1-3a spell out that historical context both in terms of international events and the circumstances of the prophet Jeremiah, and there is no reason to doubt the accuracy of this report. The time is during the second and final siege of Jerusalem by Nebuchadnezzar, following Judah's revolt against Babylonian authority. The 'tenth year of King Zedekiah', the 'eighteenth year of Nebuchadnezzar', was 588 BC, not long before the fall of the city in 587 BC. Jeremiah is 'confined in the court of the guard' (verse 2) connected to the king's palace, apparently because his persistent announcements of the city's fall and the king's exile (verses 3-5) were considered by the authorities to be destroying the morale of the people.

What transpires at this time is an almost classic prophetic symbolic action, or sign act, but it is identified as 'the word of the LORD' that came to Jeremiah (verse 6). Reports of such symbolic actions are common in the classical prophetic literature (Isaiah 10:7-20, 8:1-4; Hosea 1:2-9, 3:1-5; Ezekiel 4:1-17, 5:1-17) and may be either third person or first person accounts. Jeremiah 32:6-15 is a first person account. It includes the report of the divine instructions to perform a particular action (verses 6-8), the report that the prophet did as told (verses 9-14), and the interpretation of the meaning of the action (verse 15).

By means of the report and interpretation, a simple real estate transaction becomes a message from the Lord. During the siege, and possibly when pressure from the Babylonians had been relieved by the advance of the Egyptian army, Jeremiah, having been informed by the Lord what is about to happen, has a visitor. Hanamel, the son of his uncle Shallum (verse 7), comes to Jeremiah in the court of the guard and asks him to buy his 'field that is at Anathoth in the land of Benjamin, for the right of possession and redemption is yours' (verse 8). Behind this allusion is the traditional view of land ownership in ancient Israel; namely, that it is to remain in the family (Leviticus 25:25-31; cf. also Ruth 4), and when it is to be sold it is to be offered to the closest relative. Because we are not told why Hanamel wants to sell the field, that point must not be important to the prophet's message.

The details of the transaction are spelled out in meticulous and technical detail (verses 9-14). These verses give us the clearest picture in the Hebrew Scriptures of such legal transfers (see also Genesis 23 and Ruth 4). Everything was done according to law and tradition. Jeremiah reports that he weighed out the purchase price (seventeen shekels of silver) and handed it over to his cousin, signed and sealed the deed, and had the process witnessed. Then, in the presence of Hanamel and the witnesses, Jeremiah turned over the deed of purchase to Baruch the scribe, instructing him to put the documents 'in an earthenware jar, in order that they may last for a long time' (verse 14). The reference to two deeds, one sealed and one open, recalls the use of double documents in Mesopotamia, both containing the same terms and sealed, but one inside the other. But Jeremiah's documents would have been either papyrus or leather. Most likely there was actually only one piece of writing material with the contents written twice. One half would have been rolled up and sealed, leaving the other half open for public inspection. The sealed copy would ensure against altering the contract and could resolve any disputes.

Not only the introduction of the report as the 'word of the Lord' but also the particular instructions to Baruch begin to indicate that this transaction is more than a simple purchase of property. That he is to place the deed in a jar so that it will last a long time might not be unusual, but in this context it takes on special significance. This word of the Lord concerns the events in the distant future. The interpretation in verse 15 discloses how Jeremiah's action is a message from God: 'Houses and fields and vineyards shall again be bought in this land' (verse 15). This message is secure because the prophetic symbolic actions, like their words from the Lord, were understood not as dramatisations or as ways to make complex messages clear but as actions that set the future in motion.

As the later interpretations (32:16-34) of this message make plain, this symbolic announcement of salvation does not contradict Jeremiah's previous announcements of judgement. He does not share the wishful thinking of his fellow inhabitants of Jerusalem that the city would not fall nor the people be carried off into exile. He was convinced the end of the city was in sight, and it was. The message of the purchase of the field ws good news for the more distant future. The Lord would indeed punish Judah and Jerusalem for the sins, but that would not be the end of the Lord's history with the Lord's people. After the Exile the Lord would bring them back and settle them on the land, and fields would again be bought and deeds signed and sealed and witnessed (32:44).

Gene M. Tucker
Preaching Through the Christian Year: Year C

The more I read and ponder the life and work of Jeremiah, the more convinced I am that it was hope in God and in the better future only he could bring in, that sustained him through all his anguished prophetic ministry. So a short meditation on hope:

When hope does awaken, an entire life awakens along with it. One comes fully to life. It begins to seem indeed that one has never lived before. One awakens to life that is eternal in prospect, a life that opens up before one all the way to death and beyond, a life that seems able to endure death and survive it. Wherever hope rises, life rises. When one first enters upon the spiritual adventure, hope rises where there was no hope before, where there was a life of 'quiet desperation', and life rises too, the life of the spiritual adventure, the sense of being on a journey in time. There is *something to live for* where before there was nothing. Yet it proves not to be enough. One's heart is kindled, and yet there is a residue of darkness in it that remains unkindled. That dark residue is touched only when one discovers a new and unknown life in another person. Where one finds the other, a new hope rises and one seems now to have *someone to live for*, but that hope is disappointed. The dark residue in one's heart has been heated but not to the kindling point, the 'fire point' after which it will burn by itself. It reaches the kindling point only 'when we dead awaken', when one discovers a life that is able to live through death and loss. When the hope of living through death arises within one that appears to be the very life one is hoping for, the life that is spoken of in the words of promise 'and whoever lives and believes in me shall never die'.

John S. Dunne
The Reasons of the Heart

189

Proper 22/Ordinary Time 27

Lamentations 1:1-6

If grief, whether for death or disaster, is not expressed, it will be repressed and continue to cause pain, depression, and anger.

In the Christian canon the Book of Lamentations is among the prophetic books, following Jeremiah. This is the result of the traditional attribution of the book to the prophet Jeremiah, as early as the time when the book was translated from Hebrew into Greek. But in the Hebrew canon, Lamentations is included with the writings as one of the *megillot*, five books connected with specific events in the liturgical calendar. Appropriately, the Book of Lamentations is read in Jewish worship on the occasion that commemorates the destruction of the temple by the Romans in AD 70.

Lamentations consists of five carefully crafted poems that arose during or after the Babylonian Exile. Although Jeremiah was not the author, it is fitting to associate the book with that prophet both in terms of mood and historical circumstances. In sombre words Jeremiah announced the fall of Jerusalem and the exile of its people; Lamentations bewails the city's destruction and the dispersion of its population into foreign lands.

The first four of the five poems are alphabetic acrostics; that is, lines or verses begin with successive letters of the Hebrew alphabet. For the most part, the poetry is in the qina metre, a distinctive rhythm common to dirges. In fact, in some cases the Hebrew word means dirge or lamentation (Amos 5:1). These poems are similar in some ways to the communal complaints or laments in the psalms (Psalms 44, 74, 79, 80). They share with these songs a mood of deep sadness and describe disasters for the community. However, the communal complaints of the psalter finally are prayers, petitions to God for help in time of national trouble. These poems, on the other hand, hardly address the Lord. The various speakers seem to speak to and for the community that has experienced tragedy. Thus they are formally and functionally more like the dirges or funeral songs that express and thus try to come to terms with grief (2 Samuel 1:17-27).

In many respects Lamentations 1:1-6 sets the tone for the entire book. These verses graphically describe the disaster that has befallen Jerusalem and its people, and mourn over what has happened. Each successive verse paints a different facet of the state of the city after its destruction. Verse 1 contrasts Jerusalem's former status with the present. Once full of people, she is lonely; once great, she is now a widow; once a princess, she is now a vassal. In verse 2 the city, personified as a woman, is heard to weep with none to comfort her; her friends have become her enemies. Verse 3 is a rare instance in the book when the grief is extended beyond Jerusalem to the nation, Judah, who is now in exile. Verse 4 is filled with allusions to the temple and worship there. 'Zion' refers specifically to the temple mount, but often is a synonym for Jerusalem. The 'festivals' here would have been the great pilgrimage feasts. In verse 5 the description of the disaster of the Exile continues but now it is interpreted theologically as the Lord's punishment for the people's sins. Verse 6 uses the affectionate title 'daughter Zion' for the city, which has lost its majesty and whose princes are pursued like deer before the hunter.

Rituals of mourning and funeral songs are essential for the survival and well-being of both individuals and communities. If grief, whether for death or disaster, is not expressed, it will be repressed and continue to cause pain, depression, and anger. Thus Jewish communities over the centuries have continued to find in these ancient lamentations the means to articulate their own grief. These songs have also functioned as the confession of corporate sin, even over the generations, as verse 5 makes clear. We, too, might find in these sad songs the words to express our own pain over community disasters, whether on the level of the congregation, the neighbourhood, the nation, or even the whole world. And in the process we can lift up the community's responsibility for such disasters to one another and to God.

Gene M. Tucker
Preaching Through the Christian Year: Year C

Some years ago I read E. Annie Proulx's Pulitzer Prize winning novel *The Shipping News*, first published in 1993. It is set mainly in Newfoundland where the locals joked that they had four seasons: fall, winter, misery and summer; certainly a bleak and harsh area in which to live.

The story concerns a man named Quoyle, a slow-witted single father who, following the death of Petal his tempestuous and unruly wife in a car crash moves to an isolated old family home set on some rocky cliffs in Newfoundland. There he manages to find a job on the local newspaper reporting car crashes and the people who become fatally injured as a result of them. Later on he is promoted to writing articles about local sea-going vessels and their histories; who built them and who sailed them.

As Quoyle settles in to his new home and job he is made aware of some of the tragic stories of local people; many of whom, like his own daughter, refuse to face up to their own tragic past; all the pain and suffering that they had come through.

However, one by one, as Quoyle hears the stories, he contrives to make people admit and face up to their tragic past. He himself falls in love with a local widow who, on first meeting, says that she is still grieving over the death of her husband. Quoyle, having heard other stories about the death of her husband, confronts her and demands the truth. Only after she tells the real story of how she herself killed her husband does their romance begin to blossom and both find new life and happiness.

That happiness can also now include Quoyle's young daughter who for a number of years could not face the fact that her mother had died so tragically because she is helped by her father to face it, admit it and accept the pain of it.

As the exposition of Lamentations 1:1-6 above makes very clear, grief has to be expressed and also guilt because otherwise repression continues to cause deep pain. It has been my privilege over the last forty years to help a number of people to see the truth of all this and to be humbled in awe and wonder when they have.

For myself, I have also had to learn these lessons and be brutally frank and honest with myself and with God the Holy Trinity of Love who, even though he knows the very worst in me, nevertheless has always heard my lament with a marvellous patient love and acceptance of me. What a mercy and blessing that has always proved to be!

Ron Dale

Proper 23/Ordinary Time 28

Jeremiah 29:1, 4-7

The responsible man seeks to make his whole life a response to the question and call of God.

There is one very interesting historical phenomenon that is profoundly important to the history of humankind: the Jewish people survived the Babylonian exile. If this fact does not appear particularly impressive on its face, one need only remember that Judah's twin, the Northern Kingdom of Israel, had been carried off in substantial numbers into captivity by the Assyrians in 722 BC. Except for those people left in the land (who later came to be called Samaritans), the so-called 'lost tribes' of Israel disappeared from history. (Claims that they were ancestors of Native American people are without foundation.)

However, by the mercy of God, the Jews survived their ordeal in Babylon. Many Jews, descendants of the original exiles of 597 and 587 BC, would ultimately find their way back to Judea in the years following their release from captivity in 538 BC. Others would elect to stay in Babylon and perpetuate a vital Jewish presence there that continued unbroken until anti-Jewish sentiment virtually destroyed the Jewish community in the Mesopotamian valley a few years ago.

In a sense, it is idle to raise the question of why the Jews survived, while the community of Samaritan exiles vanished. The short answer, of course, is that such was the will of God. But in human terms, much of the credit for the survival of the Jewish exiles may be laid at the feet of Jeremiah. For it was Jeremiah who, more than any other spokesperson for God, provided those words by which the people could come to terms with the tragedy of their nation and, thus, could rise above it. If Jeremiah's enemies had succeeded in any of their several attempts to kill him (Jeremiah 26:11, for example), one might argue that God would have raised another to take Jeremiah's place. Yet while God's mercy restored the nation (note Jeremiah 31:27-34, Proper 34), Jeremiah was an essential tool by which that restoration took place.

At some time after the initial capitulation of Jerusalem in 597 BC, but before the terrible destruction of the city in 587 BC. which marked the end of King Zedekiah's fruitless revolt, Jeremiah wrote a letter to those Jews who had been forced to go to Babylon in the company of King Jehoiachin (Jeconiah of 29:2). The questions with which those captives wrestled were haunting. Many in Jerusalem, who had heard the prophetic promise of judgement from Jeremiah and others, announced with satisfaction that the exiles of 597 had been chosen to receive God's wrath because they were more evil than those who had been spared (note the account of the vision of the figs in Jeremiah 24:1-10). Could that possibly be true? The exiles wondered.

What should be their attitude toward their present confinement? Should they resist, hoping that if they rebelled, God would send a deliverer to save them. It seems evident from the record in the book of Jeremiah that some Jews in Babylon actually tried to revolt, only to be condemned to a horrible death by the government of King Nebuchadnezzar (29:21-23).

Into their confusion Jeremiah injects his coolly reasoned advice (29:4-7). The captivity of the people is from the Lord of hosts, the God of Israel, and, as such, should not be resisted by God's people (verse 4, compare 27:5-11). It will not end soon, and any who promise that it will are deluding the people. Instead, the people should 'build' and 'plant', two verbs that form part of the Lord's original commission to Jeremiah (1:10, see Proper 16). They must expand their families, so as to ensure the survival – indeed, the expansion – of the people in this hostile land (29:6).

Perhaps most surprising of all, the exiles should so identify themselves with their captors' community that they look upon themselves as its citizens (verse 7). 'In its welfare you will find your welfare' is the climax of this astonishing advice.

It is not difficult to comprehend why many of Jeremiah's Jewish contemporaries considered him a traitor to the cause of his nation and imprisoned him as a subversive (37:11-15). Even the Babylonians thought of him as their ally and offered him asylum after the destruction of Jerusalem (39:11-14).

But Jeremiah was no traitor, because his only motivation was to do and speak the will of the Lord. Because the Lord had designated Nebuchadnezzar as the divine agent of judgement, any resistance to the Babylonian king was resistance to the Lord. In due time the Lord would restore the people (29:10), but until then the people must make their peace with their situation. If that meant co-operation with the Babylonians, so be it. The will of the Lord must be fulfilled.

This text raises fundamental questions, not all of which it answers. Perhaps the most important is: When should the people of God resist tyranny? Universal statements will not stand, for each tyrannical situation must be evaluated on its own. The Jews of Nazi Germany were forced to confront that question, as were many Christians. The Jews of the Warsaw ghetto and Dietrich Bonhoeffer, to name but two examples, decided that resistance to tyranny was the godly thing to do. No one may judge them to have been in error. But the testimony of Jeremiah is that sometimes resistance is not the will of God. Sometimes passiveness is God's will (compare 1 Timothy 6:1).

Each person must decide the issue for herself or himself – sometimes, again and again – relying on scripture, prayer, and the traditions of the church (or synagogue) as guides.

James D. Newsome
Texts for Preaching: Year C

Both Jeremiah in his day and Dietrich Bonhoeffer in his, had to cope with enemy hostile forces. For Jeremiah it was King Nebuchadnezzar who not only invaded the prophet's homeland, but also carried off many of his fellow citizens to live in exile. For Bonhoeffer, the enemy was within – Hitler and the forces of Nazism and the Gestapo.

Both men were imprisoned for their beliefs and suffered for their faith; both men had to wrestle hard on how to make their response: to work with the enemy or oppose him. In the end Jeremiah though was regarded by the invading Babylonians as a friend and cared for, but as an enemy and a traitor, by his own people. Bonhoeffer, because he was involved in the plot to kill Hitler was regarded as an enemy and was put to death.

So here are two short extracts from the writings of Bonhoeffer on the need for courage and faith in harsh times:

What lies behind the complaint about the death of civil courage? The last ten years have produced a rich harvest of bravery and self-sacrifice, but hardly any civil courage, even among ourselves. To attribute this to personal cowardice would be an all too facile psychology. Its background must be sought elsewhere. In the course of a long history we Germans have had to learn the necesssity and the power of obedience. The subordination of all individual desires and opinions to the call of duty has given meaning and nobility to life. We have looked upwards, not in servile fear, but in free trust, seeing our duty as a call, and the call as a vocation. This readiness to follow a command from above rather than our own private opinion of what was best was a sign of a legitimate self-distrust. Who can deny that in obedience, duty and calling we Germans have again and again excelled in bravery and self-sacrifice? But the German has preserved his freedom – what nation has talked so passionately of freedom as we have, from Luther to the idealists? – by seeking deliverance from his own will through service to the community. Calling and freedom were two sides of the same thing. The trouble was, he did not understand his world. He forgot that submissiveness and self-sacrifice could be exploited for evil ends. Once that happened, once the exercise of the calling itself became questionable, all the ideals of the German would begin to totter. Inevitably he was convicted of a fundamental failure: he could not see that in certain circumstances free and responsible action might have to take precedence over duty and calling. As a compensation he developed in one direction an irresponsible unscrupulousness, and in another an agonising scrupulosity which invariably frustrated action. Civil courage however can only grow out of the free responsibility of free men. Only now are we Germans beginning to discover the meaning of free responsibility. *It depends upon a God who demands bold action as the free response of faith, and who promises forgiveness and consolation to the man who becomes a sinner in the process.* [Author's italics]

Who Stands His Ground?

Who stands his ground? Only the man whose ultimate criterion is not in his reason, his principles, his conscience, his freedom or his virtue, but who is ready to sacrifice all these things when he is called to obedient and responsible action in faith and exclusive allegiance to God. The responsible man seeks to make his whole life a response to the question and call of God.

Dietrich Bonhoeffer
Letters and Papers from Prison

Proper 24/Ordinary Time 29

Jeremiah 31:27-34

I will put my law within them, and I will write it upon their hearts.

The New Covenant (31:31-34)

The prophecy of the new covenant in 31:31-34 is unique in the Old Testament and raises some of the most far-reaching questions about the nature of the hope expressed in its literature. It may be stated at the outset of the exposition that it is highly unlikely that the passage, in the precise words in which it is now formulated, is from Jeremiah's own lips (or pen!). The promise is couched in the elevated language and style of the homiletical prose which marks much of the editorial and developmental material in the book. It represents a concern to express the authoritative word of hope given through Jeremiah concerning the restoration of Israel (cf. 32: 1-15) and to set this out in carefully defined theological terms. It endeavours to make clear and precise what restoration will mean for the future of Israel in regard to the nature and conditions of her relationship to God. The unspoken question that underlies what it has to declare is this: If Israel's sins in the past brought such fearful judgement upon the nation so that it came close to annihilation, what assurance can there be that after a future restoration has taken place the same fate will not befall Israel again? The theologically conceived response to this is that God will, by the very creative power of his love, write the law of the covenant upon the hearts of the men and women who make up Israel. This is to be understood as a radically new type of covenant . . . The old covenant of the law is dead; instead there will be an inner power and motivation towards obedience on the part of Israel written on the very hearts of the People of God, not on tablets of stone. Although the word 'spirit' is not used, the implication is certainly that God's Spirit will move the hearts of Israel to be obedient to the divine law.

A number of major theological issues are raised by this understanding if the full reasoning or consequences that relate to them are not fully spelled out.

1. Although the term 'covenant' appears to have deep roots in Israel's religious history, it was given fullest prominence in the Deuteronomistic literature of the late seventh and early sixth centuries BC. It is this Deuteronomistic language and theology that has so strongly coloured the thinking

of Jeremiah's editors. The term 'covenant', drawn most directly from the sphere of international relations (perhaps more properly 'treaty'), allowed for a flexible, two-sided portrayal of the mutual commitments involved in the relationship between God and Israel.

2. A sense of the radical nature of Israel's 'breaking' of the covenant implied not simply a transgressing of its demands but such a scale of transgression as to render the covenant effectively annulled. It had been 'broken' so that it was no longer in force. This radical breach is given force by the introduction of the analogy of a broken marriage (verse 32).

3. In this promise of the new covenant the concepts of 'law' and 'covenant' are treated as virtually synonomous, which is also the case elsewhere in the Deuteronomistic usage.

4. A measure of uncertainty is left over what exactly the new covenant will amount to. A new law is not properly envisaged at all, but only a new way of knowing and keeping the existing law of the covenant made on Sinai (Horeb). What is promised is not so much a radically different covenant but a renewed form of the earlier, broken covenant. Only later, in the thinking of the Jewish community at Qumran and among the early Christian community (cf. Luke 22:20), did the idea begin to emerge that a wholly new covenant was intended by God. Certainly there came to exist in Jewish thought of the later Old Testament period very different understandings of what was foretold concerning the content of the 'new covenant' between God and his people. So too, among the early Christian communities, more than one understanding arose about the relationship of the new covenant to the law of Moses.

5. The promise of verse 33, 'I will put my law within them, and I will write it upon their hearts', closely recalls the words of Deuteronomy 6:6: 'These words (of the law) which I command you this day shall be upon your heart.' The concern in the Old Testament passages, in contrast to what emerged later in Christian thinking, was not for a law that could be summarised in certain succinct, fundamental principles. Rather it was for an obedient attitude towards the law. The central attention is upon the willingness to obey the known law, not for the clarification of obscure or conflicting elements within the law. The issue is focused on whether Israel is willing to obey the law that God has so graciously given.

6. In noting the importance of the relationship between the new covenant and the Mosaic law, it should be noted that verse 33 defines the human partners to the covenant in a strikingly significant way as 'the house of Israel'. Use of the quite imprecisely defined term 'house' instead of 'nation' must be of set purpose. Israel was now no longer a nation but an emergent group of scattered communities in diaspora. Furthermore the covenant itself, with its focus on the conscious moral bond between God and the people based on a given law (Torah), stands at some distance from the parallel notion that began to emerge of a relationship between a people and their God based on genetic descent and the sign of circumcision (cf. Genesis 17:9-14). From this we can see how later Judaism gradually became conscious of a tension in the understanding of divine election between the ideas of gift and obligation. This tension became very important in the conflicts within Judaism in the first century BC and is powerfully reflected in Paul (esp. Galatians 2:15-21).

R. E. Clements
Jeremiah

The unusual story of Henry Suso (1300-1365), the German mystic, is an illustration of how one man sought to express his 'covenant' love for God, though not recommended in today's world!!

No man ever practised more painful self-torture than Henry Suso, a fourteenth-century mystic of great charm and sensibility. At the age of eighteen he had experienced a spiritual awakening, but in disburdening his heart, he laid upon it, mistakenly, heavier burdens. He lived in a Dominican friary at Constance, which was built out into the lake and is now the Insel Hotel. Here he made for himself a little cell and oratory in what was not much more than a cupboard under the stairs; and here, out of sheer devotion, he pursued that strange and austere discipline which occupied the best years of his life. He came to see, however, in middle life, that such methods were unwise and confessed his mistake in supposing that God calls for such unnecessary suffering.

He became a disciple of the great Master Eckhart and was a close associate of Tauler, Ruysbroeck, and others, who belonged to the Strasbourg group of mystics known as the

'Friends of God'. In his autobiography, which has great literary charm, he tells us how with a style he inscribed in the flesh above his heart the Name of Jesus, then went torn and bleeding from his cell to the pulpit under the crucifix, and kneeling down, said: 'Lord, look now upon my heart's intense desire. I cannot imprint thee any deeper in myself; but do thou, O Lord, I beseech thee, complete the work, and imprint thyself deep down into my very inmost heart.' So he bore the name of Jesus upon his flesh until his death, and with every beat of his heart the Name moved with it.

Frederick C. Gill
The Glorious Company

Proper 25/Ordinary Time 30

Joel 2:23-32

Judgement and mercy met on the cross.

Most likely immediately post-exilic, Joel's message is an admixture of judgement, repentance and blessings. As with the other prophets, he is a 'covenant enforcement mediator' (Stuart and Fee, *How To Read the Bible for All Its Worth*), and frequently cites other prophets and the law (2:13 quotes Exodus 34:6; 2:32 quotes Obadiah 1:17, 3:10, cf. Isaiah 2:4) He proclaims the coming of:

Renewed covenant (verses 23-26). The material blessings will be real enough, but their primary significance is in declaring that, following the people's repentance (2:12-17), the covenant with God is re-established (see Deuteronomy 11:13-17; Leviticus 26:3-5). A change of heart opens the doors to God's generous rule (Mark 1:15).

Renewed people (verses 27-29). The renewal of covenant leads to the restoration of God's presence (verse 27), a sharp contrast to the departure of the glory in the destruction of the temple. Open hearts to God's covenant love also means open hearts to the renewing work of his Spirit.

Renewed visitation (verses 30-32). The Day of the Lord was to be a moment of judgement and mercy – judgement on the nations (3:2) and also on Israel (1:15-16), but mercy on all who call on God's name (verse 32).

This passage 'bursts its original wrappings and leaps into the New Testament with wider and deeper significance' (L. C. Allen, *Joel, Obadiah, Jonah and Micah*). For Jesus' arrival was God's visitation (Luke 19:44); judgement and mercy met on the cross (Romans 10:13); the Spirit was poured out at Pentecost (Acts 2:16ff.); and God's renewed covenant re-established with a wider Israel (Acts 10:34-35). And we await the final visitation, when the fulfilment inaugurated in Christ reaches its completion.

The Revd Dr Ian Paul
The Ministry of the Word

Proper 26/Ordinary Time 31
Fourth Sunday before Advent

Habakkuk 1:1-4; 2:1-4

A spirit of trust and dependence characterises the lives of God's faithful people.

Although not all the material in the book of Habakkuk is the composition of a single hand (for example, the entire third chapter appears to have been unknown to the author of the celebrated Habakkuk commentary discovered at Qumran), the heart of the book seems to have been prompted by one of the several Babylonian invasions of Judah in the late seventh and early sixth centuries BC. Its author had every reason to be discouraged, as his nation's defences, and those of Judah's neighbours, were pushed aside. But Habakkuk also had an uncommon amount of frankness and courage, and he was bold enough to put to God those questions which must have been in the hearts of many devout Jews. Chief among these: Granted the sinfulness of God's people, why does God allow an even more sinful alien folk to oppress them? When one remembers that Habakkuk was a contemporary of Jeremiah, a prophet who went to great pains to assert that the Babylonian king, Nebuchadnezzar, was an agent of God (Jeremiah 27:6), his questioning of God's motives is all the more remarkable.

The core of the book consists of a series of conversations with God, in which the prophet first interrogates God and then God replies. The manner in which the present lection is structured captures the dialogical nature of the material, in that Habakkuk 1:1-4 represents the prophet's questioning of God, while in 2:1-4 God responds.

If 1:1-4 strikes one as similar to other Old Testament laments, that is not accidental. The opening complaint, 'O Lord, how long . . . ?' is echoed in a number of texts (compare Psalms 13:1, 62:3; Job 19:2) and is somewhat confrontational in nature. Destruction and violence (Habakkuk 1:2-4) are abroad in the land, and God seems unconcerned. Law and Justice are forfeit – disorder prevails at every hand. We learn from 1:6 that the wicked ones who 'surround the righteous' (1:4) are none other than the feared Chaldeans (or Babylonians), whose skills at terror are legendary (note verses 6-11). The prophet cannot understand how the Lord, Israel's god, would allow such horror while still claiming to be a righteous God (see verse 13).

In the face of such incomprehensible behaviour on the part of the Lord, the prophet defiantly positions himself to hear the

Lord reply to his protest (2:1). When the Lord does speak, the message is accompanied by indications that it is very, very important, as shown by the prophet's instruction to write down what he has learned in characters so large and legible that even a passing runner (a refugee from the Chaldeans?) may read it (verse 2). It may appear to ordinary mortals that the Lord takes a very long time to make the divine will known; but one must not be impatient, for the truth will come (verse 3). And the truth is this: Whereas the proud live their lives by principles of falsehood ('their spirit is not right'), 'the righteous live by their faith' (verse 4).

In other words, a spirit of trust and dependence characterises the lives of God's faithful people. The problem caused by so much evil in the midst of a world presided over by a righteous God does not admit a solution based on logic. Rather, insight into this problem comes to women and men who are confident that God has certain purposes in human life and that those purposes are full of love and grace – even if God's people do not always understand in detail what God is up to. The faith of such people is not a conceptual matter (as in the proposition 'I believe that God exists'). It is rather a casting of oneself on God in the conviction and hope that God does what is right by God's world and by God's people. The word in 2:4 translated 'faith' may also mean 'faithfulness.'

If the matter seems less than fully resolved – if all the questions have not been completely answered – that is part of the human condition. When all is said and done, the nature of life before God is one of trust, and the hope based on that trust.

This text from Habakkuk has played a significant role in the faith of the church. Quoted several times in the New Testament (Galatians 3:11; Hebrews 10:38), its most significant citation is perhaps in Romans 1:17. Here Paul cites Habakkuk 2:4 as an illustration of his assertion concerning the centrality of faith in the life of the Christian: 'The one who is righteous will live by faith' (or, as the NRSV margin has it, 'The one who is righteous through faith will live').

Martin Luther, at a critical time in his own life, was profoundly influenced by Habakkuk 2:4 when he read Paul's quotation of the text in Romans 1:17. Luther is reported to have written the latin word *sola* ('only') in the margin of his Bible beside Romans 1:17, a significant early expression of what became for him the important Reformation doctrine of justification by faith alone.

James D. Newsome
Texts for Preaching: Year C

Many years ago, when I first began to wrestle with the problem of evil and why bad things happen to ordinary so-called 'good' people, and some of the whys and wherefores of evil done on a massive scale as well as on the personal level, I began to read as widely as I possibly could about the problem. One most helpful book was *Evil and the God of Love* by John Hick. I also visited Israel a lot to guide pilgrims around the Holy Land and in doing so I visited the Holocaust Museum. There I saw some of the terrible atrocities vented on ordinary Jewish men, women and children. I was in tears as I walked through the Children's Memorial dimly lit by three million candles, one for every child who died under the Nazis. As I walked through, holding gently to the guiding rope handle, a disembodied voice read out continually the name of every child as an act of remembrance. It was one of the most moving experiences of my life and made the search for some kind of answer to the problem of evil all the more urgent.

Some time later I came across a story that was horrific, but strangely helpful. It told of how one day in one of the Nazi concentration camps two Jews were discussing the problem of belief in God in such a world as theirs. Was it possible to believe that they were part of God's chosen people when they were being sent to their deaths in such atrocious circumstances. Apparently one Jew was a believer, the other had lost all faith. The believer was trying to say that in spite of everything to the contrary, God still loved his people.

As they were having their discussion a German soldier roughly pushed a young Jewish boy to the ground and shot him dead. In his horrified response the unbelieving Jew said to his friend, 'Where is your God now?' The reply he was given was, 'Right there, being beaten and shot dead.' In other words, God so identified with the boy that he himself suffered also with, in and for him.

But in the end, there is no rational answer to the problem of evil in the world that so profoundly affects us personally and socially because evil is totally irrational, beyond all reason. The believer can only do as the prophet Habakkuk taught: 'the righteous live by their faith'; trusting God in dark times as well as good ones. In fact, I have sometimes been made aware of God's presence in the evils of prison life and riots more than when taking a stroll in a lovely garden or in the beauty of creation; and I have suddenly remembered during the bad times those words concerning Moses: 'Moses went up into the darkness, where God was.'

Ron Dale

All Saints' Day

Daniel 7:1-3, 15-18

*God will put
an end to the
worldly enemy
and will set up a
kingdom in which
the faithful will
take their place.*

The specific link between All Saints' Day and this text is its reference to 'the saints of the Most High' (verse 18, RSV). But a reading from the Book of Daniel is highly appropriate for other reasons as well – its apocalyptic vision of a final judgement day, of the resurrection of the dead (Daniel 12:1-3), and a kingdom of God in which the saints take their rightful place.

Our lection comes from the central chapter in the Book of Daniel, which was written during the Hellenistic period in a time when faithful Jews were experiencing persecution. The one responsible for their trouble was the Seleucid ruler Antiochus Epiphanes. Because so much of the symbolism of the book relates directly to historical persons and events, it can be dated with confidence to 167-164 BC.

Daniel 7 contains the first four vision reports in the book. Although similar in some ways to earlier prophetic visions, the apocalyptic visions are quite distinctive. Like most prophetic visions, they report what was seen and then give an interpretation. Often the visionary sees himself in the revelation and sometimes in dialogue with God or some intermediary. But apocalyptic visions are much longer, and their symbolism is striking, bizarre, and detailed. The more significant contrast is that prophetic visions, like prophetic speeches, generally concern the immediate future and the continuation of history, whereas apocalyptic visions set the immediate situation of the visionary and his contemporaries into the framework of world history as a whole and its imminent radical transformation. The writer of Daniel was convinced that the wars and persecutions of his time were the last throes of the forces of evil, and that God would soon act to establish his kingdom.

The verses that make up our lesson should be read in the context of Daniel 7 as a whole. The first and last verses of the chapter provide a narrative framework. The remainder contains the report of what Daniel saw (verses 2-14) and its interpretation (verses 15-27), which at points reverts to the description of the visionary scene. Today's reading thus includes the beginning of the vision and the first part of its interpretation.

Verse 1 is the narrative introduction, indicating the date of Daniel's visionary experience and the fact that he recorded what he saw. As in a great deal of apocalyptic literature, the writer has attributed the vision to a famous figure and has located it almost four hundred years before his own time. Verses 2 and 3 set the scene and summarise the vision. The four winds and the great sea in tumult provide the background for the appearance of four beasts. Then follows the detailed description of the four terrible beasts, each one composite in form and vicious in behaviour. Everything leads up to the fourth beast, which has ten horns, and then a little horn. Each beast represents a different world empire, successively the Babylonians, the Medes, the Persians, and the Greeks. The ten horns of the fourth beast are the rulers following Alexander the Great, and the little horn stands for Antiochus Epiphanes. It was common in apocalyptic literature to see the history of the world in terms of four eras, with the last the most terrible of all. Then (verse 9) the scene shifts to the heavenly throne room, with the Ancient One passing judgement on the beasts.

Daniel reports that the visions disturbed him (verse 15), so he approached 'one of the attendants' and asked for and was given the interpretation of what he had seen (verse 16). The first two sentences of the interpretation correspond to the two main scenes. The four beasts are four kings who will arise (verse 17), but the vision of the Ancient One contains the promise that 'the holy ones of the Most High' ('saints of the Most High' in the RSV) will inherit an eternal kingdom. Those 'holy ones', are the Jews who have remained faithful to their God during the time of persecution.

This text was originally written primarily for just those saints, to encourage them to endure difficult times. The writer means to communicate a divine revelation concerning the course and end of history, which end will be the reign of God in justice. God will put an end to the worldly enemy and will set up a kingdom in which the faithful will take their place. Even suffering under bestial powers has meaning, and it will last only for a short time.

For the writer of the Book of Daniel, and for the early Christians, the New Age was already breaking in. The details of that future – when, where, how? – have not been revealed to us. But the confidence that God would ultimately triumph and vindicate the saints has enabled generations of the faithful not only to endure, but to live the abundant life.

Gene M. Tucker
Preaching Through the Christian Year: Year C

My interest in the saints began at theological college when a friend strongly recommended two small books of mini-biographies of many different saints. He said he was going to use them as a basis for all his talks to children in church services. They were entitled *The Glorious Company* by Frederick C. Gill and I bought my copies as long ago as 1964, and still use them to this day (they are I believe out of print now).

Ask anyone to define a saint and they may well point to stained glass windows in old churches depicting some of them. Indeed a ministerial friend of mine had pastoral care of a church which had a beautiful window, but the inscription at the bottom of the window was what made people smile. For it said: 'To the glory of God, and in loving memory of His wife Harriet!' It became known as God's wife's window!

In the Old Testament saintliness is expressed by two words; 'Hasidh' meaning 'good', compassionate, and then holy; and 'Qadhash' that means 'to be holy', 'to be set apart for God's service'.

In the Christian Church every member is called to be a saint and in the Book of Revelation, Jesus is described as 'King of Saints'.

From earliest times the church has honoured the memory of saints and martyrs even though during their lifetime they may not have been too popular.

And of course there are many places in Great Britain that are named after saints: St Just, St Ives, St Brelade, St Albans, named after the first Christian martyr in these islands, killed for his faith because he took the place of a priest who was on the run from the authorities and who refused to worship idols. There has been a church in his memory since AD 429.

One of my own personal favourite saints is Edward the Martyr, King of England, who was murdered in AD 979. His succession to the throne had been disputed but he was chosen by the Witan in 975 under the influence of Dunstan, the then Archbishop of Canterbury. His brutal murder at Corfe Castle was caused by a power struggle among the magnates. Some wanted his half-brother Ethelred.

The Anglo Saxon Chronicle describes his death in these words: 'King Edward was slain at eventide at Corfe gate and was buried at Wareham without any kingly honours.' Miracles soon followed at his tomb, so his relics were transferred to Shaftsbury by Dunstan in AD 980. The real villain of the piece was Edward's stepmother who wanted power for her son. Apparently Edward arrived at Corfe after a hunting trip and while his servants were seeing to the dogs she 'allured him to her with female blandishments and made him lean forward . . .

while he was eagerly drinking from the cup which she presented, he was stabbed to death by an attendant. Apparently the evil step-mother expiated her crime by eventually becoming a nun at Wherwell.

It was whilst on a vist to Corfe Castle during a holiday that I first heard Edward's story and was hooked; so I went as soon as possible to Wareham Church and sat in the pew for a long time, just simply soaking up the most wonderful atmosphere. I discovered later that whenever I visited the known home or place of a saint or martyr there has, for me, been a most lovely atmosphere of peace and love and grace. I still delight to visit areas of this country where I know saints have loved and laboured, suffered and died. What a blessing they still are to me!

Ron Dale

Proper 27/Ordinary Time 32
Third Sunday before Advent

Haggai 1:15b-2:9

*Poor beginnings
do not mean poor
endings.*

The apparent failure of God to fulfil divine promises – those moments when human prayers seem to go completely unanswered – is not the only cause of spiritual despondency. Women and men of faith also experience the seeming distance of God when God's promises are fulfilled, but in ways that are less expansively proportioned than the believers had hoped for. That is the crisis that the present text addresses and, although the prophet's words are intended for a very specific historical moment, they overarch that moment and speak to the community of faith in all generations.

It would have been quite difficult to be cheerful in the Jerusalem to which the first groups returned from Babylonian exile. Ringing in their ears (or at least in the ears of some) were the grand promises of the Second Isaiah (see Isaiah 55:1-11), which would have led many Jews to expect that their new Jerusalem would be a land of milk and honey. Instead they found ruins and deprivation so vast that the most strenuous effort was required to scratch a living from the land. In addition, quarrels with their neighbours (Ezra 4:1-5) made life uncomfortable and required constant watchfulness on the part of the settlers (note Nehemiah 4:21).

The most immediate objective to which many of them bent their efforts – once their houses had been made habitable – was the restoration of the house of God. Interference from others (Ezra 5:1-5) and the poverty of the Jews themselves delayed the restoration of the Temple for almost two decades, so that it was not until the arrival of the Davidic prince Zerubbabel about 520 BC that the new Temple was completed and services of worship reinstituted (Ezra 6:13-22).

And what a shabby Temple it was – at least in comparison to the great edifice on which Solomon had lavished such treasure! When the foundation of the second Temple had been laid, it was apparent from the size of the stones and the outline of the building on the ground that this sanctuary would only hint at the beauty and grandeur of its predecessor: 'But many of the . . . old people who had seen the first house on its foundations, wept with a loud voice when they saw this house, though many shouted aloud for joy, so that the people could not distinguish the sound of the joyful shout from the sound of the people's weeping' (Ezra 3:12-13).

It is precisely to these weepers that Haggai speaks in the present text. Perhaps the prophet too is among those who feel great disappointment over the new house of worship. It was Haggai who had urged upon the newly arrived Zerubbabel that the work on the Temple must proceed as quickly as possible (Haggai 1:1-11). Perhaps in his view the new sanctuary did not come up to the standards one would expect for the house of Israel's God. Or perhaps he wished to mollify any wounds inflicted on Zerubbabel and his priestly colleague Joshua by those who were so vocal in their feelings of disappointment.

In any event, Haggai's message is basically this: Poor beginnings do not mean poor endings, when the Lord of hosts presides over the fortunes of the people. The God who brought Israel out of Egypt so many years ago still stands behind all the ancient promises (2:5). Just as the Spirit of the Lord was present in the pillars of fire and cloud (Exodus 13:21-22; 14:19-20), so 'my spirit abides among you' here and now. The Second Isaiah had been quite straightforward in comparing the return from exile with the exodus from Egypt (note Isaiah 43:15-17; 48:20-21), and Haggai draws upon this analogy also, with the same result: fear must be replaced by joy, for Israel's God is at work in the life of the nation and in the life of the world in ways that no one can quantify.

It is quite likely that the shaking of 'all the nations' (Haggai 2:7) which the prophet expects is somehow connected with the wave of social and political unrest that appears to have swept the Persian Empire during the first years of Darius' reign (1:15b-2:1a). These convulsions will upset the normal order of things so that Judah, now an impoverished vassal state, will become the centre of commerce and wealth into which the wealth of the nations pour. A particular beneficiary of this new wealth will be the Temple which, although modest and unspectacular at the moment, will ultimately exceed even the greatest expectations. 'The latter splendour of this house shall be greater than the former, says the Lord of hosts; and in this place I will give prosperity' (2:9).

The historical record makes it clear that, in materialistic terms, the promise was never completely realised (although the Temple as rebuilt by Herod the Great beginning in 20 BC was a very magnificent edifice). So it was natural that this text, along with certain others, should begin to be understood in eschatological terms. This new Temple vision is part of the biblical vision of the new Jerusalem, a city beyond time and place where the people of God dwell eternally (compare the vision of the new Temple in Ezekiel 40-48). It is in this sense that the author of the Letter to the Hebrews understands this passage (and quotes part of it: Hebrews 12:26). That which Israel's God has not done within history will be done beyond history, and of this New Jerusalem Jesus Christ is the pledge and symbol (Hebrews 12:22-29).

In the face of all those promises of God that have not come true or have come true only in fragmentary and partial ways, the prophet's word stands forth: 'Do not fear!' (Haggai 2:5). The God who is Lord of both history and beyond-history is in the midst of the people of faith. God's promises will be consummated in ways that outreach all imaginings.

James D. Newsome
Texts for Preaching: Year C

When I read in the above reading about Haggai's basic message being this: 'Poor beginnings do not mean poor endings,' it rang a few bells with my experience in the Methodist ministry. For in the course of a 35-year itinerant ministry I had eight different moves. I began in glorious Devon and had spells in Lancashire, the Midlands and Yorkshire, and I remember to this day my low emotional feelings on first arriving in each Methodist Circuit.

As I waited for the furniture and books, etc. to arrive at each Manse I would contemplate my future ministry in the place. I was always a bit depressed and in low spirits for the first few weeks due I think, looking back, to a number of reasons. For one thing I felt quite lonely because I didn't know anybody. I also felt a bit lost because I wasn't familiar with either the countryside or town where I had been planted. I was also unsure of what I could preach and do in the new situation. And in one appointment, the biggest and toughest job I tackled, it was three years before I felt settled and comfortable in the work.

But having said all of that, I never ever had a poor ending to any appointment. In fact, every one of them ended on a high note and a wonderful public send-off to the next appointment. I used to look back over each ministry and savour the wonderful things I had been able to do as an industrial chaplain, as a broadcaster with the BBC for many years and as a prison chaplain. I always felt that God in his mercy had opened many doors in his service and I was able to say and do things I could not possibly have imagined. The joy of those 35 years of ministry will remain with me for ever, and in one sense there was no complete 'ending' to any ministry because so many people keep in touch and so the past becomes a hallowed present and a hopeful future.

Ron Dale

Proper 28/Ordinary Time 33
Second Sunday before Advent

Isaiah 65:17-25

It will be a sorry world that takes a vision of God's new heaven and new earth out of its social justice equation.

We can picture the prophet closing his eyes, quietly reflecting, and then after a period of silence, replying with the words in verses 17-25, words describing the life intended by God for all creation. But please! What purpose is served by this description of 'new heavens and a new earth'? Is this not primary evidence for a Marxist analysis of religion as an opiate of the people?

It is terribly important that in answering this question one draws a clear distinction between two exercises of religious imagination. One dreams of shalom as an avenue of escape from real life with the effect of disabling people by breaking their will to act with courage and determination on behalf of God's order of justice. The other envisions shalom as an act of defiant affirmation that no power will thwart the fulfilment of God's righteous purpose. The former leads to resignation and despair. The latter engenders hope. The former undermines social reform. The latter gives reform a clear focus to sacrifice justice to the logic of expediency.

The vision of the new heaven and the new earth fosters hope even as it elicits incisive action. It is simply not true that only programmes outlining goals attainable on the basis of pragmatic logic are capable of moving people to action. Perhaps that is the case in movements that exclude a spiritual dimension, where the warning not to aim too high is in order, lest failure to reach the goal translate into a sense of defeat. For those whose identity is grounded in God's sovereignty the case is very different. No goal short of the restoration of all God's creation to its intended wholeness will satisfy the yearning of the Servant of the Lord. Shortfalls do not devastate the Servant, for the campaign for justice is not a personal project but a part of God's eternal purpose.

Our personal experience can aid us in understanding the contribution of the vision of the new heaven and the new earth to a life of involved commitment to compassionate justice. The medical doctor in Somalia, labouring in the midst of seemingly endless need, perseveres not by scaling down objectives to saving one infant out of ten but by working indefatigably out of yearning for the world in which there shall no longer be 'an infant that lives but a few days' (verse 20). The relief worker in Bosnia steers the food-laden lorry up a dangerous mountain pass in commitment to the world in which 'no more shall the sound of weeping be heard in it' (verse 19). Albert Schweitzer left the limelight of cathedral and university for the villages of Africa, Dag Hammarskjöld kept landing his United Nations plane in dangerous trouble spots, Mother Teresa maintained her ministry to the outcasts of Calcutta not out of programmes designed on the basis of human pragmatics but out of a vision of a world in which 'they shall not labour in vain, or bear children for calamity' (verse 23).

It will be a sorry world that takes a vision of God's new heaven and new earth out of its social justice equation. Of course many humanitarian efforts will continue to do their work on the basis of strictly rational criteria. The results will alleviate some human pain. But it is a sad prospect to think of a world bereft of servants who labour for no other reason than that God has called them to be agents of a love that is intended to restore the dignity and wholeness of every mortal. For them, one promise in the vision is more precious than all others: 'Before they call I will answer, while they are yet speaking I will hear' (Isaiah 65:24).

The community of faith – whether it is in the form of a church, a synagogue, a mosque, or another assembly of worship – betrays its calling if it yearns for anything less than a human family so intimately connected with its source that when it calls, God answers! Only through this communion between the divine and the human can the community of the faithful offer to the world its unique gift, the gift of hope that will not be broken until that day when: 'The wolf and the lamb shall feed together, the lion shall eat straw like the ox; but the serpent – its food shall be dust! They shall not hurt or destroy on all my holy mountain, says the Lord' (Isaiah 65; cf. 11:6-7).

Paul D. Hanson
Isaiah 40-66

I was visiting a hospital one day that I had never been to before. Unfortunately for me, I had taken a short cut and so had to enter the hospital by a side entrance, and when I was inside I was confronted with a bewildering array of signs on walls and coloured lines on floors. I hadn't a clue where the ward I wanted was located. I simply stood still and surveyed the hustle and bustle of many people who all seemed to know where they were going and how to get there. I was just saying to myself that I must ask someone for directions when to my surprise a voice spoke from behind me, and said 'Can I help you?' I quickly turned to see that the questioner was the hospital chaplain and he soon showed me the route I needed to take.

I was sitting on a chair in the very beautiful Church of the Beatitudes overlooking the Sea of Galilee, and I was getting very anxious because earlier in the week a BBC producer had asked me to give a four-minute sermon during the service I was participating in. All through the week I had wondered what I might preach about, but nothing had suggested itself, even after many a prayer for help!

Suddenly the worship leader said, 'I now call on Ron Dale to give the sermon.' I shall never forget what happened next. For it was only in the act of getting to my feet, only then did I suddenly receive every word I needed to speak, and I sat down precisely four minutes later. It was the only time in over forty years of preaching that a divine message was given me without any preparation on my part. Usually I very thoroughly researched, planned, thought through and noted what I wanted to preach. But on this unique occasion, every word was given me before I could even ask. Not only so, but many people asked if they could have a copy, it had proved so wonderful for them to hear. No copy of course, was available; for me, only the wonderful memory of it all.

There have been a few other occasions in my life when, as a poor student money has been given from totally unexpected quarters; when clothes have been bought me because I could not afford any myself; food and drink have been generously given when I had no resources to obtain them.

As I sometimes reflect on all these experiences, I remember with gratitude the words of Isaiah the prophet: 'Before they call I will answer' (Isaiah 65:24).

Ron Dale

Proper 29/Christ the King

Jeremiah 23:1-6

The prophecy expresses a future hope that a king, who will bear the name 'The LORD is our righteousness' will be 'raised up'.

Three Prophecies of Hope (23:1-8)

We now encounter a series of three short prophecies, all prose, which are hopeful in their content and concerned with the future welfare and administration of Judah. It is unlikely that any of them derives directly from Jeremiah. Rather they are in this position to amplify the picture of the future after the threatening prophecies of the preceding chapter and in particular to provide an affirmative theological stance with respect to the kingship. The first of these (23:1-4) takes up again the metaphor of 'the shepherds' which has already been used in 22:22.

In this fresh prophecy the point is made that God wholly condemns and repudiates the irresponsible and misguided shepherds of the past who had misled the people and brought them to destruction (verses 1-2). The punishment they received (at the hands of the Babylonians) was therefore wholly deserved and necessary. Over against this condemnation there is a promise that God would provide in the future trustworthy and obedient shepherds who would care for the people and lead them with safety and care (verses 3-4). It will be they who will bring the people back from the lands to which they have been driven.

The addition of this point at this juncture may appear at first to be needless and rather obvious. However it sets out a point of considerable importance. Since the preceding prophecies had presented a negative judgement upon the office of the king, it might have appeared that the role of the 'shepherds', including that of the king at the head, would disappear altogether. Yet this was not to be so; it would be replaced by a new body of responsible and trustworthy leaders. No doubt the metaphor of 'shepherd', as used of a king, is entirely self-explanatory and its use was undoubtedly very ancient. It was, however, sufficiently undefined to be applicable to leaders of many kinds, not necessarily those holding the office and title of 'king'. It is this possibility for the future that is now envisaged; it lends divine authority for the changing political structure and for the administration of the people of Israel and Judah that emerged after the debacle of 587 BC. Not only would there be new forms of leadership and government in the land of Judah, such as that which emerged under Gedaliah, but leadership of other kinds would also emerge among Jews of the dispersion. In this way the prophecies of Jeremiah provided an important step in the transition from the hitherto prevailing concept of Israel as a nation to a new but not fully developed one in which Israel would emerge as a covenant people living in dispersion among the nations of many lands. There they would remain until the time when God would bring about the great 'return' to the land of Israel (Judah).

A second prophetic comment, this time directly concerning the kingship, is set to follow in 23:5-6 and has aroused a good deal of discussion on account of the play it makes upon the name of Zedekiah. Many earlier commentators have taken it to be authentic to Jeremiah . . . Others more recently have questioned this . . . The prophecy expresses a future hope that a king, who will bear the name 'The LORD [Yahweh] is our righteousness' (verse 6), will be 'raised up' (i.e. elevated to the throne) by God to fulfil the promise attached to the Davidic dynasty. This precisely is the meaning of the name Zedekiah; the Babylonian administration placed Zedekiah on the throne in place of the deported Jehoiachin. The interpretation favoured by others has seen this as an extremely subtle rejection of Zedekiah, implying that he was unworthy of his name (and royal office) and would be one day replaced by one who would bear it more appropriately.

We must consider, however, that Jeremiah's attitude towards Zedekiah appears to have been altogether more open and equivocal than is implicit in such an interpretation and that the saying itself fails to make clear the all-important point that Zedekiah is being rejected. Much more likely, Zedekiah was already dead at the time this prophecy was composed and it has been added here to find within the name of the last of Judah's kings a word of hope and assurance for the future. It is simply taking the last king's name as a prophecy, not about this king himself but about the royal dynasty he represented. In this way it is wholly in line with the prophecies set out in 33:14-26.

R. E. Clements
Jeremiah

Because one of the themes of the above reading is about bad shepherds, here is a piece concerning God the True Shepherd, caring for even one lost sheep; but we must not lose sight of the truth that God is also the True Shepherd of ALL his people, actively working for the care of the corporate body of his flock.

Where do you begin with your daily paper? With the Births, Marriages and Deaths? With the sporting pages, or the financial columns, or with the news of national and international moment on the centre pages? Sometimes I find myself on a long journey having time for the curiosities of the Personal Column, or the very intriguing notices under 'Lost and Found'. What odd things appear to be valuable to the owner, so that when they are lost he cannot rest, but will spare no trouble or expense to find them. The fifteenth chapter of Luke's Gospel is all about losing and finding. It contains the stories of a lost sheep, a lost coin and a lost son, and each story ends with a scene of rejoicing when what was lost is found. This chapter contains some of the greatest teaching of Jesus, and has much to tell us of God's scale of values, what he holds dear and precious, what it is that, being lost, leaves an empty incompleteness in the heart of God, and being found again, produces deep rejoicing.

First, this chapter makes plain what, in the eyes of Jesus, constitutes being lost. The word is often used in the Gospel – Jesus came to seek and save that which was lost; he sent his disciples out to the lost sheep of the house of Israel; in the great Intercessory prayer he said: 'Those thou gavest me I have kept and none of them is lost.' What does it mean to be lost? Look at these three pictures. The sheep: how did it get lost? It was grazing peacefully with the rest, it noticed a promising tuft of green grass further off, the grass that is always sweeter on the other side of the fence! It went after it, and little by little it got out of the flock, out on its own, and when the sheep were folded for the night it just wasn't there. It all happens so easily.

Of how many lives it could be written, 'Lost between 13 and 25'. Some get lost during their National Service, some between leaving school and qualifying for their job in life. Some wander off while they are working for exams or building up a business, others are lost in marriage and family life, busy doing the garden or lost in a thicket of chores. Many find their own way back, but not all, for they lose the road, they get out of the habit of church-going. They are not in actual but only in potential danger, the danger being that they are on their own, they have to fend for themselves. Then the sheep gets into difficulties, crag-fast, or caught in a thicket; the man has some problem or trouble to handle, he needs security, he begins to miss the fellowship of the flock, the fold and the Shepherd. And how tragically people can be misled when that need becomes clamant! You can be lost because you are out of the fellowship . . .

A shepherd loses one sheep in a hundred. It is a pity, but you are bound to have losses, from disease, accident, attack by wild beasts and other causes.

You are doing very well if you can keep the loss down to one per cent. It is a pity about one lost sheep, but it was probably lost by its own fault, and you may as well just write it off. The shepherd, however, does nothing of the kind. He leaves the ninety and nine to fend for themselves and goes out after the lost one per cent. What a revelation of God's love for the individual, for God's sheep are people. Thank God we do not, in practice, follow this callous writing-off method. All the resources of the Navy and the RAF will be mobilised, and used at extravagant cost to search for two men missing in a small yacht, and rescue parties will toil sacrificially to find one student lost in the Cairngorms. God will do no less.

Robert Leonard Small
My Way of Preaching

Index of Authors and Translators

Acknowledgements

The publishers wish to thank all those who have given their permission to reproduce copyright material in this publication. The readings listed below are all in copyright and the addresses of the copyright owners are given at the end of this section.

First Sunday of Advent

One of the greatest . . . (John B. Taylor), taken from *Preaching on God's Justice*, published by Mowbrays, 1994. Used by permission of Continuum International Publishing Group Ltd.

These verses from Jeremiah . . . (Gene M. Tucker), taken from *Preaching Through the Christian Year C* © 1994 Fred B. Craddock, John H. Hayes, Carl R. Holliday, Gene M. Tucker. Used by permission of Trinity Press International, USA.

Second Sunday of Advent

There is a saying . . . (John B. Taylor), taken from *Preaching on God's Justice*, published by Mowbrays, 1994. Used by permission of Continuum International Publishing Group Ltd.

That Advent is a time . . . (James D. Newsome), taken from *Texts for Preaching: Year C* by Charles B. Cousar, Beverly R. Gaventa, J. Clinton McCann, and James D. Newsome. © 1994 Westminster John Knox Press. Used by permission of the publisher.

Third Sunday of Advent

Zephaniah 3:20 records . . . (Barbara Brown Taylor), taken from *The Preaching Life*, published by Cowley Publications, USA. All rights reserved.

No emotion is more welcome . . . (James D. Newsome), taken from *Texts for Preaching: Year C* by Charles B. Cousar, Beverly R. Gaventa, J. Clinton McCann, and James D. Newsome. © 1994 Westminster John Knox Press. Used by permission of the publisher.

Fourth Sunday of Advent

The prophet Micah . . . (Gene M. Tucker), taken from *Preaching Through the Christian Year C* © 1994 Fred B. Craddock, John H. Hayes, Carl R. Holliday, Gene M. Tucker. Used by permission of Trinity Press International, USA.

Christmas Day 1

The scene is a royal coronation . . . (Revd Preb. Gill Summer), taken from *The Ministry of the Word* (page 35) © The Bible Reading Fellowship, Oxford 2000.

This is one of the best known . . . (John F. A. Sawyer), taken from *Isaiah: Volume 1*, published by The Saint Andrew Press.

Darkness in the spiritual . . . (Olive Wyon), taken from *On the Way*, 1958, published by SCM Press.

Christmas Day 2

Isaiah 62:6-7 tell of sentinels . . . (Father Andrew), taken from *In the Silence*, published by Mowbrays, 1947. Used by permission of Continuum International Publishing Group Ltd.

The last verse . . . (Paul D. Hanson), taken from *Isaiah 40-60* (Interpretation Series), © 1995 John Knox Press. Used by permission of Westminster John Knox Press.

Christmas Day 3

What every man looks for . . . (Thomas Merton), taken from *No Man Is an Island*, published by Burns and Oates, 1974. Used by permission of Continuum International Publishing Group Ltd.

Because salvation . . . (Paul Tillich), taken from *The Eternal Now*, 2nd edition, 2002, published by SCM Press.

Zion stands ready . . . (Paul D. Hanson), taken from *Isaiah 40-60* (Interpretation Series), © 1995 John Knox Press. Used by permission of Westminster John Knox Press.

First Sunday of Christmas

I once read a news item . . . (Ron Dale) © Ron Dale.

Second Sunday of Christmas

The exile of Israel . . . (Walter Brueggemann), taken from *Texts for Preaching: Year C* by Charles B. Cousar, Beverly R. Gaventa, J. Clinton McCann, and James D. Newsome. © 1994 Westminster John Knox Press. Used by permission of the publisher.

Lord, in your presence . . . (Rex Chapman), taken from *A Glimpse of God*, 1973, published by SCM Press.

The Epiphany

Isaiah 60: 1-6 tells of kings . . . (Barbara Brown Taylor), taken from *Home By Another Way*, published by Cowley Publications, USA. All rights reserved.

Israel has had a long . . . (Walter Brueggemann), taken from *Texts for Preaching: Year C* by Charles B. Cousar, Beverly R. Gaventa, J. Clinton McCann, and James D. Newsome. © 1994 Westminster John Knox Press. Used by permission of the publisher.

The Baptism of the Lord
First Sunday of Epiphany

But now, this is what the Lord . . . (John Calvin), taken from *Isaiah*, published by Crossway Books. Used by permission of Inter-Varsity Press.

Isaiah 43 vs 1 and 5 . . . (Eric James), taken from *In Season, out of Season*, 1999, published by SCM Press.

Second Sunday of Epiphany

In my sermon . . . (John Killinger), taken from *Fundamentals of Preaching*, published by Augsburg Fortress, USA.
A city not forsaken . . . (James D. Hanson), taken from *Isaiah 40-66* (Interpretation Series), © 1995 John Knox Press. Used by permission of Westminster John Knox Press.

Third Sunday of Epiphany

Read the text and give . . . (N. T. Wright), taken from *Twelve Months of Sundays*, published by SPCK.

I vividly remember . . . (Ron Dale) © Ron Dale.

Fourth Sunday of Epiphany

In one fashion . . . (James D. Newsome), taken from *Texts for Preaching: Year C* by Charles B. Cousar, Beverly R. Gaventa, J. Clinton McCann and James D. Newsome, © 1994 Westminster John Knox Press. Used by permission.

When I look back . . . (Ron Dale) © Ron Dale.

Fifth Sunday of Epiphany

One of the main themes . . . (Barbara Brown Taylor), taken from *The Preaching Life*, published by Cowley Publications, USA. All rights reserved.

It is natural to assume . . . (John F. A. Sawyer), taken from *Isaiah: Volume 1*, published by The Saint Andrew Press.

Sixth Sunday of Epiphany

This is an uncompromising . . . (Revd Dr Robert Fyall), taken from *The Ministry of the Word* (pages 80-81) © The Bible Reading Fellowship, Oxford 2000.

I can still remember . . . (Ron Dale) © Ron Dale.

Seventh Sunday of Epiphany

Our capacity to know . . . (Walter Brueggemann), taken from *Threat of Life: Sermons on Pain, Power and Weakness*, published by Augsburg Fortress, USA.

Eighth Sunday of Epiphany

On a warm sunny morning . . . (Betty Schimmel), taken from *To See You Again: The Betty Schimmel Story*, © 1999 Betty Schimmel and Joyce Gabriel. Used by permission of Simon & Schuster, UK.

One senses that . . . (Paul D. Hanson), taken from *Isaiah 40-66* (Interpretation Series), © 1995 John Knox Press. Used by permission of Westminster John Knox Press.

Ninth Sunday of Epiphany

John Killinger is an American . . . (John Killinger), taken from *Fundamentals of Preaching*, published by Augsburg Fortress, USA.

First Kings 8, as the . . . (Gene M. Tucker), taken from *Preaching Through the Christian Year C*, © 1994 Fred B. Craddock, John H. Hayes, Carl R. Holliday, Gene M. Tucker. Used by permission of Trinity Press International, USA.

Last Sunday of Epiphany

Much of what has been . . . (L. H. Brockington), quoted in *A Theological Word Book of the Bible*, 1950, published by SCM Press.

Word and Body . . . (Terrence E. Fretheim), taken from *Exodus* (Interpretation Series), © 1991 John Knox Press. Used by permission of Westminster John Knox Press.

First Sunday of Lent

'The Affluent Society' (H. O. Phillips) and 'The Death Touch' (Dawn Hunt), taken from *The Book of Mini Sagas*, © 1985 Telegraph Group Ltd and contributors.

It is interesting . . . (James D. Newsome), taken from *Texts for Preaching: Year C* by Charles B. Cousar, Beverly R. Gaventa, J. Clinton McCann and James D. Newsome, © 1994 Westminster John Knox Press. Used by permission.

Second Sunday of Lent

The covenant with Abram . . . (Henry Wansbrough), taken from *People's Bible Commentary: Genesis*, published by the Bible Reading Fellowship, and used by kind permission of the author.

The Wilderness of faith . . . (Maggie Ross) © control.

Third Sunday of Lent

Just in case anyone . . . (N. T. Wright), taken from *Twelve Months of Sundays*, published by SPCK.

Fourth Sunday of Lent

The words from an old . . . (James D. Newsome), taken from *Texts for Preaching: Year C* by Charles B. Cousar, Beverly R. Gaventa, J. Clinton McCann and James D. Newsome, © 1994 Westminster John Knox Press. Used by permission.

Having worked as a stage . . . (Ron Dale) © Ron Dale.

Fifth Sunday of Lent

This part of Isaiah . . . (Revd Dr Robert Fyall), taken from *The Ministry of the Word* (pages 128-9) © The Bible Reading Fellowship, Oxford 2000.

Palm/Passion Sunday

Because Isaiah 50:4 speaks . . . (Frederick Buechner), taken from *Wishful Thinking: A Theological ABC*, 1973, published by HarperCollins Publishers, USA.

The Servant Songs . . . (Gene M. Tucker), taken from *Preaching Through the Christian Year C*, © 1994 Fred B. Craddock, John H. Hayes, Carl R. Holliday, Gene M. Tucker. Used by permission of Trinity Press International, USA.

Easter Day

The passage begins with . . . (Stephen Breck Reid), taken from *The Lectionary Commentary*, published by William B. Eerdmans, USA. Used by permission of Continuum International Publishing Group Ltd.

It seemed to them . . . (N. T. Wright), taken from *Twelve Months of Sundays*, published by SPCK.

There have been occasions . . . (Ron Dale) © Ron Dale.

Second Sunday of Easter

Verse 1-4 from an introductory . . . (Cyril S. Rodd), taken from *Psalms 73-150*, published by Epworth Press. Used by permission of The Methodist Publishing House.

The picture is that . . . (Leonard Griffith), taken from *God in Man's Experience: The Activity of God in the Psalms*, 1970, published by Hodder & Stoughton. Used by permission.

Third Sunday of Easter

A man who has been ill . . . (Cyril S. Rodd), taken from *Psalms 1-72*, published by Epworth Press. Used by permission of The Methodist Publishing House.

Why do we fast . . . (Barbara Brown Taylor), taken from *Gospel Medicine*, published by Cowley Publications, USA. All rights reserved.

I had at last become . . . (Thomas Merton), taken from *The Seven Story Mountain* (pages 163-4), published by SPCK.

Fourth Sunday of Easter

Most of the time . . . (Frederick Buechner) © control.

A friend told me . . . (Walter Brueggemann), taken from *Texts for Preaching: Year C* by Charles B. Cousar, Beverly R. Gaventa, J. Clinton McCann and James D. Newsome, © 1994 Westminster John Knox Press. Used by permission.

Fifth Sunday of Easter

Psalm 146-150 constitute . . . (John H. Hayes), taken from *Preaching Through the Christian Year C*, © 1994 Fred B. Craddock, John H. Hayes, Carl R. Holliday, Gene M. Tucker. Used by permission of Trinity Press International, USA.

Sixth Sunday of Easter

In the Bible blessing means . . . (Alan Richardson), taken from *A Theological Word Book of the Bible*, 1950, published by SCM Press.

That your way . . . (James L. Mays), taken from *Psalms* (Interpretation Series), © 1994 James L. Mays. Used by permission of Westminster John Knox Press.

Ascension

Psalm 47 is one of the hymns . . . (A. B. Rhodes), taken from *Psalms*, 1961, published by SCM Press.

The kingship of God . . . (Alan Richardson), taken from *A Theological Word Book of the Bible*, 1950, published by SCM Press.

Seventh Sunday of Easter

The closing words . . . (Kenneth Leech), quoted in *Julian, Woman of Our Day*, published by Darton, Longman & Todd. Used by permission of the author.

An enthronement psalm . . . (John H. Hayes), taken from *Preaching Through the Christian Year C* © 1994 Fred B. Craddock, John H. Hayes, Carl R. Holliday, Gene M. Tucker. Used by permission of Trinity Press International, USA.

Pentecost

The Tower of Babel . . . (Henry Wansbrough), taken from *People's Bible Commentary: Genesis*, published by the Bible Reading Fellowship, and used by kind permission of the author.

Jealousy is probably . . . (Martin Israel), taken from *The Discipline of Love*, published by SPCK.

Trinity Sunday

Believers throughout the . . . (Barbara Brown Taylor), taken from *Home By Another Way*, published by Cowley Publications, USA. All rights reserved.

The sum of our passage . . . (James D. Newsome), taken from *Texts for Preaching: Year C* by Charles B. Cousar, Beverly R. Gaventa, J. Clinton McCann and James D. Newsome, © 1994 Westminster John Knox Press. Used by permission.

Proper 4

The above passage . . . (Barbara Brown Taylor), taken from *Gospel Medicine*, published by Cowley Publications, USA. All rights reserved.

By making explicit . . . (Richard Nelson), taken from *First and Second Kings* (Interpretation Series), © 1987 John Knox Press. Used by permission of Westminster John Knox Press.

Proper 5

The trouble in Israel . . . (Walter Brueggemann), taken from *The Threat of Life: Sermons on Pain, Power and Weakness*, published by Augsburg Fortress, USA.

The full Old Testament . . . (Gene M. Tucker), taken from *Preaching Through the Christian Year C* © 1994 Fred B. Craddock, John H. Hayes, Carl R. Holliday, Gene M. Tucker. Used by permission of Trinity Press International, USA.

Proper 6

The story of Naboth's . . . (Margaret Killingray), taken from *The Ministry of the Word* (page 224), © The Bible Reading Fellowship, Oxford 2000.

Proper 7

Faced with this angry . . . (Robert Davidson), taken from *The Courage To Doubt*, 1983, published by SCM Press.

Proper 8

These verses begin . . . (Elizabeth Achtemeier), taken from *Preaching Hard Texts of the Old Testament*, 1998, published by Hendrickson Publishers, In., USA. Used by permission. All rights reserved.

This reading is a tale . . . (Gene M. Tucker), taken from *Preaching Through the Christian Year C* © 1994 Fred B. Craddock, John H. Hayes, Carl R. Holliday, Gene M. Tucker. Used by permission of Trinity Press International, USA.

Proper 9

I have never spent . . . (Barbara Brown Taylor), taken from *Home By Another Way*, published by Cowley Publications, USA. All rights reserved.

Proper 10

With this text from Amos . . . (James D. Newsome), taken from *Texts for Preaching: Year C* by Charles B. Cousar, Beverly R. Gaventa, J. Clinton McCann and James D. Newsome, © 1994 Westminster John Knox Press. Used by permission.

Verse 7-9 of the above . . . (Ron Dale) © Ron Dale.

Proper 11

Mammoth production facilities . . . (Martin Luther King), taken from *The Words of Martin Luther King*, © 1968 Martin Luther King, Jr. © renewed 1996 Coretta Scott King. Used by permission of the Estate of Martin Luther King, Jr, c/o Writers House, New York.

Put Paul alongside Mary . . . (N. T. Wright), taken from *Twelve Months of Sundays*, published by SPCK.

Proper 12

Then Moses said to God . . . (Gerhard von Rad), taken from *Moses*, published by The Lutterworth Press.

Sin, judgement . . . (James D. Newsome), taken from *Texts for Preaching: Year C* by Charles B. Cousar, Beverly R. Gaventa, J. Clinton McCann and James D. Newsome, © 1994 Westminster John Knox Press. Used by permission.

Proper 13

You must thank . . . (Eric James) © control.

This passage, for good reason . . . (Gene M. Tucker), taken from *Preaching Through the Christian Year C*, © 1994 Fred B. Craddock, John H. Hayes, Carl R. Holliday, Gene M. Tucker. Used by permission of Trinity Press International, USA.

Proper 14

The vision of Isaiah reveals . . . (Revd Dr Ian Paul), taken from *The Ministry of the Word* (page 275), © The Bible Reading Fellowship, Oxford 2000.

Proper 15

The above commentary . . . (Barbara Brown Taylor), taken from *Gospel Medicine*, published by Cowley Publications, USA. All rights reserved.

An important debate . . . (Christopher R. Seitz), taken from *Isaiah 1-39* (Interpretation Series), © 1993 Westminster John Knox Press. Used by permission.

Proper 16

The account of Jeremiah's . . . (R. E. Clements), taken from *Jeremiah* (Interpretation Series), © 1988 John Knox Press. Used by permission of Westminster John Knox Press.

As I reread the call . . . (Ron Dale) © Ron Dale.

Proper 17

This passage has an ominous . . . (Revd Dr Ian Paul), taken from *The Ministry of the Word* (pages 294-5), © The Bible Reading Fellowship, Oxford 2000.

Proper 18

Repentance, renewal . . . (Maggie Ross), © control.

We now encounter . . . (R. E. Clements), taken from *Jeremiah* (Interpretation Series), © 1988 John Knox Press. Used by permission of Westminster John Knox Press.

Proper 19

See, Christian soul . . . (Anselm of Canterbury, trans. B. Ward), taken from *The Prayers and Meditation of St Anselm*, 1973, published by Penguin Classics, © 1973 Benedicta Ward. Used by permission of the publishers.

Two words appear . . . (James D. Newsome), taken from *Texts for Preaching: Year C*, by Charles B. Cousar, Beverly R. Gaventa, J. Clinton McCann and James D. Newsome, © 1994 Westminster John Knox Press. Used by permission.

Proper 20

The first thing to get clear . . . (N. T. Wright), taken from *Twelve Months of Sundays*, published by SPCK.

Proper 21

The more I read . . . (John S. Dunne), taken from *The Reasons of the Heart*, 1978, published by SCM Press.

Jeremiah 32 marks . . . (Gene M. Tucker), taken from *Preaching Through the Christian Year C*, © 1994 Fred B. Craddock, John H. Hayes, Carl R. Holliday, Gene M. Tucker. Used by permission of Trinity Press International, USA.

Proper 22

In the Christian Canon . . . (Gene M. Tucker), taken from *Preaching Through the Christian Year C*, © 1994 Fred B. Craddock, John H. Hayes, Carl R. Holliday, Gene M. Tucker. Used by permission of Trinity Press International, USA. Some years ago . . . (Ron Dale) © Ron Dale.

Proper 23

Both Jeremiah in his day . . . (Dietrich Bonhoeffer), taken from *Letters and Papers from Prison*, the Enlarged Edition, 1971, published by SCM Press.

There is one very interesting . . . (James D. Newsome), taken from *Texts for Preaching: Year C*, by Charles B. Cousar, Beverly R. Gaventa, J. Clinton McCann and James D. Newsome, © 1994 Westminster John Knox Press. Used by permission.

Proper 24

The unusual story . . . (Frederick C. Gill), taken from *The Glorious Company*, published by Epworth Press. Used by permission of The Methodist Publishing House.

The prophecy of the new . . . (R. E. Clements), taken from *Jeremiah* (Interpretation Series), © 1988 John Knox Press. Used by permission of Westminster John Knox Press.

Proper 25

Most likely immediately . . . (Revd Dr Ian Paul), taken from *The Ministry of the Word* (pages 346-7), © The Bible Reading Fellowship, Oxford 2000.

Proper 26

Although not all . . . (James D. Newsome), taken from *Texts for Preaching: Year C*, by Charles B. Cousar, Beverly R. Gaventa, J. Clinton McCann and James D. Newsome, © 1994 Westminster John Knox Press. Used by permission.

Many years ago . . . (Ron Dale) © Ron Dale.

All Saints

The specific link . . . (Gene M. Tucker), taken from *Preaching Through the Christian Year C*, © 1994 Fred B. Craddock, John H. Hayes, Carl R. Holliday, Gene M. Tucker. Used by permission of Trinity Press International, USA.

My interest in the saints . . . (Ron Dale) © Ron Dale.

Proper 27

The apparent failure . . . (James D. Newsome), taken from *Texts for Preaching: Year C*, by Charles B. Cousar, Beverly R. Gaventa, J. Clinton McCann and James D. Newsome, © 1994 Westminster John Knox Press. Used by permission.

When I read in the above . . . (Ron Dale) © Ron Dale.

Proper 28

We can picture . . . (Paul D. Hanson), taken from *Isaiah 40-66* (Interpretation Series), © 1995 John Knox Press. Used by permission of Westminster John Knox Press.

I was visiting a hospital . . . (Ron Dale) © Ron Dale.

Proper 29 / Christ the King

We now encounter . . . (R. E. Clements), taken from *Jeremiah* (Interpretation Series), © 1988 John Knox Press. Used by permission of Westminster John Knox Press.

Because one of the themes . . . (Robert L. Small) © control

Every effort has been made to trace the owners of copyright material and we hope that no copyright has been infringed. Pardon is sought and apology made if the contrary be the case and a correction will be made in any reprint of this book.

Addresses of Copyright Holders

Augsburg Fortress Publishers, PO Box 1209, Minneapolis, MN 55440-1209, USA.

The Bible Reading Fellowship, First Floor, Elsfield Hall, 15-17 Elsfield Way, Oxford, OX2 8FG.

The Continuum International Publishing Group Ltd, The Tower Building, 11 York Road, London, SE1 7NX.

Cowley Publications, 907 Massachusetts Avenue, Cambridge, MA 02139, USA.

HarperCollins Publishers, 10 East 53rd Street, New York, NY 10022-5299, USA.

Hendrickson Publishers, 140 Summit Street, PO Box 3473, Peabody, MA 01961-3473, USA.

Hodder and Stoughton Publishers, 338 Euston Road, London, NW1 3BH.

Inter-Varsity Press, 38 De Montfort Street, Leicester, LE1 7GP.

The Revd Kenneth Leech, St Botolph's Church, Aldgate, London, EC3N 1AB.

The Lutterworth Press, PO Box 60, Cambridge, CB1 2NT.

Methodist Publishing House, 4 John Wesley Road, Werrington, Peterborough, PE4 6ZP.

Penguin Group (UK), 80 Strand, London, WC2R 0RL.

SCM-Canterbury Press Ltd, 9-17 St Albans Place, London, N1 0NX.

Simon & Schuster UK, Africa House, 64-78 Kingsway, London, WC2B 6AH.

SPCK, Holy Trinity Church, Marylebone Road, London, NW1 4DU.
The Saint Andrew Press, 121 George Street, Edinburgh, EH2 4YN.

Telegraph Books, Telegraph Group Ltd, 1 Canada Square, Canary Wharf, London, E14 5DT.

Trinity Press International, 4775 Linglestown Road, Harrisburg, Pennsylvania 17112, USA.

Westminster John Knox Press, 100 Witherspoon Street, Louisville, Kentucky 40202-1396, USA.

Writers House, 21 W. 26 Street, New York, NY 10010, USA.